Anna Hubbard

Anna Hubbard

Out of the Shadows

Mia Cunningham

THE UNIVERSITY PRESS OF KENTUCKY

Publication of this volume was made possible in part
by a grant from the National Endowment for the Humanities.

Published by The University Press of Kentucky
Scholarly publisher for the Commonwealth,
serving Bellarmine University, Berea College, Centre
College of Kentucky, Eastern Kentucky University,
The Filson Historical Society, Georgetown College,
Kentucky Historical Society, Kentucky State University,
Morehead State University, Murray State University,
Northern Kentucky University, Transylvania University,
University of Kentucky, University of Louisville,
and Western Kentucky University.

Editorial and Sales Offices: The University Press of Kentucky
663 South Limestone Street, Lexington, Kentucky 40508–4008

05 04 03 02 01   5 4 3 2 1

Frontispiece: woodcut by Harlan Hubbard, 1943, on thin paper glued top
and bottom onto dark green construction paper; the first in the long series
of woodcut Christmas cards the Hubbards sent out during their forty-three
years of marriage. The subject is their honeymoon cottage and first home—
the studio behind Harlan's house in Fort Thomas, Kentucky. (Copyright
Bill Caddell, reproduced with permission)

Library of Congress Cataloging-in-Publication Data
available from the Library of Congress

ISBN 0-8131-2189-2 (alk. paper)

This book is printed on acid-free recycled paper meeting
the requirements of the American National Standard
for Permanence in Paper for Printed Library Materials.

Manufactured in the United States of America.

To PB, who made it possible.

Contents

Illustrations follow page 120

Introduction

In October 1944 a middle-aged newly married couple with refined tastes in art, literature, and music left their comfortable house in northern Kentucky for the rough, muddy riverbank. For two months the woman kept house, immaculately, in a lean-to, while the man built a flat-bottomed, square-ended hull with a ten-by-sixteen cabin on it—a shantyboat. Two years later they cast off in their shantyboat on what became a long drifting journey down the Ohio and Mississippi Rivers. "Far from leaving anything behind," the woman wrote some years later, "we took with us all that was most worthwhile out of our previous living." Their names were Anna and Harlan Hubbard.

It was the first marriage, a midlife marriage, for both of them. Among people who know their story, it is a frequent topic of wonderment that Anna and Harlan found each other and melded their very different personalities into a harmonious, significant life. The finding was a wonder, yes, but the melding was really not so mysterious. They had in common their love of the arts and the outdoors, and, above all, their talent for unconventionality.

At the time of the marriage Harlan was an unknown artist living with his mother in picturesque Fort Thomas, Kentucky, across the Ohio River from Cincinnati. In his childhood in nearby Bellevue he had known few luxuries—his father, a housepainter, died when Harlan was seven years old—but circumstances dealt him an excellent public high school education in the Bronx, New York. (His mother lived there for a few years, with Harlan, to be closer to her two older sons.) Harlan continued living with his mother until she died, when he was forty-three—not because he wanted to but because she lacked the inner resources to succeed at living alone. Harlan followed his own way, roaming the Kentucky hills and painting the landscapes and steamboats of the Ohio River, and doing carpentry and bricklaying for spending money, all the while deflecting his mother's criticism for going about the yard barefoot and for working at manual labor; she cared deeply about middle-class standards of respectability. But Harlan did not, and he had no interest in worldly "success." Aside from the desire to spend his life painting and living close to nature, his only ambition—more dream than ambition, really—was to build a shantyboat someday and take a drifting journey down the Ohio.

Anna's parents, too, were concerned with respectability, and moreover, they had had the means to provide Anna with comforts and niceties, such as piano lessons and pretty clothes, and a college education at Ohio State University, which prepared her for teaching college-level French. But the classroom apparently was too great a trial for her shyness, and she left home—Grand Rapids, Michigan—for Cincinnati, to pursue another of the then-acceptable professions for females: librarian. Though the choice was traditional, the leaving in itself was unconventional. As the eldest daughter, she was expected to come home and take care of her mother one day, but she resisted all her mother's efforts to that end.

In the Cincinnati Public Library, sometime in the 1930s, Anna and Harlan met. The librarian-patron relationship developed gradually, and in 1941 they began seeing each other outside the library. Their ages were forty-one and thirty-eight. It was not first love for either of them, but it was a mature love that grew out of common interests and respect. Neither of them had thought they would ever marry.

In 1943 they did marry, over the objections of their mothers. Anna had assimilated Harlan's dreams as her own, and they were free to fulfill those dreams after his mother died later that same year. In their new freedom they made two long, adventurous hiking trips in 1944, but Harlan hesitated to make the final break. He might have just gone on dreaming his dreams if not for Anna. It was she who declared the time right for building the shantyboat they had talked of so often, and Harlan began work on it immediately.

They named the boat *Driftwood*, but somehow the name didn't stick. It comes down to us as, simply, "the shantyboat," because that was how they spoke and wrote of it. For six and a half years it was their home: two years on the northern Kentucky shore of the Ohio where it had been constructed; three years and four months drifting down the Ohio and the Mississippi; and fifteen months on the Intracoastal Waterway, in the bayous of Louisiana. In July 1951 they sold it to a Louisiana rancher who planned to remove the cabin and use the hull for ferrying cattle and farm implements about on his water-locked property. By then Harlan had already begun writing about the boat and the journey in what became his first book, *Shantyboat*, published in 1953.

Even as he was writing, the "amphibious race usually called shantyboaters" was dying out. Today's young readers, then, can only try to imagine a drifting way of life in "an ark which the river bears toward a warmer climate, better fishing grounds, and more plentiful and easier work on shore. . . . At one place after another the hopeful boatman lays over for a spell, until disillusioned, he lets his craft be caught up again by the river's current, to be carried like the driftwood, farther downstream. At last he beaches out for good somewhere in the south, where his children pass for natives." The drifting trip fed Harlan's hunger for that kind of rootlessness as well as his "innate longing to be untrammeled and independent, to live on the fringe of society, almost beyond the law, beyond taxes and ownership of property."

In his books Harlan told what he and Anna made of that shantyboat life, and the story of the journey itself, but he said little about its unconventionality. Some of their friends and former neighbors looked on them as if they had fallen from grace, he wrote. In fact, a step more conspicuously unconventional than becoming shantyboaters could hardly have been imagined. Most "respectable" people viewed shantyboats as cramped, messy, and dirty, and shantyboaters as shiftless, no-account water gypsies—unsavory remnants of the Great Depression of the 1930s. People did not want to be reminded of their previous hardships once the Depression had been dispelled by wartime mobilization and postwar prosperity. But Anna and Harlan ignored whatever disapproval may have been directed at them. They were secure in their identities and proud of their nonconformity.

When the shantyboat journey ended in 1951, Anna and Harlan extended their travels with a car-and-trailer camping trip through the West. And then they settled down alongside the Ohio River in Trimble County, Kentucky, at Payne Hollow. For the rest of their lives, everyday reminders of their shantyboating days were all around them—in the foods they ate and the way they prepared them; in objects that had made the trip with them, such as Harlan's tools, their musical instruments, the kerosene lamps they read by, and the box that held the firewood; and above all, in the river, especially during high water, when Anna wrote me that she remembered being tied up "behind the willows, from which safe vantage point we watched the swift muddy river rush by, full of drift."

Soon after *Shantyboat* was published, feature stories about the Hubbards began appearing in the Madison (Indiana), Louisville, and Cincinnati newspapers. The Hubbards prized solitude, but their unconventional life and Harlan's accomplishments eventually lured thousands of visitors to Payne Hollow. Harlan accepted commissions to paint large-scale river scenes for local banks and churches and began showing his paintings locally. His reputation as a painter and writer spread throughout the Ohio River valley; his second book, *Payne Hollow: Life on the Fringe of Society*, appeared in 1974, and his exhibitions grew more numerous and spread farther afield. In December 1986 he received the Artist Award for Lifetime Achievement from the governor of Kentucky. The following year he saw published the first volume of his journals, written from 1929 to 1944. His third and last book, *Shantyboat on the Bayous*, was published in 1990, two years after his death. Two more volumes of journals followed.

In all these writings, however, Anna remained a shadowy figure. Harlan's focus was on his painting and his life in nature, and by his own admission, he was emotionally reticent. Anna did virtually no public writing and left no journal or diary. And so the questions that readers of Harlan's books have always asked about Anna have gone unanswered: What in Anna prepared her for housekeeping on and alongside the river, without electricity? How did she spend her days? What did she think and feel about the life she had chosen? What was, or at least seemed to be, the nature of her relationship with Harlan? What lay behind her famed reserve?

In October 1993 I went to a funeral in Cincinnati. My parents and Uncle Dan had been dead for years, and now Uncle Dan's wife, Carleen, had died too. I had just turned fifty, and the last of my older generation was gone. Helping to empty Carleen's apartment refreshed many memories of all of them, and of friends I hadn't thought about for a long time—Anna and Harlan. When they had cast off in the shantyboat, they left their house rented to my parents, bachelor Uncle Dan, and three-year-old me. I grew up taking their presence in my life so for granted, they had seemed like family. After Carleen's funeral I returned home to Virginia, battered by waves of nostalgia, and sat down to reread my letters from Anna, all eighty-eight of them, spanning twenty-eight years. She had died in 1986, and we hadn't communicated since 1978.

Rereading Anna's letters, I felt the loss of her, and missed her, for the first time. Now I wanted to find the letters I had written to Anna.

I wanted to relive our good times and learn more about the child I had been when she was my grown-up playmate, and I wanted to find reason to forgive myself for having cut off contact with her. Almost immediately, the idea of writing a book sprang up. I began searching out other people who had known the Hubbards. By spring 1994 I knew that my letters were not in the University of Louisville Archives with the rest of the Hubbard papers and probably hadn't survived. I put away the hope of finding them, and with it the book idea. But the book idea kept simmering, and when it came to the boil again in summer 1995, I started writing about Anna.

As I researched and wrote, I visualized Anna's life as existing behind three doors. Behind the first, the outer door, was her factual life. She was born the first of three daughters to Nellie and John Eikenhout in Grand Rapids in 1902 and brought up in the strict Dutch tradition. She was very close to her two younger sisters, Etta and Nella Mae. The great joys of her youth were summer vacations on Michigan lakes, and music. After graduating Phi Beta Kappa from Ohio State in 1925 and teaching French for two years, she moved to Cincinnati at age twenty-five, worked for the next fifteen years as an assistant librarian, and married Harlan Hubbard.

Behind the second door, the inner door, I found Anna's gift for making the ordinary sacred. She crafted her daily life creatively, with artistic sensitivity, doing everyday things in a way that nourishes the spirit. This was the dignified, elegant, refined, charming, gracious Anna whom her friends described to me warmly and admiringly. It's also the Anna I knew as a child and remember with appreciation and love.

Finally I came to the hidden door, the one marked Private. Behind that door, women of Anna's generation and upbringing kept the "inappropriate" emotions: fear, passion, sorrow, disappointment, anger, depression. Getting through that last door—finding out who Anna really was, behind the mistress-of-Payne-Hollow image that has built up around her—meant brushing past Anna's reserve and privacy, which were mentioned by nearly everyone I spoke to about her.

Written sources of information about Anna are not plentiful. She left only one piece of public writing, an article on the shantyboat days for *Library Journal* in 1954, and the most revealing portions of it are not in the published version but in the surviving drafts. In 1982 she wrote a short, unpublished autobiographical sketch that is largely nostalgic. She did not reveal herself in the letters she wrote after marrying Harlan.

Of Anna's before-Harlan letters, a biographer would hold highest hopes for the ones she wrote to her two sisters, but they are few and disappointing. Anna's early surviving letters to Nella Mae are big-sisterly at best. Etta, who in her lifetime made a series of moves to ever-smaller residences and didn't save letters in general, destroyed all but Anna's 1980s letters. A few of them reveal the hidden Anna, but only if the reader knows the facts behind Anna's interpretations.

I located the adult children of Anna's intimate high school friends, Lee Holden Thiele and Hilda Bell Webber. They searched their homes for before-Harlan letters from Anna to their mothers, and three such letters were found, all written to Lee. In them Anna revealed her heart openly and poignantly. Because revealing letters written by Anna are scarce, I looked all the more carefully for reflections of her hidden heart in before-Harlan letters she received from Hilda, Lee, her mother, and her Cincinnati friend Barre (pronounced "Barry") Pritchett. However, no letters from them or anyone else dated between 1928 and 1933, Anna's first five years in Cincinnati, seem to have survived. (Perhaps Anna did not begin saving letters until the early 1930s, when she herself reached her thirties.)

Another gap in the letters Anna received falls during Anna and Harlan's courtship and first year of marriage: archived letters from Hilda and Lee stop abruptly in early 1940 and resume in late 1944. The only mention of Harlan I found from that period is in a letter from Anna's mother on the eve of the wedding. Consequently there are no archived letters to Anna from which to deduce what, if anything, Anna told her good friends about Harlan.

Few letters between Anna and Harlan survive; they seldom had to write any, because they lived just across the river from each other before their marriage. Afterward their only separations occurred when Anna was briefly visiting family in Michigan. Seven letters from such periods have been found, two written by Harlan and five by Anna.

Accuracy was important to me in putting Anna's life on the record. Though I have kept the endnotes to a minimum, everything I've written about Anna's and Harlan's thoughts, feelings, and actions (except my own clearly identified imaginings) is backed up by sources: my few explicit memories of conversations with them; their published and unpublished writings; more than seventy interviews I conducted, almost entirely by telephone, from 1995 to 1998; various writings about the Hubbards (I relied little on newspaper articles); letters they wrote and received; conversations taped by interviewers; and letters that Anna's sister Etta wrote to friends after Anna's death. In editing Anna's letters I combined short paragraphs, and rather than use "[sic]," I corrected her infrequent lapses in spelling and punctuation. As for the portions of the book in which I have relied on my own memories, the usual warning about memoir applies: this is what happened *as I remember it*.

Accuracy was important to me, but objectivity—the exclusion of personal feelings and interpretations—was out of the question. Not only is my relationship with Anna an illuminating window on her personality, it is the window through which I see her life and through which I was gazing as I wrote this book.

1

In the Studio

We want you to know that we think of you often and like to recall the fine times we all had together last summer. I look at your picture, Mia dear, and I realize how fortunate I am to have such a dear little friend.

Anna to Mia, February 3, 1952

In summer 1950 there was one more year of the shantyboat adventure yet to come. Anna and Harlan's southward drifting had ended at New Orleans in the spring, and in July they were moving west through the bayous of Louisiana on the Intracoastal Waterway, towing the shantyboat with a flat-bottomed rowboat and a cantankerous motor, when they decided to make a trip back to Fort Thomas. Their rented house needed some work, and Anna wanted to visit her family in Grand Rapids. Leaving the shantyboat and the dogs with friends in Bayou Lafourche, Anna and Harlan returned to Fort Thomas and took up temporary residence in the rustic studio in the backyard.

They had rented their house in 1946 to the McTamney family— my parents, Rose and Harry; Harry's younger brother, Dan; and me, Mia, aged three. Dan had sought Harlan out in 1942, the year before I was born, and bought two of his paintings ("Too bad there aren't more like him," Harlan wrote to his brother Frank). Dan visited the Hubbards at Brent, the sparsely populated shantyboat community on the Ohio River at the edge of Fort Thomas, where they built the shantyboat and lived aboard it for two years, and at least once he took me along. Of the thousands of names recorded in Anna's guest book from 1944 to 1986, Dan's name is the fourth, and I am close behind him, on page two. Though I was less than two years old at the time, Anna gave me first billing: May 29, 1945, in Anna's pretty handwriting, "Mia McTamney, with Dan." The following July, with the shantyboat journey due to begin in five months, we McTamneys left

Cincinnati and moved across the river into Kentucky and the Hubbards' house.

When the Hubbards came back to Fort Thomas in 1950, Anna found seven-year-old Mia looking for a grown-up playmate. My mother kept to the house and was no longer active in her own life or mine. What she was sad about, or afraid of, I never knew. I have few memories of doing things together with her after I was reading on my own and going to school, and by the time I was ten she was spending the whole day sitting at the kitchen table. To me, home was protection and love, but I wanted more—I wanted *action.*

As for Anna, little girls brought out an "elfin streak" in her, Harlan wrote, and "little Mia" appealed to her on several counts: I am a blend of German and Irish, but I could have passed for a little Dutch girl (Anna was 100 percent Dutch), with my round face, blue eyes, pale to rosy complexion, and light blond hair. What's more, I was shy and quiet, like Anna, and because I lacked playmates my own age and had not yet been exposed to television, I had learned to entertain myself. Above all other attractions I was bright; Anna liked bright children. By summer 1950 I had completed first grade at the Summit Country Day School, a Catholic private school in Cincinnati operated by the Sisters of Notre Dame, a refined order of nuns founded in Belgium. On the brink of second grade I was reading above my grade level and was about to begin receiving French and piano lessons. Anna, you see, was a book-loving former librarian, a former teacher of French, and an accomplished cellist and pianist. In short, if Anna had special-ordered a little girl to share her interests with and to nurture intellectually, she could scarcely have asked for more.

Each morning I waited with my nose pressed against our kitchen window until Anna opened the studio door, my cue to run down to her. On the go every minute in that oversized dollhouse in my backyard, Anna rarely sat down except to read a book with me, and she taught me to do the things she was doing. We swept the floor, we cooked food outdoors, we set the table, and we washed and dried the blue-and-white dishes.

When I had grown up and was visiting my parents at home in Fort Thomas, I would sometimes go down again to the studio. I would take the long black iron key off its hook inside our pantry and walk down the sloping lawn past the big maple tree. Standing on the flat stones in front of the studio, I would turn the key in the creaky lock, open the door gingerly, and stand back so that birds, raccoons, and heaven-knows-what-else could make their escape. As I stepped over the threshold, the first familiar breath of dampness and wood smoke brought flooding over me the memory of a chubby, fair-haired little girl and a tall, slim woman with a lilting voice. I still see them standing together just inside the door at an old-fashioned washstand with a rosy marble top. The woman is washing and rinsing blue-and-white dishes in two enameled basins, and the little girl is drying them carefully with a linen dish towel. . . .

For a child, the studio was an enchanted cottage in a secret garden. Near the front door of the studio was a tall hedge of lilacs, and down behind them in the studio's backyard was the wild ruin of an old-fashioned garden with remnants of iris, peonies, and hollyhocks. Once in those early years, Anna came hurrying to see the strange new flower I had spotted in the wild garden, a tall purple one. When she saw it was only a common thistle—a weed, most people would call it—she pretended to be as excited as I was, enabling me to keep seeing it as a flower for the rest of my life.

At the top of the yard, on the kitchen end of the house, were narcissus and sweet peas, and a rose-of-Sharon hedge. The other end of the house jutted out slightly into the backyard, forming a nook where a birdbath nestled in a thick bed of lily of the valley. Roses climbed on trellises in the front yard—pink roses alongside the garage and red ones at the front door. Honeysuckle grew wild all around.

When the Hubbards were occupying the studio, they seldom came up to the house. They both seemed out of place in it, even Harlan, who had built it himself for his mother and lived there with her for twenty years. After marrying Anna he had turned his back on the house with relief. He had built it in 1923, when he himself was just twenty-three, modeling it after an old Kentucky farmhouse he saw on a country road whose name he forgot, and he considered it "an attractive place of character and originality." A visitor in the early 1930s remembered it fifty years later as a "pristine, white cottage" with numerous violins hanging on the white walls. The McTamneys kept the frame exterior white but added color inside. Upstairs were a bathroom and two bedrooms. A low door in the bathroom led to a crawl space under the sharply sloping roof. Downstairs were the kitchen and pantry, the dining room, and the living room with its stone fireplace and small enclosed porch.

The house meant no more to Anna than to Harlan; her honeymoon cottage and first real home of her own was the studio. "If you can get all your things in your cello case, you can come live in the studio," Harlan had teased her. She and Harlan lived there from their wedding day in April 1943 until they began camping at Brent and building the shantyboat in late 1944.

Harlan had built the studio in 1938, of brick, timber, stone, and slate, and described it later as "a solid, harmonious structure." He enjoyed building it, because it had no wiring or plumbing to entangle him in building codes, formal plans, or additional workers. What's more, the materials pleased him. Long before the word "recycling" was fashionable, Harlan routinely used secondhand materials. The walls, whitewashed inside, were of used handmade brick, and the frame for the large north-facing window in the upper half of the back wall he acquired cheap because it had been run over by a truck. As in all his dwellings, the fireplace was the central feature. The quarter-circle fireplace with its raised hearth occupied the right-hand corner below the big window. Down beyond the garden was a wild ravine with abandoned farmland and a decaying pear orchard. In the studio Harlan was living as close to the fringe of society as his circumstances then permitted.

After the wedding Anna domesticated the studio without introducing any fripperies. Two sections of a walnut bookcase were brought down from the house and put into the back corner opposite the fireplace. An old pie safe—gray enameled tin, as I remember it—made a useful cupboard beside the washstand, and a rocking chair and the little cookstove from Harlan's camp were added. Here and there Anna placed some of her old Dutch brass things from her mother's family. After a few months she had her upright piano moved over from her shared apartment in Cincinnati. Harlan ran electrical current down from the house somehow so that they could use their record player and Anna could do her ironing, and he toted water in buckets from the outdoor tap at the lily-of-the-valley birdbath. They did their cooking on the hearth or atop the little cookstove in the studio, or over the small stonework grill out back, in the hillock below the lilacs. Harlan wrote proudly to Frank about the new domesticity, emphasizing that for all the changes there had been no interference with his painting.

The studio was the subject of Anna and Harlan's first woodcut Christmas card in 1943, and Harlan gave Anna an undated photo of the studio, taken in an earlier winter before he had planted the lilacs, which he inscribed, "To Anneke who is always with me."

In fall 1950 Anna and Harlan went back to Louisiana, and I began second grade. A few months later, my first letter from Anna arrived:

February 22, 1951

Dear Little Mia,

The lovely silk scarf you gave me for my birthday has given me so much pleasure and comfort this winter—I want to tell you how much I have enjoyed wearing it. Every time Harlan and I go on what we call an expedition, I put on your scarf as an essential part of my costume. Often we go in the motorboat, several miles, to the nearest town to shop or ask for mail. These motorboat rides are usually cold, so I put on an extra jacket, and always tie the soft scarf around my neck to keep out the chill breezes. If I am wearing my yellow sweater, I turn the golden yellow square of the scarf out; and you remember there are squares of blue and pink and green, as well, to match sweaters or blouses of those colors. And every time I put on the colorful scarf, I think of my little Mia.

We had fun together last summer, didn't we?—washing dishes, and wiping them with our Johnny Appleseed towel, and sweeping and getting lunch. Remember the day you made the corn soup, Mia? . . .

I suppose school and schoolwork occupy your thoughts and all your time now. I am sure your report card is another solid sheet of excellent grades. I know very well that you lead your class in reading; it was a real pleasure to have you read aloud to me last summer: impossible to imagine more animated or more appreciative reading. Are you still getting gold stars on your piano lessons, too? I hope so, and I hope you will go on with your study of music, because music can be a source of great joy for you all your life. . . .

I think you might like this town where Harlan and I are now. St. Martinville is the name of it. Someday you may read the story of Evangeline and how she and many other Acadians came to this very place on Bayou Têche. She came on a boat, down the Ohio River and the Mississippi River, and then through the bayous, just as Harlan and I have come on our boat. Even now, the people of this part of Louisiana speak French, as they are descendants of those early French-speaking people from Acadia.

It is time to build our evening fire now and get supper. I hear the cathedral bell ringing the Angelus. Best regards to your mother and father and Uncle Dan. And love to my dear Mia. Harlan says hello to everyone, too.

> Yours affectionately,
> Anna

Anyone else reading that letter might be surprised that its recipient was only seven and a half years old. By never talking down to me, in letters or in person, Anna gently forced me to talk up to her. She listened to me as if what I said was important. She made me feel grown up, and I tried to make everything I said to her interesting and worthwhile.

In her second letter to me, a year later, Anna developed her favorite themes, music and books:

> When I think of Mia, of course I wonder how her piano playing is progressing. You made such a fine start, Mia. Your playing last summer showed great promise. I feel sure that under the Sister's guidance you have learned much this winter. I shall be eager to hear you play when next we come home to Kentucky.
>
> I expect you are the head of your class in school, as you have always been, and way ahead of your grade in writing and reading. We find that so many people these days do not take time to read books, they only sit and stare at the television shows. I am so glad that you have discovered the joy of reading good books—it is a pleasure that will increase with your years, and make your whole life richer.

As much as Christmas and birthdays, but more frequent, Anna's letters were a constant in my childhood. The letters that began coming from Payne Hollow in 1953 were full of the currents of her daily life: birds, wildflowers, the river, changing of the seasons, blazing hearth fires, concertgoing, homemaking, and reading aloud and playing music with Harlan. Harlan's activities, too, came in for frequent mentions: his painting and gardening, the publishing of his books, and his progress with enlarging the house, building his studio-workshop, and keeping goats.

But the theme I heard loudest in Anna's letters was her praise of my accomplishments in reading and piano, and her interest in my progress. No little fish ever rose more merrily to tastier bait. I loved playing the piano and reading, and I was hungry for Anna's specific, ego-bolstering praise. When I tried to astonish my parents with my doings, the highest tribute I could extract from them was, "That's wonderful, Honey." It was as if my mere arrival on Earth, twelve years into their marriage, healthy, was all they could want. Anna was my best audience.

Anna's early letters were a drumbeat of praise and expectations. From several of the first letters, when I was nine and ten: *I didn't have a chance to hear you play your new piece. You will have __all__ of it ready to play for us by the time we come again. . . . I'm counting on hearing that newest piece next time we're in Fort Thomas. You may even have time . . . to learn another of the pieces in your red-covered collection . . . . We must learn some new* [duets] *to play. And we'll expect to hear your latest solo pieces, too, Mia. . . . It was such a shame you had to be sick with a fever. Now we will have to start counting on the next time Harlan and I get to Fort Thomas, to play duets together, you and I.*

With the arrival of sixth grade and adolescence, I told my parents I was quitting piano lessons; I wanted to do whatever it was the other girls were doing during that class period. If I didn't want to take piano lessons anymore, my parents responded, I could go to the parish school up the street instead. That was the abrupt end of my rebellion; I loved the Summit dearly. For twelve years I rode a school bus back and forth across the river to be educated in that sprawling late-Victorian edifice where the nuns, in their floor-length black costumes with veils and huge starched white collars, lived in the convent in one distant wing and boys (only through eighth grade) were taught in another.

At Distribution, the quarterly scholastic awards ceremony, medal-ribbons were handed out for the academic subjects and for conduct and courtesy as well. The nuns believed in rewarding excellence conspicuously, and to draw excellence out of us they stimulated competition by means of contests. I couldn't resist the chance to shine, and while I was earning medals and holy cards from the nuns, some of my classmates began calling me—not with affection—"the Brain."

Piano was another arena for shining. Before my feet could reach the pedals, the nuns had me playing little pieces for Distribution, and in eighth grade I began soloing in the annual spring concert. In high school my classmate and friend Susie and I played two-piano arrangements in the high-ceilinged auditorium, Saint Cecilia's Hall, facing each other onstage at two long, shiny Baldwin concert grands.

The nuns also cultivated the social graces, and in that sphere I got my comeuppance. I was a wallflower. I dreaded the semiannual grade school dances, which started, for me, in fifth grade. Nevertheless, I apparently made the boys and the dances into good reading for Anna. "I love to hear about your school dances," she wrote when I was in sixth grade, "and especially which of your pretty dresses you wore." In writing to Anna I accentuated studies and music and, to keep the admiration and approval coming, put the best possible face on my pitiful social life. Consequently Anna never had an accurate picture of my Summit existence. I was fourteen when Anna revealed why she cared so about my dances and other activities: "I was much too shy when I was your age," she confessed in a letter, "and I missed a lot of fun. I don't want you to miss anything worthwhile."

Anna didn't hear of the scare about my quitting piano until it was over. "We're mighty glad to hear you are continuing to study piano," she wrote. "You're just getting a good start; you must not think of stopping for a long time to come." She dangled a surprise, which she was keeping until her next visit to the studio and which depended "on how well you are playing the piano when we hear you again."

School was still in session when Anna and Harlan arrived in Fort Thomas for their Christmastime visit. Late in the afternoon on a cold December day, I raced down to the studio the minute I came home. The first order of business was my playing for Anna—and for Harlan, too, but he was only audience; Anna was judge. With my back to the cozy fire I sat down at her old upright piano, the one we played duets on, and played Beethoven's "Für Elise." Played it well enough to merit the surprise, which was this: the three of us were going to play trios.

I don't remember Anna *inviting* me to play trios; I believe she just propped the music book up in front of me, in the spirit of giving me the finest present in the world. With Anna on cello and Harlan on violin, we played two or three short, simple numbers. That day, and whenever we played, Anna let me choose the pieces and set the tempo, but she was in charge of quality control; if the playing wasn't up to snuff, she would call a halt and decree what spot we would start over from.

Anna wrote later that our first trio session was "more than [they] had dared hope for." I cared only that I had gotten through it without making any serious mistakes, looking bad in front of Harlan, or disappointing Anna. What I liked best about trio playing that day was the praise and the relief when it was over. I had no idea how happy I had made Anna that December afternoon in the studio, or what hopes she held for the three of us as a trio. Music, I know now, was food, water, and air to her. She liked the way it made her feel, and she liked the orderliness of its beats and measures. It was language to her, too. She wanted certain music at certain times, depending on her mood. For Anna there was no greater fun than playing music with a friend. She and Harlan played together nearly every day, and they would drop everything to play with visiting fellow musicians. Their first experience together outside the Cincinnati Public Library, where they met, had been the playing of music.

Anna told me indirectly how it was for her, playing with Harlan, when she wrote to me in 1955 about accompanying (the italics are mine): "Some people who play solos quite well simply are no good at accompanying. It takes a special something to know when to keep in the background and when to play out to give the soloist support and when, occasionally, the piano has a real solo passage or phrase. . . . The thing is to think of the piece as a whole, not as a violin part with an accompanying piano part, but as one piece of music. You feel as if you were playing the violin part yourself, *you are in such perfect accord with the violinist.*"

Trio playing became a ritual part of my visits with the Hubbards. In the beginning I was flattered to have been chosen, but as my teens came on, self-consciousness and anxiety kept me from developing into a full-fledged trios partner. I avoided the trio playing when I could, and took it like medicine the rest of the time. Because I resisted progressing beyond the easy pieces we had started with, our trio playing was never more than an exercise in nostalgia. By the time I was in high school, Anna had given up pressing me to try more advanced music.

Anna expected the best from me in everything I did, and so for as long as I knew her I tried to show her only my best self. In the 1950s young females were still being trained to please, and I had been trained well. I wanted to please Anna, but meeting her expectations became increasingly difficult with the passing years, and one day the desire to keep trying would desert me for good.

But first there would be visits to Payne Hollow. My eyes and ears would be opened to the natural world, and I would be immersed in the now-fabled Payne Hollow life. From 1954 to 1960 I spent a total of six weeks there, alone with Anna and Harlan. In my memory today, those weeks occupy the space of whole summers—my Payne Hollow summers.

2

Payne Hollow Summers

Mia, dear, I think so often of those happy times when you came to live with us for a little while in the summer—wasn't that great fun!

Anna to Mia, April 22, 1969

Anna's letter of May 30, 1954, spelled out the directions to the Indiana side of the river across from Payne Hollow. "You stay with us as long as you like," she wrote; "the longer you stay, the more fun we can have." I was not quite eleven years old, taking my first trip away from home alone, and to Payne Hollow! On a sultry Sunday morning in mid-June, Daddy set out driving, with Mom and me, down U.S. 42 through old Kentucky river towns: Warsaw, Ethridge, Ghent, Carrollton. At Milton we crossed the river bridge to Madison, Indiana, and followed Anna's directions to the O'Neals' farmhouse, where we left the car and walked down the lane to the riverbank, arriving about noon.

I was impatient as the procedure for summoning Harlan was explained to us by Bill Shadrick, who was living there in his beached-out shantyboat at a shady spot on the Indiana riverbank called Lee's Landing. For a gong, Harlan had hung from a tree a piece of sheet iron and something to pound on it with (a farm bell came later). My father did the honors, and an answering ruckus went up from across the river. Daddy chatted with Bill while I scanned the opposite shoreline. A distant speck approached as I watched, spellbound. Both literally and figuratively, Harlan came into focus for me that day, rowing toward us across the wide, shimmering river.

Harlan was then fifty-four years old, two years older than my father. Daddy had the pallor and the portly silhouette typical of a sedentary city-dwelling man his age, but Harlan—shirtless and barefoot, with the legs of his blue denims rolled up—was brown from working in the sun, and he had no spare fat anywhere. His arms were well muscled, and the veins stood out on his arms and legs. Though the river is a half mile wide at Payne Hollow and he had to row against a cross-current, he wasn't even breathing hard when he pulled in at Bill's landing. With a big smile, Harlan greeted us in his reedy, high-pitched voice and lingered just long enough to exchange a few pleasantries with Bill. Harlan assigned us our seats in the johnboat (a flat-bottomed rowboat squared off at both ends), and the McTamney landlubbers clambered aboard. In mid-river a towboat passed by, pushing its rows and columns of barges, and Harlan gauged his rowing carefully to give us the safe thrill of crossing its churning wake.

Waiting for Harlan on the dock was Sambo—big, black, placid, mostly Labrador retriever Sambo, always damp if not dripping wet. His mother, Skipper, a dainty little black-and-white terrier who avoided the water, had given birth to him on the shantyboat in 1948, and they had been companions from then on, the unlikeliest mother-and-pup combination imaginable. Now Skipper was dead, and Sambo was the only dog at Payne Hollow.

We paused with Sambo at the dock and watched Harlan pull up his fish box from the water and remove a catfish. Without any fuss he knocked it on the head and took it ashore, and there on the gently sloping riverbank, in the shade of the big cottonwood tree, Harlan made a second tremendous impression on me—so much so, that with my Kodak Brownie camera I captured the scene in my first Payne Hollow snapshot. One moment Harlan was standing, talking face to face with Daddy, and the next he was squatting on his heels, the catfish still in his hands. Folded like an accordion, he spent several minutes gutting, cleaning, and filleting the fish, and then he straightened right up again, all with perfect ease. I hadn't known a grown man could do such things.

I puffed and chuffed up the hill through the garden to the terrace, and here came Anna in her neat slacks and blouse, striding down the broad stone steps, tall, slim, straight, and full of energy. Greeting me and my parents, she was all smiles, singing a cheery hello. Anna was nearing fifty-two that summer, and there was some gray in her necklength ash-blond hair, which was pulled back behind her ears and held with combs. In the 1950s she was still getting her hair cut and permed in town. Though her hair changed over the years, her complexion didn't; her skin remained smooth and pale, almost translucent. Standing close to her, I caught the familiar scent of Anna's only cosmetic, the Noxzema cream she washed her face with.

Anna introduced us to another guest, and by the time Harlan had washed up and pulled on a T-shirt we were seated on the shady stone terrace and being served a bountiful noontime dinner, cooked outdoors, featuring groundhog. Knowing the McTamneys wouldn't be up to groundhog, Anna and Harlan had extended the menu with catfish, fried to a delicious crisp in cornmeal and dried basil. The other guest informed us that the groundhog tasted like chicken. (Some visitors, I've learned since, thought it tasted like pork.)

The Hubbards considered these vegetarian varmints tasty, particularly the young, corn-fed ones. In a sense the groundhogs were Harlan's livestock, since it was his corn they were so well fed on. The young, tender ones Anna fried, and the older ones she browned and then steamed in tomatoes in a Dutch oven (a cast-iron pot with a tight domed lid), later adding potatoes and other vegetables. The Hubbards had appreciated groundhog as delicious food and a source of protein, and counted on their dogs as groundhog hunters, since the second of their long summer layovers in the shantyboat, in 1948 at Bizzle's Bluff on the Cumberland River. There Skipper and Sambo had worked out a joint hunting method. Skipper spent hours nosing around and treed the quarry. Her barking brought Sambo, and together they barked for Harlan. If Harlan didn't come running, Sambo ran to get him. Then Harlan would climb the tree, if necessary—barefoot—and shake the victim loose.

Soon it was time for Harlan to row my parents and the other guest back across the river. Now my first Payne Hollow summer really began, when Anna and I were left in peace in the cabin. Cleaning up after a meal was no chore for Anna and me—it was a ceremony. Anna washed the blue-and-white dishes and I dried them with a linen towel, and we chatted, just as we did in the studio. Here, though, we had something to look at while we worked, a view of the wooded hillside through Anna's wide kitchen window. We glanced up often, taking in the play of dappled light, the flitting of birds, the stirring of leaves in a rare midday breeze.

I learned where the dishes and pots were to be put away, and then Anna showed me the features of the cabin. It held even more delights than the studio, because there were lots more things in it and lots more shelves, cabinets, and drawers to tuck them away in. Anna explained about the drinking water. The cool, pure water Harlan carried up from the spring at the creek was on the countertop in the copper bucket. I still remember the shivery sensation of drinking from the cold copper dipper.

Next Anna escorted me to the privy and explained how to use it, although she never used the word "privy" or "outhouse." One went "up the hill" or to the "annex." Being young and a novice in the country, I was apprehensive about these arrangements, but I took to going "up the hill" right away, when I found there was nothing about it to offend my sensibilities. Inside were a bucket of ashes and a small shovel. In lieu of flushing, one dropped in a shovelful of ashes and put the lid down. Protected inside a large tin can was a roll of conventional paper—Anna insisted on it. The only precaution necessary in the annex, and I learned it for myself, was that after lifting the lid and before sitting down, it was a good idea to give the daddy longlegs a chance to escape.

The rest of the day was typical of the Hubbards' summer days at Payne Hollow. Anna puttered indoors (I read a book), and Harlan was nowhere to be seen, and in the late afternoon he and Anna came together to play some cello-and-violin music. After supper, the lighter meal of the day, served on the terrace, the three of us and Sambo went out in the johnboat to bait the fishing line, leaving the dishes for later. While Harlan baited hooks at one end of the boat, Anna and I divided our attention between the sunset and Harlan's deft skewering of the silvery little minnows.

Indoors again, we needed the kerosene lamps to illumine our dishwashing. Through the kitchen window Anna and I watched the last light disappearing from the hillside and the first blinkings of the lightning bugs. Now it was time for the extended evening reading that was part of Anna and Harlan's routine and one of their greatest pleasures. Three times a day, after each meal and usually in front of the fireplace, they read aloud together.

From 1942 to 1978 Anna kept a list of books that she and Harlan had read together (see the appendix). With duplications omitted there are nearly seven hundred weighty titles on it. The fiction is mostly nineteenth century. ("We don't care for the modern novel," Anna declared.) There are novels, short stories, plays, and poetry in English, German, and French. (People are awed that the Hubbards not only read all the volumes of Marcel Proust's *À la recherche du temps perdu* [Remembrance of things past]—they read it in French.) Many of the nonfiction titles are from the "seven hundreds" (the fine arts classification in the Dewey decimal system used by libraries), Anna's former domain as a librarian. The great number of entries related to art, artists, music, and composers is rivaled by the number on exploration and travel. Timeless literature figures prominently, such as works of Lao-Tzu, Aeschylus, Sophocles, Erasmus, Shakespeare, Emerson, Thoreau, and Schweitzer, and Japanese and Chinese poetry, art, and thought. From the impressive list, no one would ever know that of all the world's great literature, children's literature was Anna's favorite: Harlan said so after she died.

To get ready for our reading, "each man" (Anna's phrase) had a task to do, and all was done in a jiffy. While Harlan rounded up the chairs, I pushed the reading table into position facing the fireplace. The reading table, a low drop-leaf chest on casters, did quadruple duty as table, seating, storage, and support for the bed. Meanwhile Anna assembled the reading light, which consisted of two kerosene lamps and a holder Harlan had made for them, an H-shaped wooden stand slightly taller than it was wide. The shelf crosspiece of the H was just the right size to hold the lamps. With the lamps in place, two flat, rectangular reflector shades made of sturdy aluminum were affixed, one on each side, at a slanting angle.

At last the designated reader took the current book from the bookcase, and the listeners took up their current handwork. Anna often had mending or knitting to do; sometimes she worked on netting a fishnet from twine. If Harlan wasn't shucking popcorn, he was shelling, sorting, or toasting some type of beans. My regular assignment was black-walnut picking. Anna showed me how to dig out the meat from the labyrinthine shells with a nutpick and search out shell fragments.

The names of the books we read from have escaped my memory, but the scene is still vivid. In the glow of the lamplight we were surrounded by tones and shadows of warm wood colors and, beyond the enchanted circle, by the dark and the racket of the nighttime insects. As we bent our attention to our work and to the murmuring voice of the reader, we three were alone in the world and content.

After the reading, everything was put away shipshape and the bed, an open wooden box containing rubber air mattresses, was lowered. In the daytime the bed stood upright in the corner with its underside facing out, looking like wall paneling. At night it was lowered into position under the window that faced the river, its head resting on the window seat with a certain few books supplying some necessary added elevation and its foot supported by the drop-leaf chest.

Next came the final ritual in my Payne Hollow day, getting ready for bed. At the left-hand end of the kitchen counter was the cabin's equivalent of a bathroom vanity cabinet. On the back of the cabinet door was a mirror, and inside were a towel rod, a paper-towel holder, and shelves for shaving and teeth-cleaning things. Behind the lower cabinet door was a bucket of water for washing. To the right of the bucket was what appeared to be a deep drawer, but the drawer front pulled out *and down*, sliding an enameled washbasin out of its storage place. The used water was tipped down the back of the false drawer and into a drainpipe that emptied outdoors.

Anna briefed me on all this, poured some hot water from the kettle into my washbasin for bathing—she was explicit about that—and left me a flashlight for going up the hill. Then Anna and Harlan turned their cabin over to me for the night. I wasn't curious then about where they slept, and if they told me, I have forgotten. Since they were experienced campers, they may have assembled a lean-to with a poncho, or slept in the surviving shell of the trailer they had camped in for more than a year after the shantyboating, or under the stars, as they had done behind the studio in Fort Thomas.

By lamplight I washed sketchily, brushed my teeth, poured the used water down the drain, and placed my flashlight at the ready, memorizing its position in case a nighttime sortie became necessary. I blew out my lamp. It was *dark*. Snug in my bed with its oddly comforting rubbery smell and listening to the night sounds, I felt transported into the pages of *The Swiss Family Robinson*.

Anna could steal about in silence indoors or out when she wanted to, but when she decided it was time for me to get up, the breakfast pots began to clatter on the terrace. It was chilly in the cabin, and I left my blankets reluctantly. I dressed fast and made my trip "up the hill."

The first activity in Anna's plan for me was accompanying Harlan as he "traced" the trotline. Harlan, who had been up for hours, was waiting for me down at the dock with Sambo. Sambo—all wet, of course—jumped aboard, and Harlan assigned me the role of casting off. Concentrating on not stumbling or falling into the river, I solemnly lifted the loop of rope holding us to the dock pile and dropped it into the johnboat. Mist was rising from the water as Harlan rowed out to the line. I replay the scene often: Hazy hills, a dog barking on the Indiana shore. Languid splash of a jumping fish, mesmerizing ripples. Fragrant morning, fragrant river. A veil of coolness just barely holding back the heat of the day. Harlan's rowing seemed all of a piece with the tranquil surroundings—smooth, economical of effort, harmonious and symmetrical. And wondrous, because there were no pins in the oarlocks to keep the long, heavy oars from slipping and turning. Harlan strong-armed them, not wasting energy by scooping the water, but efficiently skimming just below the surface.

Harlan shipped his oars and moved to the opposite end of the johnboat. Then he reached out and grasped the trotline buoy, a square, one-gallon can attached by a long piece of cotton twine to the trotline, which lay on the bottom, where the bottom-feeding catfish would find it. The line, too, was cotton twine, anchored by a heavy stone at the end. Each of his fifty hooks was tied onto a separate short piece of twine, and the pieces were tied to the line about three feet apart. As Harlan drew the trotline up slowly, hand over hand, the suspense was tantalizing: Would the next hook hold a fish? Would the next fish be even bigger than the one before? The day's catch flopped on the floor of the johnboat until, back at the dock, Harlan deposited the victims in the fish box.

Next came breakfast on the terrace and my introduction to the Hubbards' homemade whole-grain breakfast cereal. Since Harlan was the first one up in the morning—by star time, he said—it was his job to start the cereal cooking, which he did in the Dutch oven, used as a double boiler. It was ready in an hour and could stay on hold indefinitely. The recipe, a carryover from the shantyboat days, was a blend of coarsely ground toasted wheat and soybeans. Black walnuts, too, might be toasted along with the wheat before grinding, and the dish was usually topped off with raisins and brown sugar. Food for the gods, a local newspaper writer called it. Other young people who visited Payne Hollow loved it too, but to me, a confirmed Sugar Pops kid, it tasted—well, chewy. Anna's niece and nephews didn't like it either, when they began visiting a few years later; they were clever and surreptitiously tossed theirs over the edge of the terrace. I ate mine politely.

Before getting up from our breakfast we read aloud a bit, probably from the journal of some heroic sea voyage or expedition of discovery. Then there were the dishes to wash and the kerosene lamps to see to—refilling, trimming wicks, and washing the glass chimneys. Anna washed the chimneys every day and kept them shiny. Smoky chimneys aren't efficient, she said.

After breakfast, Anna often sent me out again with Harlan. One morning she sent me with him to get the mail, which meant hiking up the one-mile hill that led to the ridge, the farms, and the rural mailboxes. The path through the woods was pleasant going at first, and narrow as a deer trail. With Harlan leading, I could study his walk. He truly ambled, slow and steady, bent at the shoulders and the knees and completely relaxed, almost shuffling. He set his feet down one directly in front of the other, heel to toe. After we crossed the dry creek bed the trail widened and we began the climb, which even Harlan considered steep. Before long I was breathing hard and feeling prickly.

To me, breaking a sweat was a signal to stop what I was doing and regain my composure. Fortunately Harlan was sensitive to the needs of guests of all ages and physical conditions, and he was easy on me. Instead of his vertical shortcut he had taken the easier trail, the old roadbed between the ridge and Payne's Landing, where the steamboats used to stop, and he didn't seem to mind pausing often while I caught my breath. No doubt he used the breaks to good advantage, thinking and observing. Harlan is the only man I've ever climbed a hill with who didn't seem especially concerned about when, or whether, we reached the top.

Another time Anna suggested I go with Harlan to the spring to fetch drinking water—a shorter expedition, just right for the window of time between breakfast cleanup and the 10 A.M. beginning of dinner preparation. But first I had to smear a ring of Anna's homemade chigger repellent, a blend of shortening and powdered sulfur, around both ankles above my socks. Chiggers, the summertime scourge of the Midwest, are tiny mite larvae that lurk in the grass. They latch onto humans, crawl up into the places where the clothing fits snugly, and feed on their tasty hosts for days, itching devilishly.

It was leafy and cool at the spring, in the woods along the creek, but I was more impressed by the giant sunflowers that lined the path to the woods through the lower garden. I asked Harlan to pose for a picture, reaching up to bend a sunflower stalk twice his height. What on earth, I wonder, did he think about having a little girl tagging after him and posing him for pictures? Since he never wrote himself out of my morning schedule, I suppose he didn't find me too great a pest. At least I turned off the chatter when I was with Harlan, because I could tell he didn't care for it as Anna did.

I annoyed Harlan beyond endurance just once, when I was ten or eleven. Anna and Harlan were playing their music (cello and violin) in the one-room cabin, and I was the audience. The playing droned on until I was in a hot, sticky torpor. Some pesky flies had gotten inside, and I was absentmindedly flapping a flyswatter, hoping for a kill. Suddenly Harlan stopped playing, Anna stopped playing, and Harlan snapped, "If you're going to flap that thing, flap it in tempo!"

I couldn't have put this idea into words then, but I had disrupted the Payne Hollow equilibrium. The elevator behind my collarbone plunged to the cellar and was zooming back up with a fiery blush of shame, when Anna broke out laughing her best laugh. It was no belly laugh, but refined, lilting, soprano laughter projecting off the roof of her mouth like a well-produced singing voice. Her eyes were squeezed shut. What could anyone else do but join her? First Harlan chimed in with *his* best laugh, a subdued "heh-heh-heh" with a megawatt smile that made up for the lack of volume. Then I followed, greatly relieved.

The incident taught me a valuable lesson in maintaining the equilibrium without, thanks to Anna, teaching me to be wary of Harlan. When my Payne Hollow summers were behind me, my impression of him was unchanged: I was, and am, awed by the ease with which he inhabited his body and by his sure touch with everything he handled, from fish hooks to gasoline engines. He knew everything there was to know about the place where he lived and how to live there. He was *competent*, a word I use now as if I were bestowing a medal.

After the morning reading and the morning activity with Harlan, it was time to help Anna begin preparing dinner. It was puzzling to a city child like me that Anna and Harlan worked so much of the day just to put food on the table. But of course that was the point of Harlan's way of living. The work was pleasure to him, and what better use of time than to enjoy it?

Some green beans wanted picking, so Anna put on her pink sunbonnet and took me out to the upper garden to show me where they were and how to judge their size. While my little bucket filled up with green beans I grew moist and salty, and butterflies began sampling me. Instead of giving me an edifying lesson on butterflies' attraction to salt, Anna let me believe they were attracted to *me*. Out among the green beans I took a picture of Anna in her pink sunbonnet, faded from many washings and ironings. It was the same sunbonnet that had shaded her face from the southern sun during the shantyboating years, the same one Harlan had seen in a store window in a river town on the Ohio, long before he knew Anna, and bought "on a sudden impulse, thinking I might find someone who would like to wear it."

Except for conferring with Harlan over the seed catalogs, herb gardening and picking vegetables were Anna's only involvements in the Payne Hollow garden. The division of labor at Payne Hollow was clear: Harlan's domain was outside and Anna's was inside. Out of personal delicacy she shunned dirt, freckling, and sweating, but I think an even greater deterrent to gardening was her memory of the summer of Harlan's ruptured appendix and peritonitis, when she had worked like a field hand to save the shantyboat garden.

It was 1949, their third year of shantyboat drifting, when Anna and Harlan tied up in early March for the third and last of their long layovers, at a spot on the Mississippi River called Bisland Bayou, six miles above Natchez. As they had done twice before, they would plant a garden and can food for the winter, then resume drifting in December. Providing his own food was vital to Harlan's vision of his life in nature. Without gardening and canning, the Hubbards would be dependent on store-bought food. The thought was intolerable to Harlan and therefore to Anna too.

An early garden was well under way in early May when Harlan's pain and fever began. As he set out to drift and row downstream to Natchez and medical help, he told Anna to stay behind and plant the sweet potatoes, which she did. Later she joined him in the hospital and stayed with him, and by the time he was released, the garden had died of neglect. Another week later he was declared cured and began digging up bottomland for a late garden, but the fever returned, and Harlan was hospitalized again. This time, however, Anna didn't stay with him; she spent every possible minute working in the garden.

When Harlan was released the second time, in early June, he was forbidden garden duty for nearly a month. Meanwhile Anna kept at it, and Harlan continued the writing of *Shantyboat* (his working title was *"Driftwood"*), which he had started in the hospital. Later, in *Shantyboat*, he gave Anna the credit she deserved for managing the housework and cooking, plus nursing him, sawing and splitting firewood, and single-handedly reclaiming the garden, but in comments he made at the time, he seemed to take her effort for granted: "Anna has done well in keeping [the garden] going," says his journal for June 18. "She takes a real interest in it." A week later he wrote to a friend, "As you know, Anna can handle any situation. You should see her cut wood and work in the garden."

Heat, humidity, insect bites, sun, dirt, and fatigue must have tormented Anna that June. (If she suffered, in addition, from a lack of praise, I'm unaware that she ever said so.) Surrendering to the bugs and the weeds just that once would have been reasonable, but Anna refused to give up. Focusing her powers of determination on that garden, she showed how tremendous was her commitment to Harlan's chosen way of living, and to Harlan himself.

Besides picking vegetables I was privileged to have other food-preparation assignments as well. Being admitted to Anna's kitchen was no automatic thing even for adults. Some of the grown women who visited Payne Hollow weren't permitted to do anything but dry dishes, and one of Anna's good friends had been visiting for ten years before Anna allowed her to dry even the pots and pans. But Anna had trained me herself from age seven, and she knew I would do things *her* way.

My unfailing task was to set the table with the blue-and-white dishes. And in those first few years before the goats came to Payne Hollow, there was powdered milk to be mixed. I would whip up the cool spring water and the milk powder with an old-fashioned eggbeater and put it on the table in three sweating, brightly colored aluminum tumblers. I might also be dispatched to bring things in from the cool place. By summer 1956 the cellar below the big new lower room was serving that purpose, but in 1954 Anna was still using the desert cooler method. On the bench in the breezeway behind the cabin stood a kind of rough open cabinet covered with burlap. Keeping the burlap wet kept the contents of the cabinet cool through evaporation.

If there was a cabbage salad or a salad of fresh lettuce and, for instance, Anna's own canned pears, Anna would want a mayonnaise dressing. She showed me how to combine a dollop of Hellman's mayonnaise and some lemon juice, add a little sugar, drizzle the mixture over the salads, and sprinkle some chopped walnuts or toasted soybeans on top. Only Hellman's would do. Her voice dripping with mock scorn, Anna once described the time Harlan went shopping without her and "came home with [another brand], con-found it—a whole quart of it! He ate it all himself."

Harlan thought Anna's homemade mayonnaise was just as good, but she insisted on store-bought; he never figured out why. I suspect that at first she wanted the empty jars for storage, and the purchase became habitual. Anna soaked the labels off and used the jars for storing her array of seeds, nuts, raisins, honey, flours, tea makings, and herbs. She always drew oohs and aahs from visitors when she raised the door-cover of the cupboard where she stored her recycled Hellman's jars chock-full of good things.

I might also get to mix the biscuit dough. The biscuits were Anna's everyday bread until Harlan built the cookstove at Payne Hollow. In later years she said serving them made her feel as if she was having a picnic, because they were from the time when she and Harlan had done all their cooking over a fireplace. Anna showed me how to chip flakes of peel off a lemon with a paring knife—it was the lemon peel that "made" the biscuits—and how to plop just the right number of spoonfuls of dough into a pie pan. Then she set the pan down inside the Dutch oven and placed it on the coals in the fireplace, with another pie pan on top holding coals to brown the surface. A nice pebbly texture developed during the baking as the biscuits spread together. They broke apart neatly, and their perfection was completed by Harlan's honey or Anna's strawberry preserves.

After living in the studio, at Brent, and on the shantyboat, Anna was able to cook on practically any kind of contrivance. Harlan assembled grills out of whatever was at hand, such as the chassis of the junked Model T Ford he unearthed while digging the Natchez shantyboat garden. At Payne Hollow, Anna cooked in the indoor fireplace and on the terrace, on a kind of rangetop-size griddle Harlan fashioned by building up a stone foundation to standing height and placing a flat piece of junked metal over a shallow cavity that held the wood. Anna's cooking options reached their pinnacle when Harlan enlarged the house and built a stone cookstove and oven into the new fireplace-chimney unit in the big lower room.

Harlan was building the stone foundation for the new room when I visited in 1955, and in 1956 the room was finished. The original cabin was a spare upper room from then on, with its metal fireplace removed and replaced by more storage cabinets and drawers. When I visited, I had my same bed in the upper room, now the "guest bed" in the "guest room." When no guests were present, Anna dressed there each morning and did her hair at the vanity cabinet. Anna and Harlan's bed, a duplicate of the original, was downstairs in the big room now, stowed away in a corner beside a bookcase.

I was too young then to appreciate that the two rooms were a unified work in which the decisions about materials and design had obviously been made by an artist desiring to please the senses as well as make his living space useful and efficient. Excepting Anna's Steinway, the furniture was minimal, nearly all of it made by Harlan. In the new room he used stone and many different woods in a harmonious composition, the huge stone fireplace-chimney-stove unit counterbalancing the wall of glass facing the river. Meals were taken in front of that view now, at a big new table made by Harlan and polished to a fare-thee-well by Anna.

When Anna showed visitors around the house, she displayed the cookstove proudly. She liked to tell the story of how Harlan got the stones up from the creek to build the fireplace and stove; she said it showed how he was "always thinking." First he prepared a road between the creek and the house, and then built a stoneboat, a sled made of wood. Then he asked one of the six Barnes boys to come down from the ridge for a day with the Barnes's horse, Old Joe. For a bit of pay and a hearty dinner at noon, the boy spent the day loading, hauling, and unloading. The other five brothers wanted a go, too, as Harlan knew they would. By the time all six boys had had a turn, Harlan had all his stones.

Harlan completed the cooking unit with a rangetop he made from two junked stoves. At first the draft didn't work well and the rangetop smoked. The oven, which was tucked into the chimney, overheated on one side, and the bread or cake fell flat unless Anna turned it. But Harlan worked and worked on the cookstove, fine-tuning it until it performed up to Anna's standard. With firewood furnished by Harlan and stashed in the Russian ammunition box, a holdover from the shantyboat days, Anna learned exactly how and when to feed her new stove, and it became another virtuosic instrument in her hands.

Anna admitted freely that Harlan taught her to cook; she had done no cooking at home in Grand Rapids or in her shared Cincinnati apartment in the before-Harlan time. Harlan's fervent interest in food, which shows clearly in his journals, probably made him a good teacher. He was a practical camp cook, and master of the one-pot meal, such as macaroni-cheese-beef-and-tomatoes.

After they married and began living in the studio, they gardened out back and cooked in tandem for a while. Elderberries were featured in one September dinner, five months after the wedding, when the wild elderberry bushes were in fruit. First came sweetened elderberry juice laced with lemon. Pork chops followed, accompanied by acorn squash, and red bell peppers stuffed with corn and tomatoes, all from the garden behind the studio. For dessert Harlan concocted elderberry bran muffins.

Elderberry, in bloom as well as in fruit, was high on the Hubbards' foraging list. The common elder (*Sambucus canadensis*) is a shrub eight to ten feet high that produces small, flat-topped circular clusters of tiny white flowers in early summer. Dipped in batter and fried, the blooms had a delicate, unusual flavor something like anise, the Hubbards thought. The dish was known to the Hubbards as elderberry pancakes—an Elysian food, Harlan called it—and Anna presented it to me in my Payne Hollow summers as a great treat. To prepare it she snipped off most of the main stem, dipped the flower cluster in thin batter, head down, and laid it in the sizzling fat. Before flipping the cake she snipped off all the little remaining stems.

Foraged food was important in the Hubbards' diet. They tapped maple trees and made syrup. They dug ground nuts, strings of smallish tubers that are a palatable alternate for potatoes. They gathered nuts and wild berries, and fruit fallen from trees in neglected orchards. And they gathered wild asparagus and salad greens—how they did relish a good "mess" of greens. Shantyboater Andy Detisch's wife, Sadie, tutored the Hubbards in greens during their first spring at Brent. The first time Anna and Harlan went foraging with Sadie, they came back with nine kinds in their sack, and dandelion was the only one Harlan recognized.

Of all the wild greens, poke (pokeweed) was the Hubbards' favorite. They particularly liked to cut and split the tender pokeweed shoots, dip them in cornmeal, and fry them. The handsome pokeweed (*Phytolacca americana*) endures even on the fringes of today's suburban lawns. Its sturdy central stem and graceful arching branches are bright magenta, and in fall its leaves turn red and the branches droop with grapelike clusters of chartreuse berries that turn glossy black. It can reach a height of six feet or more. The fleshy root is poisonous, as are the leaves when they have turned red; novice foragers should seek expert advice.

On the shantyboat Anna was still mastering the fine points of cooking all sorts of foods over open wood fires and in coals indoors and out, and then indoors on the little wood-burning cookstove. On Thanksgiving Day 1944, Harlan wrote, the little cookstove "was too zealous and scorched the roast and mince pie." By year-end the meals were sumptuous. Anna's wheat bread earned a commendation in Harlan's journal the following February, and her cornbread, in July. (They ground their own cornmeal, a mixture of sweet and field corn with a little soy flour and no sugar.)

Mastery of open-fire cake baking took a bit longer. When the Hubbards made a birthday cake for Sadie in 1946, Harlan called cake baking "a job for all hands, one with such trouble and difficulty that each time we say we will never try it again." Six months later he made a birthday cake for Anna. It rose up marvelously, then cracked open and got scorched. As Harlan was removing it from the heat he gouged it with a screwdriver. But he and Anna patched it and covered its faults with icing and sixteen ivory-colored candles they had hand-dipped themselves. The experiments continued, and Harlan recorded that the chocolate cake Anna baked for his forty-eighth birthday, January 4, 1948, was the best that had thus far been baked aboard the shantyboat and "could not be improved." Yet they both continued improving, until Harlan was matching his chocolate cakes with chocolate-colored candles; he wouldn't tell Anna how he did it. They went on baking birthday cakes for each other for many years.

If Anna's instructor was Harlan, her master teacher was Adelle Davis, author of *Let's Eat Right to Keep Fit* (1954) and Anna's favorite cookbook, *Let's Cook It Right* (1947). Davis laid out principles of good nutrition, emphasized retaining the nutritive value of foods, and strongly advocated steaming vegetables. To keep the nutrients and flavors in leafy salad greens, she advised thorough drying by the "whirling" method—briskly twirling the greens in a cheesecloth bag or an old pillowcase until all the water has spun out. (Anna taught me to whirl greens in a thin linen dish towel.) Davis believed that meals prepared by a beginner could be as delicious as those prepared by cooks with fifty years' experience. Anna was proof of that theory.

Following Davis's advice to use soybeans as a meat substitute and a source of protein, Anna and Harlan used soybeans every possible way. Toasted soybeans were sprinkled whole on salads and eaten as snacks; ground coarse, they went into the breakfast cereal, and ground finer, they were combined with vegetable oil to make a spread resembling peanut butter. Raw, they were broken into pieces and cooked in stock for Davis's "soy grits." After the goats were gone, the Hubbards made soy "milk" by straining ground cooked soybeans. For years Anna and Harlan used soy flour in Davis's "tiger's milk," a concoction with milk, brewers' yeast, and fruit or black strap molasses. Soy flour also was an ingredient of Anna's highly praised dense whole wheat bread, which was exceptionally moist because she steamed it double-boiler fashion in the Dutch oven.

Anna's cooking involved no complicated sauces or recipes. The impact of her meals came from the proper cooking, wise flavoring (her favorite herbs were sweet basil and summer savory), and bountiful serving of wholesome, fresh, and varied foods. "It's what goes into the pot that counts," Anna said. Guests or no guests, her meals were hearty; Harlan needed fuel to do his hard work, and she trained him to believe, as she did, in the importance of balanced nutrition.

The daily menus always included whole-grain bread and cereal and plenty of vegetables. In winter they had Anna's canned produce, and fresh greens from Harlan's cold frame. In season they enjoyed a broad range of garden vegetables—excluding cucumbers, which Anna didn't like, and onions and garlic, which she wouldn't use because they made the breath offensive. For protein they had fish, groundhog, and for more than twenty years, goat. Chickens and eggs were mainstays in the early years, when Harlan bartered fish for farmers' provender, and in the later years, when they used more store-bought food. (Harlan didn't keep chickens. They were "too noisy and flighty for me," he said, and less economical than goats.) Before and after the goats, and when the goats were dry, the Hubbards drank reconstituted powdered milk, and Anna cooked with canned evaporated milk as well. During the goat years, in addition to fresh milk there was hard cheese, cottage cheese, and yogurt. For fruits there were both wild and cultivated berries. Harlan grew melons. Anna bought raisins, lemons, and bananas. Etta sent citrus fruit from Florida. They gathered peaches, pears, and apples from the trees of friends on the ridge.

In July 1977 *Organic Gardening and Farming* magazine printed a story by writer Gene Logsdon about a visit to Payne Hollow. He had been impressed by Anna's table. Her salad contained Jerusalem artichokes, violets, parsley, Bibb lettuce, comfrey, black walnuts, and foraged greens he didn't recognize. The flavorful soup was from three-year-old stock Anna had canned. Asparagus accompanied shredded and creamed smoked goat meat. Also there was Anna's whole wheat and soy bread, goat milk (Logsdon found it sweet; others called it oily), and herb tea made from comfrey, spice bush, stinging nettle, sassafras, pennyroyal, and parsley.

Of all the elements of the artful life Anna created at Payne Hollow for herself and Harlan, her table was her principal work of art: tasty, abundant food beautifully presented. Her everyday table, set with the blue-and-white dishes, was a ritual for her and Harlan, elevating their daily life to another plane. When company came, her table displayed reverence not only for food but also for her family. It was then she brought out from deep inside the kitchen cabinets the special plates and delicate hand-etched crystal goblets, milk glasses, and juice glasses from her mother's family—her Old Country treasures, she called them.

It wasn't until years after my Payne Hollow summers that I first truly saw, in pictures, the other Old Country treasures Anna kept on permanent display. Now I know that the curious long-handled round copper pan on the rangetop was a poffertjes (pronounced "puffer-jis") pan, unique to the Netherlands, for making little molded pancakes that are sprinkled with sugar after baking. A brightly polished brass pot, maybe a foot wide and nearly as high, sat on the floor, propping up the brass dustpan at the spot where the hearth curved back to meet the base of the stove. A smaller companion pot rested above on the rangetop. In a special niche at the bottom of a bookcase was a tall copper vessel that long ago had held live coals. On the mantelpiece were two plain brass candlesticks, and perched overhead above the kitchen countertop were brass irons and an inlaid wood tea chest. All these were Anna's Dutch things, brought to the United States in 1893 by her mother's mother, Anna Wonder Ross. Up in the attic were still more treasures—fragile glasses, cups, and other things that had been sent down to Payne Hollow in trunks from Grand Rapids after Anna's mother died. Even though Anna didn't use them, she wanted them there with her.

The most remarkable of Anna's household treasures was her piano. It was an ebony-finish, six-foot one-inch Steinway grand of the type called Model A, with massive carved legs. Today its style is called Victorian, and its size, baby grand. Its situation on the slope of a primitive hollow, perched at the river's edge a mile straight down from the nearest surfaced road, was a marvel. The Steinway was fifty-five years old when it arrived at Payne Hollow. The building of it was completed at the Steinway plant in Long Island City, New York, in 1901, and it was shipped to Lyon and Healy, a now-defunct dealership in Chicago. How it made its way to Grand Rapids is unknown. Anna's father bought it secondhand there for five hundred dollars in 1924 while Anna was away at Ohio State, and in the family album Anna's mother captioned a photo of it "Daddy's extravagance." The Steinway stayed in Anna's home in Grand Rapids until Anna's mother died in summer 1956, and just then the big new room at Payne Hollow was ready to receive it.

The dismantled Steinway was shipped to Madison, where the Hubbards' friend Weston Powell took it on his flatbed trailer and hauled it by tractor across the river bridge to Milton and out onto the ridge.

The day was November 28. On that same steep gravel road I hiked with Harlan to get the mail, Powell hauled the piano down to the lower-garden level of Payne Hollow. Harlan was waiting there with a crew of eight strong men—four farmer neighbors, two fishermen from across the river, and two Hanover College professors, Dan Webster and Alvin Bailey. The crew carried the piano up the steep path to the house and tipped it on its side to take it through the front door, and then Alvin Bailey lay on his back and slipped the legs in place while the others held the piano over him. At least that's how Anna told the tale in her autobiographical sketch. She'd had to tell it often, she wrote Etta in August 1985, "and I make up a good story. Wonder how close I come to the actual move."

Anna had surrounded herself with things that were precious to her, and she saw emotional meanings in them, even in the everyday objects. When she was in her seventies a visitor commented one day on the kerosene lamps, the ones I helped her wash and refill each morning of my Payne Hollow summers. Anna pointed out one in particular: "This very lamp was on the shantyboat," she said in a nostalgic voice, as if she were telling a cherished story, "this very one."

During my Payne Hollow summers, the Hubbards took me along on what Anna called their "expeditions," which involved crossing the river in the johnboat to their car on the Indiana side and driving the eight miles or so upriver around Plowhandle Point to the state highway. Because the road around Plowhandle Point was dry and dusty, Anna wore a gauze mask over her nose and mouth; she was prone to nosebleeds and hay fever. In fact, I remember Anna having a drippy nose all summer. She seemed oblivious to it as we worked together at the kitchen counter. I would steal glances her way, fascinated by the quivering pendant dangling from the end of her nose. The snuffle and the furtive swipe with the back of the hand were beneath her. With superhuman control she would finish her task, then grab a tissue just in time. If Anna had gone to elementary school at the Summit, she would have earned high marks in "Shows delicacy in the use of her handkerchief."

Sometimes my visit coincided with the Hubbards' monthly expedition to Hanover and Madison. Anna and Harlan always had a load of books to return to the Hanover College library and a list of others to borrow, and sometimes they visited their professor friend Alvin Bailey to play trios. After the important things, books and music, had been seen to, we went on to Madison to shop. Anna and Harlan had tied up at Madison for a week in 1947 during the shantyboat journey and found the town appealing, "clean and prosperous looking," and the people friendly and energetic. It "surpasses all river towns," Harlan wrote to his brother Frank in January 1947; "a beautiful old place, with many of the original buildings . . . well kept, and in use."

Our shopping destination was Hammack's Superette, the Hubbards' favorite store, where Harlan would later display his paintings, and where Anna and Harlan liked to buy their supplies—the paper towels, bathroom tissue, mayonnaise, margarine, detergent, salt, sugar, matches, and various other things that couldn't be found, grown, or caught at Payne Hollow. But first we had a riverside picnic lunch on the sloping back lawn of the Lanier Mansion, a gracious Greek Revival house dating from Madison's heyday in the 1840s. In 1947 the shantyboat had been moored for two weeks right there, along the shore below the mansion. Nine miles downstream, Anna and Harlan had discovered the ideal spot for their first long layover—a notch in the rolling, wooded hills, called Payne Hollow.

If Harlan had been asked what was the most significant of the expeditions we made during my visits, he surely would have named the 1957 founding of the Payne Hollow goat herd. Harlan wrote matter-of-factly about acquiring the goats, two females "of Toggenburg breeding, each with a good-sized kid, all for ten dollars. We hauled them to the river in . . . our old camping trailer, for which I had made slat sides. We were a little uneasy about ferrying them across in the johnboat, but the water disturbed them not at all. . . ." By day's end they were installed in the quaint two-story goat stable Harlan had built below the terrace.

Harlan didn't bother mentioning that the hauling was done in a steady rain. I have a snapshot—underexposed, and spoiled by raindrops on the lens—of Harlan looking a perfect clown in black-rubber rain gear complete with hat and boots, striding through the mud of the goats' native barnyard, escorted by a couple of frolicking dogs, holding a goat upside down by the legs, two in each hand, and laughing at the sight he knew he was.

The expedition of ours that Anna reminisced about most often in the years afterward involved music. In my first Payne Hollow summer I shamelessly wangled an invitation for a second week-long visit. Daddy drove me down again one Sunday in August and didn't even cross to Payne Hollow with Harlan and me. The Hubbards were headed for a concert in Louisville, and there was no time to spare. The objective was a string quartet concert outdoors in the rose garden of Gardencourt, the elegant turn-of-the-century mansion then occupied by the University of Louisville School of Music. My arrival at Payne Hollow had somehow been mistimed for meals, and though a quick stop at Hammack's yielded some bananas to carry me over, I was still famished. To my delight, the concert featured refreshments. For years Anna recalled that concert in her letters to me, usually mentioning my great hunger. Much as she loved music, I think she was even more impressed that day by my performance at the refreshments table.

Anna and Harlan's concertgoing was achieved through Harlan's rowing and driving, and Anna's resolve. Getting to concerts in Louisville meant crossing the river in good clothes—rain was no deterrent—and driving the eight miles of river road plus an hour to Louisville and back again. Sometimes they didn't regain the riverbank until dark. Eventually the Hubbards gave up concertgoing in Louisville, but they were still attending concerts at Hanover College, considerably closer to home, in their eighties. One such evening concert took place during an unusually cold winter, when ice was floating in the river. To get to their car, Harlan rowed across the river (and back again) by lantern light while Anna wielded a pole and pushed chunks of ice out of the way.

In July 1960 I was visiting Payne Hollow for a week again, after skipping a couple of years. I was nearly seventeen and about to begin my last year of high school. Harlan had finished building his studio-workshop. Sambo had died the year after Skipper, and now there were two Payne Hollow dogs again—rambunctious Snapper and shy Curly, frisky young female littermates, medium size, toasty colored, with shepherdlike muzzles. Otherwise not much had changed.

For our after-dinner reading one day, Anna selected a French short story. (She and Harlan often read French or German literature at midday.) I was doing all right with French academically, but my interest never caught fire. I think Anna realized that by now. ("What are you reading now in your French classes?" Anna had written when I was ten years old. "Do you ever read any French stories, outside of class for your own amusement?" Read a French story for amusement? I would just as soon have worked a few extra long-division problems!) That hot summer day in 1960 there was no fire blazing indoors, but tradition summoned us to our places at the hearth. Anna asked me to do the reading. Concentrating on my pronunciation, I barely caught the gist as I stumbled through the story. I tried not to notice that Anna's eyes were full and her lips compressed. I finished reading and we put the book away. Thirty-five years later I remembered the title, but I had to search for the story and reread it to find out why Anna had been moved by it.

The story is "La dernière classe" (The last class), by Alphonse Daudet (1840–97). The narrator is recalling one particular day of his childhood in a village in Alsace, a province of France that borders on Germany. It is 1871, France has been defeated in the Franco-Prussian War, and Alsace has been ceded to Germany. Having dawdled to school as usual, the boy learns that from now on, only the German language will be taught in the schools of Alsace. Unable to bear the tragic defeat, Monsieur Hamel, the village schoolteacher for forty years, is leaving France forever the next day. Several old men of the town have taken seats at the back of the schoolroom to hear the last French lesson along with the children. The students have never paid better attention, and M. Hamel has never been so patient or explained the lesson so clearly. The grammar and history books that once were so boring now seem like old friends. At the end of the class M. Hamel is unable to say farewell; he turns away from his students and writes with all his force on the blackboard, "Vive la France!"

Pawn of France and Germany through repeated wars, Alsace permanently reverted to France after World War I. Thirty years after reading Daudet's story to Anna, I saw Alsace for myself, with its perfect vineyards and picturesque wine villages, and the meaning of its history sank in through my senses: Alsace looked German, with its quaint half-timbered houses out of a Grimm's fairy tale, yet it tasted and sounded French. The loss-of-freedom aspect of Daudet's story moves me now, because it involves the French people's being denied the elegant, musical language that is the cornerstone of their proud culture. Anna was touched, I think, by the idea of the students, both the children and the old men, realizing that they had lost precious opportunities for education, perhaps forever.

When I was reading the story to Anna, missing the point and the chance to cry over it with her, I didn't know it was my last Payne Hollow summer.

3

"She's So Dutch!"

*Almost I believe that clorox in your hands might change the
leopard's spots. . . .*

Barre Pritchett to Anna, March 4, 1937

Anna was a Dutch housekeeper. If any higher praise of her housekeeping is possible, I don't know what it may be. Suspicious of stereotypes, I looked into the meaning of Dutchness as interpreted by Dutch writers, and I found . . . Anna.

In 1928 a Netherlander named Jacob van Hinte wrote a history called *Netherlanders in America,* describing life in Dutch-American communities of the early 1900s, like Anna's in Grand Rapids. Dutch settlements were "extremely neat and tidy," he wrote, and the transplanted Hollanders upheld the Dutch housewives' reputation for being exceedingly particular about their floors. An untidy Dutch homeowner might be dealt with as one in Orange City, Iowa, had been: a committee of local women might "take it upon themselves to have the streets and alleys made spic and span and charge the cost to the negligent resident." As van Hinte drove through another Dutch settlement, he was struck by the contrast between the Dutch homes, with their "clean, bright, and attractive exteriors," and the Scots-Irish homes, which were "generally unkempt and neglected!"

Anna herself verified the Dutch housekeeper profile when she compared her housekeeping with her sister Etta's. After a visit from Etta, Anna once complained that Etta thought everything, even the walls, ought to be washed every day. "I have too many things to do," Anna said, "and she just doesn't understand. She's so Dutch!"

No matter where home was at the time, Anna applied Dutch standards to its upkeep. She was the designated housekeeper in the before-Harlan apartment she shared in Cincinnati for ten years with Etta and with Barre Pritchett. Anna's standards persisted in the rustic studio in Fort Thomas, and at Brent. "The roughest was at the beginning," Harlan wrote, "when we lived in a shack on the riverbank. . . . Yet we never had happier days, and under Anna's management the shack became an inviting, cozy dwelling." Her standards carried over to the shantyboat. "Fortunately Anna has an inherent love of order and neatness," Harlan wrote. He described how it was, coming home to the boat after doing some rough work in the cold and rain: "Each time I marveled again—how neat and clean it was, so insulated from the chaos of the riverbank. What good living there in that small enclosure, floating on the wild river, against the inhospitable shore."

At Payne Hollow, Anna scrubbed, waxed, and polished everything! Though Anna adapted remarkably to the conditions of the life Harlan wanted to live, there was a point where she quit compromising. The store-bought bathroom tissue and mayonnaise rested square on that point. So did the sawmarks on the wallboards. When Harlan added onto the cabin in 1955–56, the only practical way to obtain enough suitable wallboards was to buy them new from a sawmill. The rough sawmarks pleased him; they were the best possible expression of naturalness under the circumstances. But Anna worked for a long time at smoothing and polishing those sawmarks so they wouldn't catch dust.

Anna's housekeeping was not only rigorous, but thrifty as well. For example, she had a system for reusing paper towels: before throwing one away she used it three times for successively dirtier purposes, rinsing it and hanging it to dry after the first two uses. She trimmed the good bits from mostly spoiled fruits the ordinary homemaker would have thrown out whole. (So exacting was her trimming, Harlan called it whittling.) She once upbraided a visitor who was helping prepare the green beans for dinner; instead of cutting just a small piece off the stem end, he was snapping both ends off and wasting good food.

She mended, of course, and she knitted socks, mittens, and sweaters. She needed no electric sewing machine to make slacks for herself, repair bedding, and remake bought garments. Anna even made by hand, with tiny stitches, the white blouses with Peter Pan collars she favored in her later years. Anna always liked pretty clothes, and Etta sent her many nice things. But Anna, deeming them too fine to wear on the riverbank, put them away and stitched up another little white blouse.

Anna mended and re-mended Harlan's work clothes. At breakfast one day in May 1981, Harlan asked her "very casually" (she wrote

Etta) to cut the collar off a shirt for him. (She was glad he had asked rather than try the job himself and botch it, as he'd done once before.) Harlan left the shirt "lying conspicuously on the day bed!" Anna had had other plans for the morning, but instead she spent it working on the shirt collar, annoyed with Harlan, because she had interpreted his placing the shirt on the day bed as a message to get right to it. She was incapable of postponing the job for her own convenience. And she would have been just as annoyed if Harlan had thrown the shirt into the rag bin instead.

During the week of my summer visit Anna either postponed her heavier chores or, more likely, did them while I was out and about with Harlan. At any rate, her housekeeping was invisible to me except for the sweeping of the floor a couple of times a day. For example, I never saw her iron with the old Dutch brass irons that held live coals. And I never saw the all-day production that was washday, but Harlan wrote about it in *Payne Hollow*. Once Harlan had perused the early morning sky and predicted fair weather, water was heated and four tubs were filled, two for washing and two for rinsing. While Anna rinsed, Harlan scrubbed on an old-fashioned washboard. "By good fortune," he wrote, "Anna enjoys the rinsing while I prefer to rub. Both occupations leave the mind free to wander. . . . This is one of the joys of washday," he rhapsodized, "and new, influential thoughts may turn up." He liked the "carnival air" of the yard while the clothes were hanging to dry.

According to Harlan, the washday system was Anna's, but I surmise he had much to do with it. He had been thinking about washday methods long before they met. In 1931 he wrote in his journal about Lou Gander, another beached shantyboater at Brent, and Gander's washtub on a bench, his washboard, and his rinsing the clothes in the river, off the end of a johnboat. Harlan admired Gander's "simple, easily explained life." One aspect of washday in which Anna certainly set the standard, however, was the detergent. She would use only good-quality store-bought detergent, and she shunned Harlan's experiments with homemade soap.

It was "an eventful day" in February 1945, four months into the building of the shantyboat, when Harlan recorded that Anna had done "a full-time washing of clothes." Exactly when Harlan joined in, I haven't discovered. It was at least by 1948: "We are quite pleased" with how the washing went on November 23, Harlan wrote. "We do enjoy it, and are proud of our system." I wonder whether Anna asked him to help. Or could he simply not resist the allure of washday?

At Payne Hollow, Harlan eventually made water more accessible by building cisterns near the house, but it was easier to go on washing blankets and woolens at the riverbank and rinsing them from the johnboat. "Great fun!" wrote Anna to friends, of such an operation one day in September 1982, when she was eighty. Laundry continued being done entirely by hand until Anna was eighty-three, when the Hubbards started taking the heavy wash (the sheets and Harlan's work pants) to the coin laundry in Madison, one of Harlan's energy-saving compromises to keep the Payne Hollow way of life going. I'm suspicious of Anna's "Great fun!" Over the years, she wrote to me about the satisfactions of preparing meals, baking, canning, even sweeping the floor, but never washing. Seems to me she would have preferred everything washing-machine clean all along. I think Anna, in much the same way she had refused to give up on the shantyboat garden at Natchez, went through with washday Harlan's way for Harlan's sake.

Unlike washing, canning was a chore that couldn't be postponed while I was visiting at Payne Hollow. It had to be done when the crop was ready, never mind heat, humidity, or in Anna's later years, weariness; wasting good food was an unthinkable alternative. I helped Anna can tomatoes once. She let me do the scalding (the plunging in hot water to loosen the skins) and make the official entry in the small loose-leaf notebook that was her canning record. In my best handwriting I noted the date and the number of quarts we had canned. Anna surveyed the results of our work with pleasure.

Anna was especially proud of her display of canned fruit in the cellar, shelves of blackberries, raspberries, peaches, pears, rhubarb, elderberries, gooseberries. . . . I understand so well how it pleased her to see the jars fill up one after another, to write the labels neatly, and to apply them just so—not crooked! To arrange the jars on the shelves by color. To see the rows of sparkling jars lining the shelves, witness to her thrift and organization. To revel in the smug feeling of preparedness.

The canning notebook was just one of Anna's records. From 1926 to 1939 she made and saved Christmas card and gift lists, which have survived, written in a tiny hand with a fine pen point on index-card-size pieces of paper. To count all the entries she had squeezed in on a sample page of her 1934 Christmas card list, I had to make an enlarged copy.

On one side of the page, in two columns, are seventy-three names. In addition Anna had used a coding system to record the exchange of cards: a check mark meant *sent*, an X meant *received*.

Anna also kept accounts on the house in Fort Thomas. From 1943 to 1974 she entered every rent check, starting with the short-term tenants who preceded the McTamneys, and she recorded every penny my father held out from the rent as reimbursement for repairs and maintenance.

In 1964 Anna began keeping a Payne Hollow gift list, noting every dozen eggs, every jar of jam, virtually every fruit and vegetable imported by visitors, who were legion. When I first saw the gift list, I feared I had found evidence of Anna's recordkeeping turned compulsive. But to her credit, she lost patience with the gift list. It didn't taper off—it came to an abrupt end one day in 1971, when Anna wrote across the page, large and underscored, one final, abbreviated word: "etc."

And of course there was the guest book. During my Payne Hollow summers I would thumb back through it, looking for my own name. The guest book is a revealing clue to Anna's personality: An educated, refined, city-dwelling woman moves with her husband to the primitive riverbank. The neighbors are of a sharply lower social class than her own. She must keep "house" in a squatters' shack and then a shantyboat. She washes clothes in river water and mops the mud off the floor each day. And into this markedly unconventional life she introduces the ritual of a formal guest book. The guest book remained a fixture of Anna's homemaking and recordkeeping. At first she entered all the names herself, but gradually, in the 1950s, she began having the guests sign, probably because of the sheer numbers. From about three hundred visitors a year in the late 1950s, the annual count gradually rose to a thousand and more by the late 1970s.

Or perhaps something more than the mere quantity of signatures was involved. In a contemporary book on the characteristics of the Dutch, author Han van der Horst writes that in general the Dutch dislike receiving uninvited guests and aren't shy about letting them know it's time to leave. Letting the conversation die out is a common ploy. A more direct host might stand at the window and remark that the skies and the streets have dried up and the visitors can be on their way—a method that is most effective, the author notes, when the sun has been shining all day. There may have been some Dutch in Anna's invitation to sign the guest book, coming, as it did, at the *end* of the visit.

During my Payne Hollow summers, unexpected visitors were routine. To me, as a child, the frequent arrival of company was just another of the many differences between life at my house, and life at Anna and Harlan's. Now I see the irony in visitors being drawn by the annual hundreds to two people living their solitary life on the fringe of society. Anna and Harlan's lifestyle had become a popular attraction, dispelling the solitude that was the lifestyle's foundation.

At first, in the 1950s, the droppers-in were mostly from nearby, on both sides of the river—Madison and Hanover, Indiana; and Milton and Trimble County, Kentucky. During the Hubbards' shantyboat layover at Payne Hollow in 1947, both of them had commented on the great friendliness of the local people. When people offered to buy fish, Harlan preferred to give them away or barter for chickens, eggs, milk, ham, and bacon. "We give away more [fish] than we sell," he wrote, "but how much have we received from these people."

Remembering the Hubbards from that time, the local people liked and esteemed their new neighbors, though many thought it strange that they had chosen to live without modern conveniences; local farmers remembered growing up without those conveniences and were glad to have them. The bartering soon fell off as the small, self-sustaining farms began disappearing and farmers started buying their groceries in town like everyone else, but the friendships with the Hubbards endured. Families grew and word spread. Payne Hollow became a popular destination for church outings, school field trips, scout expeditions, and extended-family excursions. One weekend afternoon during my second 1954 visit, the number of drop-in visitors from up on the ridge reached fourteen, plus three dogs. Anna wrote me that the Fourth of July crowd had been even larger.

From the beginning, other friends came too. Friends from earlier days, friends who respected the quiet of Payne Hollow, friends who offered to help with some work, friends who came for congenial conversation or to play music—these were welcomed wholeheartedly. Anna especially enjoyed visits from her women friends. She was hungry for girl talk, Harlan said. When Madison and Hanover friends Anne Horner, Marcella Modisett, Helen Spry, and Nita Webster visited, conversation might run to birds, wildflowers, herb gardening, and news of mutual acquaintances. Best of all, Anna loved having Etta and their grown-up niece, Susan, visit. When the girl talk reached a certain pitch, Harlan would leave the house. "Where's Harlan going?" Susan asked Anna once. In a voice of perfect unconcern Anna answered, "Oh, he's going off to think."

In the late 1950s the ranks of visitors swelled to include Hanover College students. Anna and Harlan became known at the college by borrowing books and scores from the library and playing music with faculty members. An annual field trip to Payne Hollow became a fixture of some professors' courses. "To our dismay," Harlan wrote to friends in 1983, "we have become a revered local institution." Harlan's dismay was only halfhearted. Several Hanover professors speak warmly of the Hubbards' willingness to make themselves available to students who were sincerely interested in their way of life, and one professor remembers Harlan always genuinely encouraging him to bring his students. The Hubbards formed enduring friendships with several of their student visitors, particularly during the 1960s.

Visits by friends were interruptions, Harlan said, but they were interruptions he and Anna enjoyed. Visits by drop-in strangers, however, were another matter. That brand of visitor became more numerous as word of Payne Hollow spread up and down the river. Many strangers came in the appropriate spirit and for various legitimate reasons: to meet the author of *Shantyboat* and *Payne Hollow*, for example, or to find out what "living simply" means. Some became true friends. But the merely curious, who behaved as if Payne Hollow was a public attraction and Harlan's studio a commercial art gallery, were a trial.

The Hubbards developed a routine for receiving strangers. Anna showed off the cabin, demonstrating how the bed stowed away, describing how the cookstove and oven worked, and praising Harlan for the artistry of his construction and for providing her with running water and central wood-burning heat. If Harlan approved of the visitors, he would invite them to his studio to see his paintings, even though he dreaded their inappropriate comments and disliked having to put a price on his art. If the guests were special, Anna would tell him to be sure to show the older paintings he considered his best, the ones he kept hidden away and would not sell. But if the would-be buyers were patronizing or pushy, Harlan showed only his newer paintings, and, he told a friend, he added "naughts [zeros] to the prices."

The decision to let the visitors come was Harlan's, but it was left to Anna to make hospitality actual, through her style and hard work.

She kept the house clean, orderly, and company-ready at all times, an effort that was lost on one wealthy group that came by motor launch. A friend overheard the visiting women talking inside: "This isn't so hard to keep clean," one of them said; "she doesn't have wall-to-wall-carpet."

Even when strangers were rude or their arrival was ill timed, Anna put away her exasperation and received them with no sign of resentment. Few of Anna's friends knew of her real feelings about the more intrusive visitors. One such friend saw the warm reception Anna and Harlan gave a boatload of strangers who broke their floating beer party with a stop at Payne Hollow—and then heard the Hubbards' sharp comments after the group had left. Another friend saw Anna's reaction as a large, unfamiliar pleasure boat pulled in at the dock one afternoon. Anna rose from her seat on the terrace with an "Oh, dear" look on her face and went down to say hello. Harlan stayed behind, grumbling, "Just like a state park, except we don't charge admission." He had sized up the group accurately. The kids were rude, demanding Cokes with ice, and so forth, but Anna showed them the cabin anyway. They were not invited to the studio.

Once, tells another friend, a woman sashayed off a motorboat and up to the house in a bikini. Anna was gracious as always, but afterward she said scathingly, "I think *I'll* just put on a bikini and waltz around!" Another time she told about an acquaintance who had come down the hill, unannounced, with a new wife. Anna was offended that the man seemed to expect her and Harlan to accept instantly the breakup of his former marriage and welcome the new person who was now filling the role of wife. Anna went on at some length about the incident, then concluded, "Well, of course we don't really care about any of those people."

The great annoyance of strangers dropping in might have been allayed if Harlan had had something of Scott Nearing in his makeup. Nearing (1883–1983) and his wife, Helen (1904–95), wrote books on their homesteading life in Vermont (*Living the Good Life,* 1954) and Maine (*Continuing the Good Life,* 1979). By the 1970s they were handling up to twenty-five hundred visitors a year, often dozens in a day. Tolerating no interference with his routines, the austere Nearing organized visitors into work parties. Those who did not wish to work were welcome to sit around and talk with one another, but Scott and Helen went on with what they were doing. At last, though not until Nearing was more than ninety years old, they posted a sign at their farm entrance limiting visiting time to the hours between three and five P.M. One year they refused all visitors except by advance notice.

Harlan might have taken similar steps, or at least curtailed invitations and quit granting newspaper interviews, but he made no such efforts. He didn't like to say no to people, and he felt obliged to be hospitable: "Whoever comes to see us, college professor or riverbank camper, we try to let them have what they came for." Eventually he came to appreciate the sincerity of many of the visitors and found that "the most unpromising person will turn out to have something very interesting to say, if you just give him a chance. . . ." Nevertheless, he continued to resent the interruptions to his work and his painting; he never resolved that conflict. Perhaps Harlan's desire for solitude was not strong enough to override his need for human contact and attention. Until middle age he had been odd man out; his feelings of differentness and social unease are a theme of his published 1929–44 journals. If he was secretly pleased that, in the second half of his life, people sought him out to learn from him and admire his achievements, who could blame him?

Not Anna, certainly. Nor would she blame him for failing to notice how the years of uninvited company grated on her. Even though solitude had been a clause in their marriage contract, so to speak, still her policy was to support Harlan, not to try to change him. She resigned herself to being prepared to receive visitors at any time, and she was unfailingly gracious, no matter the cost to her peace of mind. But her gracious-hostess demeanor was often a skillful performance, one that cost her more and more emotional effort as the years went by.

Anna's fidelity to "the record" applied above all to her correspondence. In December 1958 Anna wrote praising my choice of Christmas card because, she said, it had so much of me in it. "I think I should hunt up all your Christmas cards from years back and keep them with your letters," she wrote, "as a part of the record." When the attic and the drawers, nooks, and crannies of the Payne Hollow house were full of the letters she was saving, Harlan built still more drawers for her in his workshop. She was keeping "the record," yes, but more than that, she was keeping relationships alive. Letters kept her connected to the people she loved. She taught me to treasure letters too, by saving all of mine and bringing them out for me to read when I visited. It was fun to read about my own past and see how I had changed.

"It seemed to us," Anna wrote in her 1954 *Library Journal* article (see the appendix), "that we had the best part of our distant friends in the letters they wrote to us, that we came nearer an understanding of their ideas and their problems than we had in many years of personal association, with conversation so often confined to the most trivial matters." In fact, it was Anna who kept conversation trivial. She liked face-to-face girl talk, but mostly she preferred writing letters, even with her sister Etta, whom she considered close and dear. Living temporarily in a modern cottage in Madison during 1985, Anna wrote Etta on April 25 that she now had a telephone—"Though, frankly, I don't know what you and I could say to each other, Et, that we couldn't just as well write. I like writing, myself." Etta planned a visit to the cottage that summer, and Anna wrote on May 29: "My, but you and I are going to have a lot of fun talking, Et. So many little inconsequential things that we'll hash over. We get the important things written in our letters. . . ."

That explains why I don't remember Anna ever *telling* me anything memorable or important. She gave me the best of her thoughts and words in her letters. And in her letters she gave me the best of her affection, too. When we were together there was distance between us, perhaps because she had learned the Dutch aversion to physical contact. I don't remember hugging Anna at any age. Others remember her that way too, as somehow making it clear that she didn't want to be touched. When saying good-byes, Anna might hold her sister's hand or put her hand on the shoulder of someone else particularly dear, but the full body hug was not in her everyday repertoire. In her letters, however, much of Anna's emotional reserve fell away. Love poured out in her letters to family, friends, and acquaintances. Even in simple thank-you notes, she praised the thoughtfulness and ingenuity of the sender more than the gift.

Anna began writing frequently to her niece and nephews in the voice of a mother after Nella Mae died, lavishing praise and love on them in letter after letter. To George, the youngest, who at the time was aspiring to corporate success, she wrote: *I know you are doing a great job. You have the qualities that make for success in this position and in any position—intelligence, personality, a fine attitude of wanting to do the job well, wanting to be helpful. We admire you no end. . . . You are such an outgoing, genial person, such good company, and with that special quality of taking an interest in the other fellow.*

To Susan, a dancer, Anna wrote over the years: *Sweetheart, you are such a wonderful person, . . . so animated, so quick in your thinking and acting, and of such a sweet temperament—a joy to have around. . . . You are managing your affairs so capably. . . . Your new dress is <u>beautiful</u>! And you are beautiful in it! . . . your ability and your intelligence. . . . wonderful girl. . . . beautiful dancer. . . . wonderful girl. . . .*

When Anna expressed sympathy in letters, it was clear that she felt wounded too. Susan had been disappointed in her bid to join a certain dance company in 1979 when Anna wrote: "With all my heart I love you. And more than anything we want you to be able to go on and do what you want so much to do. So Tetta's [Etta's] last letter which tells of this temporary setback, your not passing the big tryout, made me heartsick. I haven't been able to think of anything else." Several pages of encouragement followed.

In a letter Anna comforted me in my first sorrow. When I was eight years old, Anna and Harlan had given me one of Skipper's puppies. I named her Cindy. She went untrained and stayed as wild as if she'd been brought up on the riverbank herself. Only four years later she died, and these are Anna's words of consolation:

> We are so very sorry to hear about Cindy. Of course you loved her. She was a lovable dog. And then you had taken her into your home, she was really a member of the family. You and Rose and Harry made a wonderful home for Cindy. Her life, though it was short, was happy. . . . I like to think, too, how much Cindy enjoyed the morning walks back on the hill with Harlan and Sambo and Skipper.
>
> Yes, we will want to think about Cindy just as we always have, just as we think about Skipper and talk about her. Dogs who have been such good companions we will never forget. Thank you, Mia, for writing to us. You knew that we would want to be told right away about Cindy. In a way she was our dog, too, since she was Skipper's puppy. And we loved her, too.

At Payne Hollow, though, little sympathy was given in person by either Harlan or Anna. One day in summer 1957 I went to the stable with Harlan to get acquainted with the newly arrived goats. As I was petting one, I put my thumb in its mouth. Harlan was watching, but he didn't warn me. Naturally the goat chomped down. I received no sympathy from Anna or Harlan for the chomp or the ensuing blood blister under my thumbnail. I took the incident personally and formed a lasting resentment against all goats, down to all generations, but I didn't say so. The qualities of goats were esteemed at Payne Hollow, and it seemed inappropriate to express a minority opinion.

Something similar happened to Ed Lueders (pronounced "leaders"), who became friends with the Hubbards as a Hanover College professor in the 1960s. Ed came to visit one day, arriving on the Indiana side. He rang the bell, and Harlan rowed over in the johnboat, but rather than be ferried across, Ed decided to swim. It was no more in Harlan's nature to advise a grown man against swimming the river than to tell a youngster to take her thumb out of a goat's mouth. Ed knew how to deal with the swift current when he was manning oars, but he found that swimming against it was harder. In mid-river he began drifting downstream, as Harlan had known he would. For a "joke" Harlan rowed away and left him to drift. When Ed got back to the house at last, after a hard swim and a long walk barefoot through the rocks and brush, no sympathy was offered.

Many visitors to Payne Hollow, both adults and children, sensed that there was a correct way to do things and that a high standard of decorum prevailed. The visitors who fared best were the ones accustomed to doing and being what someone else wanted, the ones whose emotional radar could pick up the faintest signals and who were in the habit of performing automatic course corrections. When Anna's niece, Susan, was a rebellious sixteen, her radar failed her. She had brought along her friend Tuni on a week-long visit to Payne Hollow, and time hung heavy for the active, outgoing teenagers. One day a walk in the woods took them all the way to the top of the hill, where, miracle of miracles, they encountered a couple of cute farmboys with motorcycles. Time flew, and the boys and girls were back at the trailhead laughing and talking when Nella Mae and her husband, Stan Bartnick, lately arrived to take the girls home, appeared with Anna and Harlan, all four of them carrying flashlights and looking worried. Anna and Harlan were polite; Nella Mae and Stan were furious. Nella Mae's words under stress captured the essence of Payne Hollow decorum—transgressions were unfitting, unseemly, improper: "You've embarrassed me in front of Anna and Harlan!" Nella Mae fumed.

Anna and Harlan prided themselves on efficiency and had worked out systems for their regular tasks. Visitors who were on their wavelength knew it was important not to keep them from their work. Through no fault of my own, I broke that rule once. I was an unsophisticated not-quite-twelve, and it was my first time away from home as a "woman," when my period caught me unprepared. No one had told me about planning ahead, and I was without supplies. In tears and deeply embarrassed, I went to Anna. "My period started," I said, "and I don't know what to do-o-o!" Anna reacted as if I had complained of cramps: "That can be so uncomfortable, can't it?" she said, and arranged a trip to town. Sitting in the front seat of the car between Anna and Harlan, I was ashamed that Harlan knew exactly what my predicament was, and that they had had to drop everything because of me. If Anna felt any sympathy for my embarrassment, I saw no sign of it. My emotional distress seemed not to register with her at all.

In taking care not to create any disturbance at Payne Hollow, even the best of Hubbard friends might experience actual symptoms of physical tension. Judy Moffett, an academic and a published novelist, poet, translator, and literary critic, had visited Payne Hollow often as a Hanover College undergraduate and later. Anna loved Judy's visits and had repeatedly urged her to come anytime: "It isn't important for us to know what day you plan to arrive," she wrote to Judy in July 1973. And in July 1974: "Please, Judy, we are never too busy to welcome a visit from you. You are a member of the family, I might say." That October a feature story by Judy on the Hubbards appeared in the *Cincinnati Enquirer* Sunday magazine, and Anna and Harlan wrote her in praise of it. Soon afterward, Judy was due to visit Payne Hollow overnight. Confident of a warm welcome anytime, she was unconcerned about the change in her schedule that caused her to arrive a day early.

Judy walked down the hill to the house. Anna and Harlan were inside talking, and the moment Judy knocked, she saw from their faces that she was interrupting. Through the ritual exchange of greetings and catching-up chatter she was terribly uncomfortable. She had always tried to be acutely sensitive to the Hubbards, because remaining welcome there was extremely important to her, and now she was shocked to realize that she had angered Harlan and upset Anna. There was no possibility of talking openly. Judy couldn't say, "I'm sorry, shall I come back tomorrow?" because she knew Anna and Harlan were incapable of replying, "Yes, thanks, tomorrow would be better." Judy's distress brought on a migraine headache, the only one she's ever had. From Anna she received two aspirins, but no sympathy.

Looking back at Anna and Harlan in this light, I feel sorry for them, and the feeling is disturbing; I want them unfailingly strong and competent in my memories. But in this regard, it seems to me now that they were two insecure children themselves, finding relief in temporarily being able to feel stronger than someone else. During my Payne Hollow summers, though, the absence of sympathy was nothing more to me than a quirk of the place. Likewise, the intermittent atmosphere of politeness under pressure. Thanks to the nuns, in conduct and courtesy I was a medal winner, and adjusting to other people's personalities was second nature to me. Only now, looking back, do I see how the combination of Anna's lack of openness and my desire to please flawed our relationship and made it fragile in the years ahead.

4

Little Dutch Girl

As I get older and look back, seeing so many places where I have failed in getting my children's confidence, I have wondered if it might not be excused a little because I did not have my Mother to confide in during the growing up years.

Anna's mother to Anna, January 18, 1939

There was a great deal of Dutch in Anna's character and personality. Vigorous housekeeping, thrift, recordkeeping, love of home and family, dislike of unexpected guests, aversion to physical contact and displays of emotion, and lack of sympathy and openness—all are typical Dutch traits. So are aversion to nonsense, preference for hard facts, and emphasis on accuracy, precision, arithmetic, clear handwriting, and foreign languages. These traits, stemming from the Dutch tradition of commerce, were the norm in Anna's world and are still descriptive of the Dutch today. Some of those traits are almost visible in Anna, in the Eikenhout family photo album. There she is, in high-top shoes with eight buttons, sitting on the porch steps with Etta. It's around 1910; Anna looks about eight years old. She has a firm whole-arm grip around her doll's waist, and she and dolly are staring the camera in the eye. Her little brow is knitted, her jaw is set.

When Anna was born in 1902, the reserved, practical, home-loving Dutch were the largest immigrant group in Greater Grand Rapids (Kent County), Michigan. They constituted more than one-quarter of the county's foreign-born population, and they were more numerous there than in any other U.S. metropolitan area, including Chicago, Paterson, and New York. The Dutch had done well in Grand Rapids. In the mid-nineteenth century, Michigan had been 95 percent pine forest, and immigrants of various nationalities, fully one-third of the Grand Rapids population in the mid-1880s, were good craftsmen. The simple, lightweight furniture Grand Rapids began producing around 1860 sold well among the settlers of the Midwest and the Plains states. By the 1920s, twice-yearly furniture markets would be providing an enormous boost to the local economy, causing hotels to overflow and night life to flourish as manufacturers' representatives wined and dined buyers in high style.

The prosperity of Grand Rapids rippled out to the Eikenhout family's roofing business and provided a secure economic cushion during Anna's childhood and youth in the early 1900s, but the downtown high life had little direct effect in her Dutch world. There, family and social life was firmly rooted in the Reformed Church, a Dutch form of stringent Calvinist Protestantism. The Dutch communities were tranquil on Sundays, wrote Jacob van Hinte, because both the husbands and the wives attended *two* church services. In contrast, the "genuinely American" cities and villages were noisier, because only the women went to church; the men might even be out on the sports fields. Seven days a week, the Dutch religion ruled out dancing, card playing, drinking, smoking, and moviegoing.

The family roofing business was started by Anna's paternal grandfather, Henry (Hendrik) Eikenhout (1852–1934; in English, "Eikenhout" means "oak wood"). Henry was born in the Netherlands, in the northern coastal province of Groningen. Having emigrated to Grand Rapids, he was married by proxy in 1873 to Anna (Aanje) van der Broek, who was still back in Groningen and whose father would not permit her to sail off to America until a marriage had taken place. In our Anna's time the family business was called H. Eikenhout and Sons. The oldest of Henry and Anna Eikenhout's six children (two others died in childhood) was John, born in 1877. After finishing eighth grade, John went to work as office boy and salesman for the Herman Dosker fire insurance company. Two years later he began working for his father, and in another two or three years at roughly age eighteen, he became a partner. Unlike his two younger brothers, who later bought their shares in the business with IOUs, John bought his with $250 cash.

No one wanted to deal with Henry, because he was so grumpy. When the personable John became a partner, customers and employees began turning to him, and the business thrived. In 1939 John's wife, Nellie, wrote of him (to Anna) that in his youth he played the organ and was an usher in church and was "an all around pleasing young man. A curl, if not in the middle of his forehead, at least some curl in his hair and not bad to look at."

In the genealogical charts Anna made in the 1970s with Nella Mae's help, she devoted most of her efforts to her mother Nellie's side of the family, the Rosses and the Wonders, the source of her Old Country treasures. She was proud of their standing as prosperous rural people of Holland. Nellie's father, Jan Ross (Ros, in Dutch), was born in 1840 in Koog on the Zaan, in the coastal province of North Holland. His father and grandfather had been shipbuilders. Jan Ross, that "gentleman farmer," as Anna pointedly identified him in her charts, eventually had a dairy farm in Ede, in the inland province of Gelderland, where Nellie was born. He was a director of the local cheese factory. Less was known about Nellie's mother, Anna (Antje) Wonder, who was born in 1842 in the farming village of Old (Oude) Niedorp, North Holland, in a fine two-story house. Our Anna was named after her.

Old Niedorp is still there, about forty miles north of Amsterdam, at an inconspicuous turnoff from the main road. Just over a small bridge and beyond some trees, the narrow lane begins curving through a picture-book village. No two of the immaculate little houses are exactly alike. Some still have the traditional partly thatched roofs. All are of brick with intricate ornamentation, and all have well-kept gardens billowing with plants and flowers. About four hundred people live there today, and only two small farms are left.

On a summer day in 1996 I visited Anna Wonder's house, at Dorpsstraat, number 7, junction of Zuiderweg. Just as in the old photo I'd brought with me, the house still had the same recessed front door, the same little balcony, the same fleur-de-lis ornaments flanking the upper windows. The care that had been taken in restoring the house was obvious from the way its ornaments and trim had been painted jauntily but tastefully in white and green with accents of red and yellow.

The current owners, Mr. and Mrs. Jacob Blokker, were gracious. As the Blokkers and I told one another through my Dutch friend, Gerrit de Gooyer, what we knew of the house, I thought of Anna. Her two sisters and even her mother visited the Old Country. "How I would have loved to do that, too!" Anna wrote to friends in 1979, but after settling in Payne Hollow, Anna and Harlan did no more touring for pleasure. While talking with the Blokkers, I learned a piece of information that somehow had been left out of the Rosses' story in Anna's branch of the family: from 1859 to 1880 Anna Wonder's father, Arien Harkzoon (son of Hark) Wonder, was the village mayor. (If Anna had known, she surely would have noted it on her charts.)

For the Blokkers' accidental discovery that they were living in a former mayor's house, the credit belongs to the practicality of the Dutch. While restoring the house, Mr. Blokker excavated the front stoop to shore it up, and underneath, face down, he found a flat, engraved stone. A municipal expert told him the engraving matched that on the Wonder family gravestone in the churchyard, except that the stone in the churchyard also noted Arien Harkzoon Wonder's death in 1888. They deduced the following: When Arien died, the family gravestone had already been completely covered with the names and dates of his little son (who died in 1841); of his first wife, Reinoutje Met (Anna Wonder's mother, died 1844); and of his second wife, Neeltje Koorn (died 1877). Consequently the municipality provided a large new stone, copying the engraving from the old one and adding the former mayor's death date. The old gravestone was then given to Anna Wonder's brothers Dirk and Jan, who inherited the house. When the practical Dirk and Jan restored the house in about 1900, they used the old gravestone as a foundation for the front stoop. Both stones are lying side by side now in Old Niedorp's beautifully tended churchyard.

Jan Ross and Anna Wonder married in 1862 and moved to Ede. Jan's dairy farm prospered, he was a respected member of the community, and then at age fifty-three he left and took his family to America. Obviously his motive was not economic. Nor was it escape from religious persecution; Protestants hadn't been persecuted in the Netherlands since Catholic Spain ruled there in the sixteenth and seventeenth centuries. But since it is said in the family that his motive was religious, perhaps he, like many of his countrymen, was following some esteemed former pastor who had heeded the call to the New World.

The Ross family left the Netherlands from Rotterdam on May 27, 1893, aboard the steamship *Rotterdam* via Boulogne, France, traveling first class. They were in elite company: the 108 first- and second-class passengers were outnumbered more than six to one by the steerage passengers, about half of whom were Russians. Two weeks later, on June 10, the ship arrived in New York. With Jan and Anna came the youngest eight of their eleven living children: all five daughters—fifteen-year-old Nellie and her sisters, Alice, Gertrude, Kate, and Grace, ranging in age from seven to twenty—and three of their six sons—Nick, Andy, and William, aged six to sixteen. Two other grown sons, John and Peter, followed later.

The Rosses brought with them all their household goods, our Anna wrote in her autobiographical sketch: "brass utensils, their silver, china, linen, even the featherbeds, their pictures and books, the children's games, my grandmother's piano music, everything." They even brought the library of theological books that had belonged to Jan Ross's father; Jan Ariezoon Ross (1793–1864) had been a lay preacher as well as a shipbuilder.

Four of the five Ross sons who came to America left Michigan and scattered across the United States. The firstborn, John, died of pneumonia in a silver mine in Colorado in 1903. Nick, the one Etta called her "sailing uncle," scorned the noisy, modern steamships, but in time he sailed on them anyway rather than never go to sea again. Nick settled in San Francisco, Andy in Seattle, and William in Washington, D.C. Four of the five daughters, on the other hand, stayed in Michigan. Alice, unmarried, moved to Milwaukee and died in 1936 in a hit-and-run automobile accident. As a young girl, Nellie worked for a time as a ladies' maid to a wealthy French matron. In their maturity the four Michigan sisters—Grace, Nellie, Kate, and Gertrude—appear in Nellie's photo albums looking like their mother, four peas in a pod, four stern muses.

Nellie Ross married John Eikenhout in 1900, when John had been a partner in the roofing business about five years. When Jan Ross died in 1920, he had been living for some time with Nellie and John. Etta remembered "Opa" Ross's room upstairs filled with pipe smoke, and she recalled how a crony of his came visiting after every church service to discuss the sermon.

Nellie and John had three daughters: Anna Wonder, born September 7, 1902 (she was called Ann, sometimes spelled *Anne*, when she was young); Henrietta (Etta), November 3, 1907; and Nella Mae, May 16, 1916. In 1920 the family moved from 565 New Street to 1006 Madison Street, SE. It was the Dutch side of town, solidly middle class and not far from the neighborhood where the lumber barons had their big homes. The girls' grade school and high school were in the Dutch neighborhood, and they went to their parents' Dutch church, the Fifth Reformed Church at Church and Pleasant Streets, SW. Religious faith was a living part of Nellie's and John's lives. Nellie often attended the prayer meetings that were held at church most nights of the week. While John was working for the U.S. Army Quartermaster Corps as a roofing inspector in the last months of World War I, he attended Sunday church services wherever he was, and in his diary he commented on the sermons.

There are no "little Anna" stories on the record to explain how, in a Calvinist household run by a perfectionist homemaker, Anna managed to develop a keen sense of fun. Her early letters to me were sprinkled with a little girl's ideas of fun—playing with puppies, making a snowman, cutting out cookies, braiding a doll's hair, splashing in a wading pool. . . . Later she wrote often about the grown-up fun in her own life: appearing on television in Grand Rapids with Harlan in 1953 after *Shantyboat* was published, going backstage after a concert, visiting her dear friends the Staeblers, surprising Harlan with a special Christmas present, watching the capering of the baby goats, reliving with Harlan the shantyboat years, making an expedition to dig wildflowers for transplanting near the back door, and many other things. Boating was great fun, too. All her life Anna loved being out in boats, and the faster the boat and the rougher the water, the better. Better still if the day was dry and sunny with a cool breeze, the kind of day she spoke of, glowing with pleasure, as "Michigan weather."

Another form of fun for Anna was baseball. She was a fan of the Cincinnati Reds and the great, yet-unsullied Pete Rose. Watching the Reds on television at the grown-up Nella Mae's house, she would lean forward intently, elbows on knees, chin on hands. In summer 1985, when she and Harlan were staying temporarily in the modern cottage outside Madison, she listened to them on the radio. On June 22 she wrote Etta that the Reds had just won the game: "And what a game! They were tied 3–3 in the 9th. Then the Reds won in the last half of the 9th. They put a man on base. Then Pete Rose himself went in to bat and got on. It was Parker who made a line hit bringing in the winning run. Great baseball!" Etta sent her Pete Rose's book, and Anna read it at least three times.

Her sense of fun did not extend to practical jokes, though. Harlan once found washed up on the Payne Hollow shore a large glass container, a big orb with a long neck. For a joke he inserted some wire to simulate light bulb filament and stuck the container neck down in the ground near the front door. He told a visitor it was his new yard light and that the energy to operate it came from composting garbage. He was so pleased with his yarn, he could hardly keep a straight face as he told it. Meanwhile, says the witnessing visitor, Anna only looked "withheld."

Always at the top of Anna's "fun" list, of course, were reading good books and playing music with a friend. Anna grew up surrounded by music. Her first toy was a music box. Nellie sang the girls' school songs with them at twilight—"our children's hour," Anna wrote in her autobiographical sketch. When the Rosses gathered on New Year's Eve—Old Year's Night, the Dutch called it—they sang Dutch folk songs and the children sang along. John Eikenhout played the piano, and as a young man he had played the bass viol and the baritone horn. He also had a fine baritone voice. At one time he conducted six singing schools around the city, but when Anna was about eleven, the pressure of business forced him to cut back to two. In addition he sang in a Presbyterian church choir and was a member and a sometime officer of the Schubert Club, a long-standing men's singing group prominent in the cultural life of Grand Rapids.

All the Eikenhout girls played piano. Details of Anna's musical education are unknown, but she did have formal instruction; her mother alluded to it later in letters, and to the sacrifices that had been made to provide it for her. Still very young, Anna played piano accompaniment when neighborhood men came to the house to sing quartets with her father. She played piano in the high school string club with her friend Hilda Bell, who played cello, and she played bass viol in the school orchestra. (Etta played bass viol too, later, in the Grand Rapids Symphony and the Chicago Women's Symphony Orchestra.) By age seventeen Anna's identity as a musician was established: she composed the class song—published in her graduation yearbook, South High School, 1920—and along with the class officers and the humanities titleholders, such as Historian and Poet, Anna is named Musician.

Around then Anna began playing trios with Hilda and her younger brother, Charles. Their coach was Leo Cayvan, first cellist with the Grand Rapids Symphony Orchestra. The trio gave an annual recital and played for community events: they played background music for silent movies, they played at the Masonic temple, and they played dinner music at many local eateries in return for a meal. Charles, retired from medical practice, recalled that they could play Brahms's Hungarian Dances nos. 5 and 6 "at a dizzying, whirlwind pace" and that Anna's musicianship was "beyond belief." Music, he said, was Anna's first love. Anna's music studies continued with Cayvan and at Grand Rapids Junior College, with a teacher named Kate Baxter. At Ohio State, Anna sang in the girls' glee club and played bass viol in the orchestra.

Others have described Anna's piano playing, in maturity, as controlled and cool, the obvious result of formal instruction in the European tradition. As a child, though, I thought her style anything but controlled and cool, because of the way she moved as she played. From the hips up, her body gyrated, and she rotated her arms, too, as if she were doing what one of my piano teachers called exerting the "singing touch"—that is, trying to get some vibrato into a sustained sound after the key has been struck.

Anna's mother, an expert seamstress, made beautiful clothes for her daughters. Year after year the three sisters posed for snapshots in the yard after Sunday school in their stylish coats and dresses. Nellie documented each sewing project in a hefty scrapbook, recalled by Anna in her autobiographical sketch. On each page were pasted "the pattern in its envelope, samples of the material and the trimming, a careful detailed account of the cost of the materials, and a snapshot of the little girl wearing her new dress."

As Anna grew up, she developed decided ideas about styles and fabrics, and she and Nellie conferred over every detail. In an undated letter from Ohio State, sometime between 1923 and 1925, Anna told her mother about some yard goods she was sending home. She wanted a dress made from the pattern in "the new June Journal" (perhaps she meant the *Ladies' Home Journal*). Anna went on for five hundred words, emphasizing the style's new features and murmuring deference to her mother's judgment while specifying her own requirements: "The ribbon in the front too, is very new. Make it the width and length of the picture in the Journal. Whichever color you think best—brown or white, brown I expect. Now the sleeves. Look at the views marked 1 . . . . Use your own judgment. Short sleeves would be cool, and they are very stylish."

Later, Anna's everyday clothes were practical for her riverbank life, but she still gave thought to her wardrobe. These were her plans for the navy blue cardigan my mother and I sent her for her birthday in 1954: "I'm thinking of all the things I can wear it with," Anna wrote. "The gray shirt, yes. And gray slacks, tan slacks, or blue slacks. Under the sweater I can wear my sheer white nylon blouse with the little collar. Or another white silk blouse with no collar, just a round neckline. I wish you were here to see all these combinations. I feel as if I had a whole new wardrobe!"

Anna eventually lost her yen for new dresses at Payne Hollow, but

her neatness kept her looking well turned out. (Though she had a pe-
culiar blind spot for shoes. With her trim figure and regal bearing she
could look very nice in a carefully pressed dress, no matter how out-
dated, then finish off the outfit with her current everyday shoes, even
her 1950s black high-top sneakers.) One particular dress of Anna's
became familiar to her friends as the one she wore to openings of
Harlan's exhibitions. It was a well-kept relic, a silky purple two-piece
outfit with a mid-calf-length gathered skirt and an overblouse top, or
jacket, with a self-belt and buttons down the front. A pale lavender
satin bow at the neck matched the satin lining of the turned-up three-
quarter-length sleeves. With the money accumulating in the bank, Anna
could have bought any new dress she wanted, but evidently no such
desire seized her. The Hubbards' car was once flooded on the riverbank
with the purple dress inside, but Anna reclaimed it with dry cleaning.

When Anna was young, the Eikenhout family rented a cottage on one
of Michigan's small lakes each year from the Fourth of July to Labor
Day. The first favorite spot was Diamond Lake in Ramona, Michigan,
and their cottage was named Linger Longer. Later came Black Lake,
Crystal Lake, and Pickerel Lake. Etta was her father's fishing pal. Anna's
passions were swimming and canoeing. Anna bristled in later years
when Harlan persisted in saying she was a city girl when he married
her. Roughing it was nothing new for her, she pointed out. The living
had been rustic at all of the Eikenhouts' lake cottages: the family cooked
with kerosene fuel, used kerosene lamps and an outhouse, and toted
water. Anna's family vacations prepared her for riverbank life with
Harlan—and for the greatest flood in Cincinnati history.
    At the time of the 1937 flood, Anna, Etta, and Barre had been
working and sharing an apartment in Cincinnati for several years. In
nineteen days of flooding there in January and February, the Ohio
River reached a record crest of eighty feet. Electric power supplies
failed, and about 15 percent of the city was under water. On the day
gasoline storage tanks broke loose in Mill Creek Valley, huge fires
erupted and the waterworks pumps shut down. The flooded city lost
its ready supply of potable water. But for Anna, Etta, and Barre, in
their hilltop Clifton neighborhood situated high above the flood waters, the loss of utilities was only a minor inconvenience. The experienced campers had stored plenty of drinking water, and they had enough
electricity for one light at night and the radio during the day. There
was gas for cooking, and since the city was still accessible from the

north, there was no food shortage. They had offered their services to the Red Cross but were never called on, so all they had to do was keep occupied until their low-lying downtown workplaces reopened. Nellie Eikenhout, who signed herself "Mam" to her daughters, wrote: "I have thought more than once how your cottage experience of roughing it will stand in good stead now. Some people are much more helpless than we are."

Music, stylish new clothes, lakeside family vacations—these were Anna's happy reminiscences of her childhood. But Anna's nostalgic writing about the "children's hour" at her house seems chilling to me. Was twilight the only time the girls received special attention? How quiet, how invisible, were they expected to be for the rest of the day? In Nellie Eikenhout's house the cleaning and cooking had to be done to perfection, and so Nellie didn't want little Anna's help. Instead she would send Anna to the piano to practice. Anna learned very young to block off her hurt feelings, burying the hurts deep and putting into her music the feelings she couldn't express any other way. When she grew up she retained a certain vulnerability. Mam referred to it indirectly when she wrote in 1940 to Etta about John Eikenhout's failing health: she thought seeing the change in him might be too hard on Anna. Years later Etta told their niece, Susan, that Anna's feelings had always been tender; she took sorrows hard, and she worried.

Anna had learned from her mother that playing the piano was the only thing she did well, and for the rest of her life she remained certain that she was uncreative. In the revealing drafts of the *Library Journal* article she wrote in her fifties, she described herself in negative, unnecessarily harsh words; her idea of herself seems distorted and unrealistic: "I am not one of those with a creative mind," Anna wrote; "I am rather inept but I have always been deeply interested in all forms of [the arts]. The more so since I myself lack the imagination and the impulse to create. . . . I'm not good at doing things myself, but I've always been deeply interested in those who can, in how they think and how they work. If I can do anything at all it is play the piano, and here again I'm no soloist, I'd much rather accompany someone else. As a pianist I have no interest in playing solos."

Of course it would be unfair to hold Nellie to today's standards of parenting, because her mother-daughter tradition was rooted in the mid-nineteenth century. Nellie's mother, Anna Wonder Ross, had been only two years old when her own mother died in 1844, and for an unknown number of years she was raised by a stepmother. Her marriage in 1862 at age nineteen was the beginning of a life of hard work and exhausting pregnancies. Nellie, born in 1878, was her ninth child (the fourth and fifth children had died as infants, and the seventh would die in her teens). Fifteen more years and five more children later, Anna Wonder Ross emigrated to the United States, and in six months she was dead of pneumonia.

Jan Ross didn't remarry, and Nellie's older sister, Grace, wasn't inclined to be motherly. At age sixty Nellie wrote to Anna and Etta in January 1939 that she regretted having so often failed to win her children's confidence and hoped they would excuse her, because she had lost her mother at a young age. Hurt by that loss, she had kept her pain to herself: "Opa always seemed at a distance, until we had our children and we understood him better. Grace was only five years older than I, and never very sympathetic. So naturally, we younger ones kept things to ourselves and missed out, all around."

Nellie Ross Eikenhout became the only kind of mother she knew how to be, keeping an immaculate home, teaching her daughters the rules of proper conduct, and maintaining a blameless reputation in the community. Nellie needed her daughters' love, but not knowing any better, she tried to hold on to them by dominating them. Her letters show how she used guilt and shame to try to control them even after they had grown up and moved away. She felt betrayed and withheld love when they behaved in ways she considered disrespectable. Nellie assumed that Anna, the oldest and most obedient of her three daughters, would take care of her in her old age. But that typical Victorian expectation was one of several that Nellie would not see fulfilled by the strong-minded Anna.

5

Independence

I had hung my coat in locker nineteen every morning for some fifteen years. . . . How glad I was that the Library had not yet moved into its handsome new quarters; this old building had the feeling of home for me.

Anna's Library Journal drafts, 1954

Anna's love of home kept her in Grand Rapids until she was nearly twenty-six. From 1920 to 1922 she attended junior college in Grand Rapids with her high school friends Hilda Bell and Lee Holden. Her curriculum was heavy in English and history. Afterward, still calling Grand Rapids home, she went on to Ohio State University with Hilda (Lee went to the University of Michigan), and they shared a room there, in Columbus, during the school terms from 1922 to 1925.

In the arts-education program at Ohio State, Anna simultaneously pursued a bachelor of arts degree and a bachelor of science degree in education. Having transferred her French credits from junior college, she was able to complete her class work in intermediate French language in just two quarters. The rest of her work in French at Ohio State was in literature, drama, and literary criticism, plus phonetics and the teaching of French. As for German, she followed the elementary and intermediate courses with one called "Easy Classical Reading" and two in advanced German, one concentrating on writings of Lessing, and the other, Schiller. Anna made Pi Lambda Theta (the women's honorary education fraternity) and Phi Beta Kappa, graduating "with high distinction" in 1925.

Then Anna went back to her Dutch world. She accepted a position teaching French and German twenty hours a week for twelve hundred dollars a year at Hope College, a small coeducational institution in Holland, Michigan, about twenty miles southwest of Grand

Rapids. The atmosphere at this small college affiliated with the Reformed Church contrasted sharply with the openness of Ohio State. The 1926–27 bulletin proclaimed that Hope College "inculcates gospel truths and demands a consistent moral character and deportment," aiming to develop the "high moral culture and character of the student no less than to advance his intellectual development."

Anna resigned in 1927 after two years of teaching and never taught again. Years later she admitted that she "didn't especially enjoy it." The problem may have been her shyness: facing people in the classroom may have been too great an effort. Whatever the reason, its effect on Anna was such that Nella Mae changed her mind about becoming a teacher like her big sister.

There is no record of how Anna spent her last year at home. According to Etta, writing sixty years later, the "stifling atmosphere" at Hope College and in Grand Rapids was too much for Anna. The two sisters had "felt terribly restricted—even sanctioned to some extent—in G.R. which is the reason we both got the heck out of there—almost as soon as possible!" Etta implied they had been stifled by community attitudes, but there is little doubt they also wanted to escape their mother's control. "As soon as possible" finally came for Anna in July 1928.

Anna chose Cincinnati, Etta said, because a friend of hers had encouraged her to apply for a job with the Public Library of Cincinnati and Hamilton County (the Cincinnati Public Library). That friend was probably Catherine (Kay) Learned, who went to Cincinnati with Anna and shared an apartment with her for about five years. Kay, who became a teacher, was one of Anna's former Hope College students, a 1926 graduate from Plymouth, Michigan, and five years younger than Anna. In later years Anna said she went to the Cincinnati library because of its in-service training program, after which trainees were obliged to work for two years in the Cincinnati library system. Anna was asked to stay on afterward, and she did so until 1943, a total of fifteen years.

The hilly, picturesque Queen City on the Ohio River was ideal for Anna. German immigrants of 1840 to 1880 had toned down the sober Presbyterian influence and toned up the boom-town atmosphere of the riverfront. The Germans' "Over-the-Rhine" community, with its beer gardens and saloons, became a cultural and political center. First steamboats, then the railroad, brought prosperity and the refinements that accompany a city's growing up. By the early 1900s German culture had been thoroughly assimilated, flavoring Anna's Cincinnati of 1928 with as much tradition as Grand Rapids had, and at the same time more open-mindededness.

Cincinnati was flourishing in 1928. For two years the Cincinnati Street Railway Company had been buying motor coaches to augment the streetcar service. The corrupt political machine of the late Republican boss George B. Cox had been swept out in 1924, and many civic improvements were being introduced under an innovative city-manager form of government. A construction boom during the prosperous 1920s gave Cincinnati many new landmark buildings as well as one of the two signature skyscrapers of the Cincinnati skyline, the Carew Tower. Occupying the block from Fourth to Fifth Streets and from Vine to Race, the Carew Tower project was the forerunner of New York's Rockefeller Center when it opened in late 1930 with its office tower, department store, shopping arcade, and thirty-one-story hotel. The hotel, the Netherland Plaza, became Cincinnati's finest. Other fine hotels, such as the Sinton and the Gibson, and out-and-out speakeasies furnished nightclub life during Prohibition. The Gayety burlesque survived the other downtown vaudeville theaters, and in the 1920s several ornate movie palaces went up. My own girlhood favorite three decades later was the Albee on Fountain Square. The marble mantelpiece from the fireplace in one of its three ladies' lounges is preserved now in a reception room of the administrative offices of the "new" Cincinnati Public Library at Eighth and Vine.

Anna was drawn into Cincinnati's lasting love affair with music, another Germanic legacy. The success of decades of German-style choral festivals led to the erecting of Music Hall, dedicated in May 1878, and the permanent establishment of the Cincinnati Music Festival, today called the May Festival, Cincinnati's most important musical event. Anna became a Music Hall regular at concerts of the Cincinnati Symphony Orchestra, and in the 1930s Etta, an accomplished soloist, and Anna, with her small, high, clear soprano voice, sang in the festival chorus. In the summer they attended opera performances at the Cincinnati Zoo. (Cincinnati's opera lovers, steeped in the Germanic summer-garden tradition, were used to the quacking of the ducks and the barking of the seals during the quiet arias.) Even more than these large-scale musical opportunities, however, Anna cherished her association with an informal group of music-making friends who gathered in one another's homes to play. In later years, on the rare occasions when

Anna shared reminiscences of her before-Harlan life, it often was those "musical evenings" she spoke of.

Anna and Kay lived about three and a half miles north of the downtown riverfront, in Clifton, which at the turn of the century had been an exclusive suburb of large estates. Now many of the mansions had given way to smaller residences. Anna and Kay's one-room apartment at 3502 Clifton Avenue was a block north of the corner of Clifton and Ludlow, Clifton's recognized center. The late George B. Cox's mansion was just across the avenue and down a shady street along the edge of Burnet Woods park. To get downtown to the library, all Anna had to do was hop onto the Vine-Clifton streetcar.

When Anna began working in 1928 at the old public library at 629 Vine Street, concerned citizens had already been calling for a new building for nearly forty years. In 1868 Truman B. Handy—contractor, builder, grain speculator, and grandson of John Marshall, former chief justice of the U.S. Supreme Court—began to build an opera house on the site. When no more than a facade and entrance had been erected, he went bankrupt. The opera house architect, James W. McLaughlin, was employed to remodel the front and redesign the rest of the building as a public library. It opened in 1874, and by 1890 it was overcrowded.

Seen today, photos of the interior seem to show a theater whose tiers and galleries had been modified to hold bookshelves, but in fact the design was intentional and resembled that of a half dozen other libraries of the period. The central atrium-hall was the public's reading room and the Circulation department, and surrounding the atrium were the four open floors of stacks. Shelvers and other employees working in the stacks walked along a catwalk with only a hip-high iron railing between them and a drop to the ground floor. Those who needed extra height to reach the top of the seven-foot shelves stood on a two-step stool called a "cricket," specially constructed with a built-in pole for use as a steadying handhold.

The shelves constituting the stacks were supported by an integral grid of cast iron. In other words, the shelves *were* the structure, and interior renovations were impossible; the space couldn't be redesigned short of tearing down the building—precisely the step heatedly advocated by many Cincinnatians throughout the decades of failed bond issues, court cases, and factional wrangling over site selection that continued during Anna's years there. Time and again the approaching bond issue was heralded by a crescendo of newspaper articles about the old library's deplorable conditions: poor light and ventilation; insufficient fire exits; mold and mildew in the basement and subcellar, where newspapers and books were piled up; and debilitating summertime heat on the top floor, under the metal roof. Seating and shelf space were at a premium. Some years later Anna wrote that working in the old library had given her the best possible training for keeping house in the crowded quarters of a shantyboat.

In summer 1928 Anna took, and passed, the library's challenging entrance examination in history, current events, literature, and general information, a requirement for applicants who didn't have a library science degree. Anna was hired in September as a library apprentice for a six-month training period at the rate of $600 a year, and after the appointments were made in April 1929, her salary rose to $1,260.

The examination and the training were, from 1926 to 1956, the bailiwick of Miss Alice Dunlap. As a career girl in New York City, Miss Dunlap had trained for three years at the New York Public Library, and when that program was absorbed later by Columbia University, she was accredited with a master's degree. In the program she created at the Cincinnati library, trainees took classes in the morning and worked in the various departments in the afternoon from fall through spring. Summer training was out of the question, because the only space available for holding class was on the top floor, under the metal roof.

Anna took impeccable notes during her library training and saved them. The instructors stressed the importance of discovering exactly what the patrons wanted, even when the patrons themselves didn't know. On January 16, 1929, Anna heard a lecture she titled "Traits of a circulation librarian, as given by Dr. Charters." The list of traits she recorded, each followed by three or four tips, is a profile of the professional Anna: accuracy, adaptability, belief in your work, courtesy, dependability, forcefulness, health, imagination, industriousness, initiative, intelligence, interest in people, judgment, memory, mental curiosity, neatness, patience, pleasantness, poise, professional knowledge, speed, system, and tact.

The library staff created an atmosphere in which ladies could work respectably. The Staff Association had an active program of social events, including teas on Mondays and Fridays in the Tea Room. The tradition of serving springele, lebkuchen, pfeffernüsse, and other German cookies at the Christmas tea endured long after the staff ceased to be mostly German. Special affairs, such as the 1935 spring tea at which the Junior Staff Association entertained the graduating training class, were held at the Netherland Plaza. On that particular Sunday afternoon, reported the *Cincinnati Times Star*, Miss Dunlap announced the engagement of one of the staff members, and "Miss Miriam Rothenberg, soprano, entertained the assembly with vocal selections." Taking for granted that the accompanist was of German extraction, the *Times Star* reported that Miss Rothenberg was accompanied by "Miss Anne Eichenhaut."

The days of the old library and the teas were running out when, ten years after Anna resigned, the Staff Association honored the Hubbards with a tea. It was 1953, and Harlan's *Shantyboat* had just been published. Tea was served "in the little informal lunchroom with its old-fashioned wooden lockers lining the walls," Anna wrote in her *Library Journal* drafts. "I had hung my coat in locker nineteen every morning for some fifteen years. . . . On this special occasion the tea table was beautiful with lace and lighted candles, shining silver and a centerpiece of chrysanthemums. I noticed that the sink and the old gas stove were discreetly hidden behind a folding screen. How glad I was that the Library had not yet moved into its handsome new quarters; this old building had the feeling of home for me."

In late 1929 or early 1930 Anna became assistant librarian in the Fine Arts department under department head Miss Sophie Collman, and except for one or two brief assignments in Reference, she remained in Fine Arts until her resignation. In her *Library Journal* drafts Anna wrote about the pleasure of working in Fine Arts and serving its cross-section of interesting patrons:

> I was assigned there originally because I had some knowl-
> edge of music, but I soon became engrossed in learning about
> all the other fascinating subjects covered by the seven hundreds.
> Since part of my work was writing notes on the new Art Room
> books for the Guide Post [the library's newsletter], I first
> became acquainted with the latest books in each field; from
> them I worked back into the older literature finding a wealth of
> material and no end of treasures. We gave time, in the Art
> Department, to studying the books, for it was Miss Collman's
> conviction that only by knowing the books personally could we
> be of the greatest help to our patrons.
> The patrons were every bit as interesting as the books. It was
> a pleasure to wait on the housewife who was doing her own

redecorating, to bring out the best books of plans for the
couple that was going to build a house, to find just the right
lettering for the commercial artist. Some of our patrons returned so often they became our friends. . . . There was the
vivacious young teacher of modern dance. . . . The designer for
the local stock company might need period furniture, or
interiors, or costumes. . . . There were the young string players
from the symphony who regularly borrowed the chamber
music scores. The writer of program notes for the symphony
concerts came in to use our index. . . . Among the Art Room
patrons I remember, too, a young architect who had studied at
Taliesin [Frank Lloyd Wright's home and architecture school in
Wisconsin]. And there was the sculptor who was making the
huge figures for the Times-Star building; for him we searched
out portraits of his subjects. It was a joy day after day to work
with these people who were doing things.

Prosperity crashed with the stock market in October 1929, usher-
ing in the Great Depression. Unlike many less fortunate American cities, Cincinnati had only one minor bank failure. Well into 1930 the
Queen City continued being cushioned by its diverse economy and by
numerous large construction projects, including Union Terminal and
the Carew Tower. Cincinnati construction declined only 6 percent between 1928 and 1930, while the nationwide average was down one-
third. But the building energy of the 1920s finally trickled out, and
bread lines, strikes, bankruptcies, and hardship gripped Cincinnati too.
Unemployment and demands for private and public relief were massive problems by 1932 and 1933.

The library also was affected. Employees' salaries were reduced
by 8–1/3 percent until 1934. In 1932 the library began offering a program of free classes where people out of work might learn a new trade
in fields such as airplane mechanics or architectural and mechanical
drawing, or just forget their worries with activities such as tap dancing and basketball. Book circulation increased. In demand were books
that would help people pass the time, stretch their dollars, or learn
new ways to make a living.

Throughout the Depression the Eikenhout family still gathered at
a lake cottage in Michigan in the summers. In familiar surroundings
where the living had always been rustic anyway, everyone could forget
the prevailing hard times—or so it seems from the happy faces pictured in Mam's photo albums. Though the Great Depression lasted

more than a decade, it did not dominate Eikenhout family letters. Habits of thrift in good times sustained the family through the most severe economic and emotional shock the country had ever experienced.

Anna's first five years in Cincinnati are lost to the record along with all but two letters she wrote, both of them to Lee Holden. In them Anna sounds lonely living as an independent career girl. If Kay's newsy, unemotional letters to Anna in later years are a reliable indicator, Anna and Kay were chums, but not kindred spirits. My guess is that the summer lakeside vacations were what Anna lived for above all else in those first Cincinnati years, because her heart was still at home with her family. But the years of loneliness would soon be over.

6

~∂~

Turning Points

Write to me, Lee. Tell me all about everything. I'm really very sentimental—to a fault—and I just adore to know all about things. Very likely this will be the nearest I'll ever come to an engagement and a wedding.

Anna to Lee Holden, September 18, 1932

Anna was still at home in late 1926, graduated from Ohio State and teaching at Hope College, when Hilda Bell wrote out in a little loose-leaf booklet a number of poems about love and loss and gave it to Anna. There were poems by Yeats, Walter de la Mare, Robert Browning, Edna St. Vincent Millay, Robert Frost, and others, and some by Hilda herself. In the booklet is this note: "My Annie dear, Just a tiny note to you to tell you your own Hilda is loving you and to put here a most precious kiss. Goodnight darling. Your Hilda."

Hilda's romance with her college sweetheart, Johnny, had gone awry. The memory of him was still with Hilda years later, when she wrote Anna that busy hands and heart had cured the old hurt: she had married Bob Webber, and she adored him and their two boys. But the hurt had been still fresh in November 1926, when Hilda gave Anna the little booklet. It was an expression both of her heartache over Johnny and of her loving friendship with Anna. In the shockingly sophisticated Roaring Twenties, the gift of the booklet and the wording of the note were innocent echoes of the nineteenth-century era of rigidly prescribed moral behavior and gender roles known as Victorianism. Though technically Anna and Hilda narrowly missed being born Victorians, they were raised by Victorians and brought up in a Victorian community.

Victorian women were trained to be emotionally reserved with men, but with one another they could share their emotions openly.

Loving friendship between young single women was considered enno-
bling, a practicing of the devotion and fidelity that would be part of
marriage. Women could travel together; give each other gifts; write
each other poetry; hold hands; share kisses, a bedroom, a bed—all
with society's approval. Women also could live together permanently.
In nineteenth-century America a long-term, loving relationship between
women living together was commonplace and acceptable, and was
called a "Boston marriage." Henry James, chronicler of proper Boston society, wrote about one in *The Bostonians*. Louisa May Alcott,
the ultimate writer of moral stories for girls, wrote of one in *An Old-
Fashioned Girl*.

Some of the poetry and letters women exchanged then seem obviously erotic to modern readers, but at that time it was assumed that
"good" women didn't experience sexual desire. Women's feelings for
one another were considered spiritual and emotional, not physical.
Then the late-nineteenth-century writings of Sigmund Freud and others began influencing American social attitudes. By the end of World
War I, Americans knew that loving relationships between women might
be unions of bodies as well as souls, and approval was shut off abruptly.
But in the 1920s Anna and Hilda still belonged more to the nineteenth
century than to the twentieth.

Anna and Hilda remained friends all their lives, and the great bond
between them was music. In letters during the 1930s Hilda wrote Anna
about ensembles she was playing in, and about concerts she had heard
on the radio. Many years later Hilda wrote to Anna after her husband
died, telling Anna about her two musical sons and their children. Anna's
response summed up her love of music and of Hilda:

June 2, 1969

Dearest Hildy,
    Your dear quiet letter, written May 24, is so reassuring. . . .
It is good to be able to think of you with your precious family,
especially those wonderful grandchildren. . . . It is good they
are involved in music, and best of all is their studying with you,
Hilda. You have so much to give them. Music is the most
precious inheritance. The music we played together in our high
school years and then in our college years has been a live thing
for me and is still a wonderful part of my experience of life.
    Last Saturday afternoon a group of young friends, Hanover
College students, came here to see us once more before school
is over. . . . You can imagine how it turned my thoughts back to

the Glee Club singing at Ohio State. And you, Hilda, were the very special high point of the concerts, playing your 'cello. ᐧ . . . All these fine things go way back to the days when you and Charles and I played trios. Uncle Leo [Cayvan] was there trying to help us play better. Kate Baxter was always talking, in her harmony class, about the golden thread—in the inner voices. It seems to me that music has been the golden thread through all my life. And that is inseparable from my love for you, Hildy dear.

Know that I am thinking of you, loving you always.

Your Annie

Anna's friendship with her other dear friend, Lee Holden, was no less intimate or long lasting. "Some friends, like you Lee," Anna wrote Lee in 1933, "whom one has known intimately and since younger days, one never loses. Whether I go, or whether you get married and go to live in Green Bay, doesn't matter. We still have each other. I feel almost that I have had more of you (the real you) since we have had to depend on letters and a few precious hours snatched at holiday times. I wonder if you know how much you mean to me, Lee. And always will."

Though Lee was less fanciful and romantic than Hilda, it was Lee to whom Anna wrote a long, starry-eyed letter at the end of summer 1922. The girls had finished their second year of junior college, and Anna had spent the summer working as a music counselor at Keewano, a Campfire Girls' camp on Lake Michigan about thirty miles west of Grand Rapids. With her twentieth birthday only days away, her heart was still tied to home, and she was unsure about her future. The campers had left, and some of the counselors were staying behind to strike camp. For fun they took a nighttime motorboat ride to nearby Fruitport.

The camp motorboat was tied up at the Coast Guard station. As everyone was getting settled, the Coast Guard vessel *Alabama* passed by, churning up the water. "The waves were wonderful," Anna wrote. Lowell, the head counselor, brought the motorboat around the *Alabama* at the dock to gas up "and made a perfect landing, of course," Anna noted. "And then we started up the river [the Grand River]. Oh, Lee, you can't imagine how wonderful the night was, and how beautiful the water and the hills mirrored in the deep dark river. The moon was shining, and there were thousands of thousands of stars. . . . there is something irresistible about water and stars and night—the spell is fatal."

For telling about Lowell, Anna described herself in the third person, and the scene in the present tense, as if she were writing fiction: "She can just see the outline of broad shoulders and a firm chin and a little white hat. That is enough. To sit there and know that everything is all right. Such a sense of security, but not without reason. Steering by the stars. It is almost too great a privilege to be sitting there." Anna was enthralled by Lowell's boat-handling skill as he shut the engine off and drifted in to the dock at Fruitport. "He jumps out and fastens the rope—same as he always fastens that rope, but the girl never tires of watching this simple action. Perfect control. Such ease."

Anna wrote all the details of the action and the dialogue. They bought snacks in a little dockside store and reboarded for the return trip. "The girl is glad that the other three have taken the back seat again. And in her heart she thanks her two chums for giving her the same seat across from him." Soon they were landing. "Perfect again. He jumps out just as we drift alongside, and ties the boat fast to the pier."

In the bittersweet conclusion of the letter, Anna showed that she wasn't taking her crush on Lowell seriously. She even seemed amused by it. She would have liked to stay with her family and continue with junior college, but somehow she felt she should leave home for Ohio State and gain broader experience. She knew she was at a turning point:

Well, Lee, you have had enough of this I'm sure. But I had to take it out on somebody. You really don't mind so very much, do you? And think, it is almost over. "And then," as the line in the play goes. And then—But nobody will ever know what comes next.

Lee, what if I should go to Columbus with Hilda? Everyone thinks it is the best thing to do—Miss Baxter and Mr. Cayvan and my folks and Diddle's [probably Hilda's] folks. If I am going to do French there would be no point in staying another year at J[unior] C[ollege]. I should have been perfectly content at JC another year. Somehow after this summer at camp I would like to be with my family for a while. But I suppose we can't always stay at home.

We don't know just when we'll leave camp. . . . Anyway I will see you very soon.

How are you, Lee? How is your work? And your family? And how many more names of people you have met? Oh, everything? And do you still love me? I shall be so glad to be

with you again, for longer than just one afternoon. Loads and
loads of love,

Yours as ever,
Anne

Ten years later, in summer 1932, Hilda had been married for two
years and living in Bronxville, New York, and Lee was planning her
wedding to Art Thiele, when Anna visited Lee at home in Grand Rapids. Back in Cincinnati again, Anna wrote Lee about the fun she and
Kay had had, sprucing up and reorganizing their one-room apartment.
But Anna had begun longing for a home of her own: "When I was
upstairs with you that evening at your house, and saw all your lovely
linen and heard about your plans for the things you would need, I
wished I were going to have a whole house to keep, too. One room is
fun, but a whole house or even apartment with all your own things—
I think that would be wonderful. I felt the same way when I saw Hilda's
lovely apartment in Bronxville."

So much of Anna is in the next few lines: the tenderness, the sentimentality, and at this time in her life, the loneliness. She thought she
would never marry: "Write to me, Lee. Tell me all about everything.
I'm really very sentimental—to a fault—and I just adore to know all
about things. Very likely this will be the nearest I'll ever come to an
engagement and a wedding."

Anna's tone was sad again when she wrote to Lee the following
February, 1933. After mentioning certain recent losses that friends of
theirs had suffered, Anna confided that she was about to lose a new
but dear friend, Barre Pritchett: "Changes are always hard. You will
forgive me for mentioning this as if it were of the same proportions as
these other sorrows. But I have felt that Barre's leaving us will change
everything for me. She will be leaving Cincinnati in a few months,
perhaps sooner. And I feel somehow that I shall never see her again.
When she leaves she goes out of my life." But Barre didn't leave Cincinnati after all, not until ten years later, when Anna was married.

Barre Pritchett came to Cincinnati in 1932 as supervisor of the
Home Service Section of the Hamilton County chapter of the American Red Cross. She had worked for the Red Cross since 1927, first in
Charlotte, North Carolina, then in New Orleans. She was born on
July 25, 1900, in Greensboro, North Carolina, and earned a bachelor
of science degree from Meredith College in Raleigh in 1923. In 1923–
24 she did graduate work in social science and community health at

Columbia University. Over the years Barre developed a career as a researcher and writer-editor in health and medicine.

Anna and Barre met in 1932, but how and exactly when are unknown. Sometime in 1933 Kay moved to another address in Cincinnati, and Etta moved to Cincinnati after being laid off in New York and spending a while at home in Grand Rapids. Barre resigned from the Red Cross in April, and by Christmas, if not sooner, the Anna-Barre-and-Etta trio was installed in the red-brick Rockdale Apartments at 538 Rockdale Avenue, a few blocks east of the Cincinnati Zoo. With Barre as cook and Anna as housekeeper, the three women would stay together for ten years.

Barre resigned from the Red Cross because of an illness unnamed in surviving letters, and it was several years before she resumed full-time work. Her health was precarious all the while she lived with Anna and Etta, and after. Sometime in 1933 she had surgery, and Anna cared for her. At various times in the 1930s Barre wrote to Anna of having headaches, using an inhaler, wearing a harness, and having pain in her back and in her neck and shoulder muscles. She struggled constantly with fatigue, weight loss, and inability to gain weight. In a 1944 letter to Anna, Barre alluded to having had lumps in the breast in past years. Two of Barre's workplace associates in later years thought she had had cancer at least once and might have had a double mastectomy.

In August 1936 Anna, Barre, and Etta moved to an apartment at 3027 Clifton Avenue, a boxy, two-story stucco building a few blocks south of where Anna and Kay had lived. The locale is still much the same. A few doors north is the oldest Jewish theological school in the Americas, the Hebrew Union College of the University of Cincinnati (UC). Across the street is the property line between Burnet Woods park on the north side and the UC campus on the south (Etta earned her college degree from UC in eight years of night school). The summertime band concerts in Burnet Woods were probably popular with the 3027 trio, and by walking its trails, Anna kept her love of the outdoors alive between summers. In 1933 Barre joined the Eikenhout family for the annual lakeside vacation, and they accepted her as one of their own. It was the first of six consecutive summers she would spend with the Eikenhouts at Pickerel Lake outside Newaygo, Michigan. Barre would take her part-time editing work to the lake and stay there all summer, trying to regain strength and weight, and Etta's friend Fran Bailey stayed at the apartment while Barre was gone. Family members came and went at the lake, and Anna and Etta went up in

July for their vacations. These summertime idylls went on through 1938, and then John Eikenhout's failing health put an end to them.

Many letters Barre wrote to Anna in Cincinnati from the lake and elsewhere in 1936, 1937, and 1938 have survived. They are full of relationship-rich stuff, flowery, verbose, intense, moody, and shot through with humor, Appalachianisms, poetry, and metaphors involving sun, clouds, mist, and rain—anything but the terse, prosaic letters that might be expected of a technical writer-editor. Over and over, Barre wrote that she was longing to talk with Anna again: *Dovelette— I've missed you just as much as you have missed me* [May 1936]. *So many things I have to tell you—so much in my heart—that wants to be told—even my favorite words are not enough—could never be* [June 1936]. *Each day I know you nearer and dearer than ever before—I wonder what I did without you all those years* [August 1936]. *I never really knew before I found you the true meaning of love and friendship and trust and confidence* [March 1937]. *Am I crazy Dove—or just too deeply touched with the essence of a spiritual contact?* [June 1938].

Mysterious, the attraction that brought Anna and Barre together. They did share an interest in children's books; Barre left a large collection when she died. But what Barre knew of classical music she learned from Anna and Etta. And if Barre's reaction to reading *Gone with the Wind* in March 1937 is indicative, great literature wasn't a bond either: she was "overwhelmed at its power—its tragedy—its beauty. . . . I shall have to tell you of it later when I have recovered from the stupendous effect."

What is clear is that Anna and Barre shared the gift they both had for emotional intimacy. Yet Barre felt that she and Anna couldn't stay together always. She knew that society now considered her unconventional. "I do not believe that Lee has exactly ever approved of me," she wrote to Anna in 1944. "Oh yes Dove—I know, or have an idea, how rigidly conventional ideas can be." Anna's mother also sensed the impossibility of Anna and Barre staying together. In a letter the day before Anna's wedding Mam wrote: "There was bound to be a change, sometime, Ann, and parting with Barre for a long time, perhaps, has been hardest for you. So I am very glad that your plans have taken this shape."

Barre had always feared losing Anna, but not to community opinion; Anna stayed with Barre regardless of how middle-class society might view their relationship. Rather, Barre feared losing Anna to Anna's desire to love and be loved by a man, to marry and have a home of her own. In a letter from the lake in 1938 Barre wrote: "To this day—my blindly prophetic words of some six years ago haunt me in the night! . . . Today I hear the echo of my gentle warnings resounding in my own ears—reminding me I must not expect the impossible. . ." (June 23). The year after Anna married, Barre wrote: "It must be wonderful to have always someone with you who means more than anyone else and to whom you mean everything—without the constant knowledge and eternal fear that someday you will of circumstantial necessity go each a separate way" (April 23, 1944).

When Anna thought, in 1932, that she would never marry, her stored-up emotions had nowhere to go but to other women. But by 1938 Anna's marrying was Barre's greatest fear. Obviously life had changed for Anna in the meantime.

A patron seeing Anna at the Fine Arts desk in the library in the early 1930s, with her ash-blond hair parted in the middle and gathered into a nineteenth-century bun on her neck, might have thought her a spinster. But that label was quickly dismissed when her words and smile revealed her charm. That quiet charm of Anna's is summed up in a reminiscence by one of her former library patrons, who as a young man went to Fine Arts to borrow the score of *Rigoletto* in preparation for attending the Zoo Opera. When he couldn't find the score on the shelves, Anna told him it had been checked out. "My disappointment must have shown on my face," he wrote many years later, because "a smile lifted the corner of her mouth and her eyes took on a soft look. Leaning over she opened the lower drawer of her desk and handed me a bound score with the word <u>Rigoletto</u> stamped on the spine. 'Here,' she said, 'I had planned to take this home overnight but you may have it.'"

The outward pattern of Anna's life, by 1934, seemed set: she had companionship, satisfying work, and music. But Anna was unhappy. She was attracted to one of the Fine Arts patrons, an architect named Charles E. Young, and he was not taking notice. She wrote to Lee and Hilda about her unhappiness. "By the way, do you see the young architect at all?" Lee asked in January 1935. "Isn't there some way you can get acquainted with him," Hilda wrote in May, "or is he married or in love with someone?" In November, Lee advised Anna to keep busy and happy. "If Charles Young is <u>your</u> man, your paths will cross and you will get acquainted. . . . While you are upholding him as your ideal perhaps you are missing some other more accessible gentleman!"

For much of 1936 Charles Young was still on Anna's mind. Lee wrote in September that she was glad Anna's temporary assignment in the Reference department was over, because only in Fine Arts was she likely to see Mr. Young. "I do wish you could find out if he is married before you waste so much thought on him," Lee wrote. "I don't want you hurt." Again Lee advised being "interested in and interesting to all the nice men" who patronized Fine Arts. "Above all else you must keep happy!"

Anna's next letter brought Lee thrilling news. Lee's advice had been prophetic; Anna was going out and having fun now, but not with Charles Young. She had fallen in love with Paul Briol.

The well-known Cincinnati photographer Paul Briol was born on September 18, 1889, in Spencer, Massachusetts, to parents who were French-Swiss immigrants. The family moved often as Paul was growing up; his father was a Presbyterian minister and missionary. Paul's first job, after graduating from high school in 1908, was as a newspaper journalist in St. Louis. A year later he went to Cincinnati, and he stayed there the rest of his career.

His first professionally credited work appeared in November 1909 in the Cincinnati *Commercial Tribune*, a photograph of Leopold Stokowski conducting a rehearsal of the Cincinnati Symphony Orchestra. From 1910 to 1920 Paul was a staff photographer for the *Cincinnati Enquirer,* and for the last eight of those years he was also author of the *Enquirer*'s column "Old-World Chitchat." He left the *Enquirer* in 1920, and in 1921 he began managing a downtown bookstore called The Book Shelf, at 112 Garfield Place, the elegant former home of Cincinnati's prominent Seasongood family. Paul and his associate, Howard Henderson, made the store a center of local culture and literary discussion. In 1925 The Book Shelf published Paul's small book of Cincinnati photographs titled *The City of Rivers and Hills.*

When the store closed in 1930, a victim of the Depression, Paul opened a studio in the nearby Doctors' Building at 19 Garfield Place and began building his reputation as a freelance commercial, architectural, and scenic photographer. Portraits helped pay the bills, but Paul's real interest was in being on the go with his eight-by-ten camera, photographing the sights and the people of Cincinnati and environs. Paul's photographs made an artistically historic record of the fine old city— the river, steamboats, scenic views, houses, gardens, and landmarks of all kinds. He and Anna may have met while he was photographing the library inside and out.

Paul's first appearance in the record of Anna's life is in a letter from Barre at Pickerel Lake on August 19, 1936. The letter seems to be a reaction to a letter from Anna containing the news about Paul—"seems to," because the metaphors are particularly dense. But Barre implied in two phrases, at least, that she had lost Anna: ". . . all those beautiful realities that have slipped beyond my fingers . . . the love that almost belonged to me. . . ." Barre's fear had been realized: her love hadn't been enough for Anna. Nevertheless, her letters to Anna never lost their loving quality, never were marred by jealousy. In fact, in March 1937 Barre wrote warmly of Paul. From her mother's home in Charlotte, where she was spending a few weeks to rest and gain weight, she wrote to Anna that she was pleased about Anna's "parties and doin's" and anticipated enjoying good times again with her, "except—I like you to be with Paul alone sometimes—and then again my heart outraces my every ability to speak or to write!—That thought—My feeling for your great love for love and Paul—but it strikes me dumb and humble!"

Though Anna's heart had gone a separate way, Anna and Barre continued living together, with Etta, until 1943. Barre left Cincinnati afterward and ultimately settled in the Washington, D.C., area, where in 1958 she became a medical copy editor in Bethesda, Maryland. Her co-workers found her a great talker about books and politics, but she revealed nothing of her personal life, not even to those she shared an office with for years. When Barre retired in 1970 she moved to Fort Wayne, Indiana, to live with her sister, and she died there in 1981.

Lee and Hilda responded very differently to Anna's news about Paul; maybe Anna had tailored her news for her two friends, with their different emotional makeup. To Lee she evidently wrote about having a good time, how interesting Paul was, and her new hairstyle. Falling in love had spurred Anna to drop the nineteenth-century look at last and have her hair cut. Delighted, Lee answered in November: "My dear, you can't know how glad I am you are having a good time at last! And you have had your hair bobbed!! I can't imagine how you must look. . . . Bobbed hair does make one more carefree but in your case that is not objectionable. Keep on being carefree and keep on having a good time. Oh, I'm so glad for you." In December, Lee wrote: "I'm so thrilled for you for I've wanted you to have a real good time for years. And now I feel that at last some one is seeing your true worth and really appreciating you. . . ." Anna finished the year in a whirl of Christmas parties. "I'm so glad you are having such a good time," Lee wrote the following February. "It is surely due you."

With Hilda, Anna's fellow romantic, Anna apparently emphasized love and romance. Hilda answered in December: "What a beautiful letter! It has made me so very glad. Always I have wanted you to find the someone who could love you and whom you could love enough. Yes, I have always known you would find him. I hoped the silence meant that you were happy, and I expected that kind of a letter, but not one telling me of this great happiness, Nan. I am so glad."

Now Anna was happier than she had ever been, meeting Paul's wide circle of intellectual and artistic friends, confident of her attractiveness, and enjoying herself in the company of a man who admired and wanted her. Anna's friend Rosalind (not her real name) at the library saw a great change in Anna after she fell in love with Paul. She seemed to come to life, becoming happier, warmer, and less reserved. Paul shook her loose, says Rosalind, and showed her there was more to life than the library. In early 1937 this happy, self-assured Anna caught the eye of "the young architect" Charles Young at last. They went to a symphony concert together on the eve of Valentine's Day.

And now Anna was confused. She was in love with Paul, yet she had dreamed of Charles for so long. Her heart was in turmoil, trying to sort out her feelings. It's plain from her confusion, and from Lee's letters, that romantic involvement was new to Anna, and Paul was her first beau: *You have finally met someone. . . . You are having a good time at last! . . . At last someone is seeing your true worth. . . .* Anna wrote about her confusion to Barre, who was still in North Carolina, and Barre answered on March 15: " . . . your own heart has so many fingers clutching at its vitality—confusing the already complicated issue. . . . I don't doubt you wonder how you can feel the same about Charles when your heart is so full of Paul." Anna's confusion apparently cleared up quickly, though; Charles Young disappears from the record after March 1937. He couldn't hold the stage once Paul Briol had made his entrance.

Sometime early in 1937 Anna received a blow: she learned that Paul was married. Anna did not write to Lee for several months afterward. It appears from Lee's letter dated June 13, 1937, that Anna had somehow known both Paul's wife, Mary, and his twelve-year-old daughter, Jan, without realizing that Mary and Paul were married: "I don't believe that Mary is Paul's wife!" wrote Lee; "What did his little daughter call Mary?" Lee's letter seems to imply that it was Paul who told Anna he was married: "I'm so sorry for you," Lee wrote, "but am proud of you that you 'came back' with chin up and a smile on your face. It doesn't pay to let a man think he means too much to you—unless of course you are married to him!" Anna had longed for love, found it at last, and given herself over to it with the stored-up passion of adolescence and the tenaciousness of maturity. Yet in the moment when her great happiness collapsed, from the blow delivered perhaps by Paul himself, she was able to smile and keep her "chin up."

Paul had been married since 1920 to Mary Emerson, a 1909 graduate of Wellesley College and daughter of Mary Adelpha Simpson and Dudley Emerson, members of two wealthy and prominent Cincinnati families. Five years older than Paul, Mary had the spirit, intelligence, and elegance Paul found attractive in women. They shared love of literature, nature, and music, and Mary thought Paul was the most interesting man she had ever known. The 1920s were a happy time for them, with an active social life and the birth of their daughter, Jan, in 1923.

In the 1930s Paul began pursuing his own interests and having intimate relationships with other women. The women he found stimulating were not necessarily beautiful or physically striking; they were capable, intellectual single women who were free to go along on his photography expeditions. They were somewhat boyish and outdoorsy and didn't flirt or dress alluringly. All were interesting but at the same time submissive. "Seducer" is too vulgar a word to describe Paul. Jan suggests "missionary"; he didn't see anything wrong in "releasing" repressed Victorian women "and helping them to enjoy life," says Jan, and he went about his mission with zeal, "a missionary with a subversive approach."

The Briol marriage had already become remarkably unconventional when, in about 1935, Paul acquired a small Japanese-style cottage on the steep bank of the Little Miami River near Foster, Ohio. He called the cottage "Camp" and went there most weekends for the next fifteen years. On Sundays he held open house for lively gatherings of university intellectuals, symphony musicians, foreign expatriates, and political reformers. Liquor was abundantly available. Guests would listen to music, dance, play the Steinway upright piano, swim in the river, walk in the woods, and sunbathe on the roof. Mary went there on Sundays. Saturday, however, was Paul's private day, the day reserved for his specially invited guests.

Rosalind also was seeing a married man, and they too were part of the Camp scene. In a foursome at Camp one weekend, Rosalind observed Paul, the "missionary," trying to convert Anna. He was facing formidable obstacles: virginity, Victorianism, and restrictive religious upbringing. Since Anna and Paul continued seeing each other, and since Paul wasn't known for having exclusively spiritual relationships with women, I have to assume that in the romantic Camp atmosphere Anna's intense feelings yielded to Paul's compelling appeal. Whether this happened before Anna learned Paul was married, or after, is impossible to say. The conventional Catholic schoolgirl in me thinks Anna would not have begun an affair with a man she knew was married, but I see now that once she had fallen in love with him it was too late for making rational decisions. Nothing else mattered, not even the rules of respectable behavior as taught by Nellie Eikenhout.

Guilt was the motivator in Nellie's brand of training. If Anna felt guilty about having an affair with a married man, maybe that guilt was tempered by Mary Briol's declining to play the role of deceived wife. Mary tolerated her husband's extramarital affairs because she wanted him to be happy. She offered him a divorce and he turned it down. Relations between Mary and her husband's women friends, including Anna, were open and cordial.

When Lee learned from Anna that Paul was married, she assumed that Anna would now want to find someone else: "Best just to try to forget all about the past. . . . One man often leads to another!" But Lee had no notion of Paul and Mary's unconventional marriage, and apparently Anna, once she had accepted it herself, didn't explain it to her. At any rate, there are no more mentions of Paul in the rest of the numerous archived 1930s letters from Hilda and Lee. But though Anna seems to have stopped writing to her friends about Paul, she continued seeing him. He gave her Christmas gifts through 1939: framed prints, French graphic-art magazines, an etching, a lamp, a book on world religions, and several of his own photographs, including one of a night baseball game at Crosley Field. At Christmas 1938 he gave her a nun's costume to wear to his popular New Year's Eve party at Camp. Paul went as the Pope, in flowing robes, tall miter headdress, and, hanging around his neck instead of the traditional cross, a corkscrew. Midnight came, and the celebrating went on into a new year that would bring Anna unexpected joys and heartaches.

In late 1936 the Eikenhout roofing business had been feeling the effects of the Great Depression, and Anna loaned the business seven hundred dollars, characterizing the loan as an investment. That same year, John Eikenhout's health began to decline with high blood pressure and headaches, and by the end of 1937 he had given up all his music activities. Mam had to learn about business matters and take over some of the decision making. In 1938 John's mental confusion accelerated. The diagnosis today would be Alzheimer's disease, and everyone would know what to expect, but in 1938 the family was baffled and alarmed. Mam found caring for her husband difficult and frustrating. By year-end she couldn't talk things over with him anymore, nor could she share the worry with easygoing Nella Mae. She wanted Anna to come home.

But Anna wouldn't leave Cincinnati. A struggle ensued between Anna and her mother, and rather than confront it directly, they talked about it at first in terms of library school. Without a library science degree, Anna was restricted to an assistant's title and salary. Mam railed against Miss Collman for holding on to Anna's "cheap help." In a letter on January 11, 1939, Mam prodded Anna to assert herself "and get through with some of that wishy-washy stuff. How many more years have you the chance to enroll in school? Time marches on. As for a school, why would not Ann Arbor be as good and not the most expensive in the country."

In her next letter, on January 18, Mam was more direct. She believed that Anna was staying in Cincinnati because of Paul, and continuing to go out with him was a disgrace: "Now Ann, once for all, understand me well," she wrote. "I would be the last one to deny you your friends, but also, girls [Anna was thirty-six] can not be too careful in choosing them. Families as friends, young men as friends, women as friends are fine, and every one needs them. But some are absolutely out, as we not only do not want to ever feel ashamed, but we want to always be proud of our girls."

Because the "girls" always shared their letters, Mam inserted a small enclosure just for Anna, marked "Ann—personal." It was an extreme effort to get Anna under her control again, and in it she used all her skill at inflicting guilt:

> Next morning:
> Questions which came up during another sleepless night:
>   Why has Ann changed her mind, and wants to stay in Cin[cinna]ti?
> Is it devotion for Miss C[ollman]?

Is it because she is still carrying on with that man, even
tho[ugh] everything fine and decent tells her how wrong it is?

Does she care that little for poor Dad and me?

Has she forgotten how we have given up much for her music
and education?

Didn't we talk it over on that street car ride and we agreed,
no decent girl should go out with a man who has a family?

As Grandpa said: "what would the people say?"

Can I cover it up much longer if that is the case?

Do I care to go on lying, a thing I have always despised?

If she wants to break away, what better chance than to go to
library school?

Haven't I saved every dollar possible, for several years, to
pay off what Dad borrowed?

Does she owe us anything for all we have done for her?

Didn't I sit up till midnight many times to finish a dress for
her?

Is all that forgotten? Will my head hold out much longer:
Please answer.

I wish this note had made Anna angry, but I think instead she
buried it deep in her heart, just one more in a long line of hurts she
denied having received from her mother. Maybe it did bolster her resolve, though. Anna did not go back home, and she did not go to
library school. She would not submit to her mother or to the stifling
Victorian principle that self-sacrifice is a woman's greatest virtue; she
kept her independence.

Whether, or how much, Mam's disapproval contributed to Anna's
breaking with Paul is impossible to say. She appears to have continued
seeing him until about 1940. In the end perhaps Anna's attraction to
Paul had faded. Perhaps Sunday open house at Camp, delightfully novel
in the beginning, had become repugnant with its drinking, dancing,
smoke, and noise. And Anna surely had learned that gregarious, free-
loving Paul would never love her exclusively. On the other hand, perhaps Paul tired of the relationship first. Either way, the ending could
not have been easy for Anna. The loss of him, and the loss of her
image of herself as a woman loved and in love, must have grieved her
deeply.

About ten years later, on Saturday afternoon, June 3, 1950, Paul
was seriously injured in a collision between a Greyhound bus and the
car he was driving while on an excursion from Camp with a woman

friend. The story was given a banner headline in Sunday's *Cincinnati Enquirer*. Paul received head injuries and, after a week in a semicoma, was never the same again. In 1962 Paul and Mary moved to Katonah, New York, to live with Jan and her family. Paul died there in 1969, about a year and a half after Mary.

Mam was worried about Anna's health in 1938. On February 18 she cautioned Anna: "If not for your sake, or ours, then for Barre's sake take care of your own health, so you can stand by when she needs you." (Barre had had another health crisis.) Mam wrote to Etta around the same time: "I hope Ann is feeling better; she is too thin for her size, Tet, and works mostly on her nerves, I fear." Anna's distress was so great during this time, until the summer, that she shunned her music-making friends and the musical evenings.

On April 5, 1939, Anna underwent a hysterectomy. No word from her about it survives, except her reporting of it nearly fifty years later to a physician in a medical history, which states that the cause (unnamed) was benign. That cause may have been the fairly common uterine tumors called fibroids, which can be painful and can cause alarmingly heavy out-of-cycle bleeding. If Anna did have debilitating physical symptoms, they must have added greatly to her burden of worry about the decline of her father's health and reason, the demands and harsh criticism from her mother, and the stressful relationship with Paul.

Anna did not write to Hilda or Lee about her surgery until after the fact, apparently saying only that she had had a tumor removed. "I want to know more about it all and just where the tumor was," Lee wrote on April 10. To cheer Anna, both Hilda and Lee wrote her about the good outcomes of their recent hospital experiences, Hilda's tonsillectomy and Lee's sister-in-law's appendectomy, comparisons that would have been absurdly trivial if Hilda and Lee had known the full extent of Anna's surgery. Several of their letters over the next few months also contained remarks about babies, childbirth, and parenthood that would have been unthinkably insensitive had they been fully informed. Anna apparently kept the name of the operation, and her feelings about it, private from her two dear friends. There is only one triple-veiled suggestion of Anna's feelings during that spring, in a letter from Lee: Lee wrote that Etta had written that Anna had said she didn't want much company.

Mam wrote Anna concerned, affectionate letters and traveled to

Cincinnati to see her. Nevertheless, one of the letters contained a thoughtless and revealing remark, another failure of Nellie's mothering skills. A literal interpretation would have been too hard for Anna to face: "I guess I didn't know how much you really mean to me," Nellie wrote, "but I am finding it out."

I can only imagine what Anna was feeling. Her body had sustained enormous insults from the anesthesia and the cutting. She had arrived at menopause overnight, abruptly and traumatically circumventing a natural biological process that takes years; she was prematurely old. Since that 1932 letter to Lee in which Anna had expressed doubt that she would ever marry, seven more years had passed. And the refrain running through all her thinking surely had to be Paul. She was in love with a man who would never be hers. What could she do but walk across the street to Burnet Woods again and again, and sit in the spring sunshine until the hurts began to lose their sharp edges.

The news about Anna's father continued worsening. As Mam went about acquiring power of attorney and taking care of business, she consulted with the girls. She wrote on January 24, 1940: "If I had it to do over again, I would go to night school and learn about business administration instead of sewing. I would let my girlies wear ready made things, and improve my mind." After five more months of family heartache, Anna's father died on June 12, 1940, aged sixty-three.

One summer day in 1939 a library patron from out of town came to the Fine Arts desk and spoke to the librarian about the "cabbage rose." Anna gently chided Robert Basye for demeaning the noble *Rosa centifolia,* and he fell in love with her. Robert Basye (rhymes with "Casey") of Kansas City, Missouri, was an instructor in mathematics at Texas A&M in College Station, with a bachelor of arts degree from the University of Missouri, a master of science degree from Princeton, and a doctorate from the University of Texas. He loathed teaching mathematics and longed to devote all his time to breeding roses.

Anna's friend Rosalind remembers "the young man with the roses" and thought he seemed, not exactly to satisfy Anna, but to give her some relief. Anna told Rosalind she had some feeling for the young man, a feeling that Rosalind thought might break Anna's worrisome attachment to Paul. It was good that Robert came into Anna's life in 1939, the year that dealt her so much unhappiness. She was thirty-six when she and Robert met; he was thirty. His eager, sensitive admiration and touching love letters must have had the effect of healing.

His first letter to Anna was dated February 24, 1940. Spring had come to Texas, and the cardinals and mockingbirds, wrote Robert, seemed to be singing more sweetly that spring than ever before. As a reminder of Anna he had ordered from London a set of the books on roses by Ellen Willmott that Anna had showed him at the Fine Arts desk, and the order had been filled at last—by the bookshop proprietor's widow. Europe was at war; in the London blitz a Nazi bomb had destroyed her shop and killed her husband.

Robert went on to tell Anna of the spring blooms in Texas: flowering quince, redbuds, peach and plum blossoms, violets, and bluebonnets. His planting bed of rose seeds was edged with a row of narcissus, he wrote, "and each time I kneel down and breathe in their fragrance I wish that you might kneel beside me and help me hunt for that first seedling to push through."

Anna's father died that June, and for long months, apparently, Anna didn't answer Robert's letter. I imagine her keeping it tucked away in a special place, rereading it every so often as she came to terms with parting from Paul, and carefully considering whether and how to respond. Then one day she made a decision of the heart and wrote her first letter to Robert. His response is dated October 5, 1940. "I have read and reread your little letter," he wrote, "which has stirred me more than I can say. I have wondered what feeling drew me toward you almost from the first moment we met. In small measure it might have been the interest you found in the roses, which during the past few years have become the guiding passion of my life. But more than this it was the native sincerity and charm which lighted up your face and eyes and was apparent in every word. And I could not help but feel the presence of your poetic sensibilities. I will confess that the second time I came in was more to see you than the rose books."

"I am sure that if you play the piano as poetically as you write letters," Robert wrote on October 24, "I would never let you quit playing. You write exactly as I knew you would the first time we met. When you were distressed at hearing me call Centifolia the cabbage rose, in that instant you revealed half your soul to me." On November 17 he addressed her, "My Anna," and his letter concluded, "I think of you often, Anna. I think of you as a beautiful, noble chord of music which I heard for a brief instant and now hunger to hear again." On the "cold, drizzly, miserable night" of December 3, Robert wrote that school was out early and he was longing to go north, but he could not. "You know how impatient I am to see you again," he wrote. He hoped he could get to Cincinnati "before the month of roses has departed. . . . How much happiness there is in just anticipating the future! . . . And so I have my eyes on the beautiful month of June."

When Robert wrote next in January 1941 he had received three letters from Anna, forwarded to him in Baton Rouge. "I cannot finish reading them," he wrote. "They have all the quaint charm and poetry of a harpsichord, and their music too, lingers on and will not fade." Anna had written to him about her Christmas in Grand Rapids: "Your pretty picture of how you trimmed the Christmas tree, 'green with lights of many colors,' Aunt Grace's Christmas stockings and your attachment to the same ornaments year after year—this is a picture of you, too. Be as old-fashioned as you please, Anna, and I will love you more for it. And in every Christmas season that comes hereafter I shall see you—somewhere—'arranging the holly and evergreens wherever they would look festive.'" In his last surviving letter to Anna, dated February 2, 1941, Robert wrote that he was still dreaming of June.

The last item from Robert in the archives folder is a postcard dated two years later, a farewell. It was mailed on February 16, 1943, when the United States had been at war for fourteen months and Robert was a lieutenant junior grade in the U.S. Naval Reserve stationed in Norfolk, Virginia. "Some of my roses will be gone when I return," he wrote, "but there is one whose memory I shall hope to keep forever fresh and unfading. Soon now they will be my guiding stars. Goodbye, Anna."

Robert survived the war and continued teaching mathematics at Texas A&M. He never married. He died in 1999, having devoted his retirement years to his hobby and his passion, roses, but advancing age robbed him of the memory of Anna he had hoped would be "forever fresh and unfading." Whether Robert ever returned to Cincinnati to see Anna a second time is unknown. My guess is that the February 1941 letter was Robert's last because Anna wrote him that someone else had come into her life.

The someone else, of course, was Harlan.

7

"And Then There Was Harlan"

"If you leave it to me, you know where we'll end up—on the riverbank."

Harlan to Anna, quoted by Anna
in her autobiographical sketch

"And then there was Harlan," Anna wrote years later in her *Library Journal* drafts. But *when* was Harlan, exactly? Before starting to go out together in 1941, Anna and Harlan both said, they had known each other in the library for several years. They may have met in 1934, when Harlan did research in Fine Arts on the steamboats he was painting for the Federal Public Works of Art project. But it was 1939, two years before their first "date," when Anna entered Harlan's name and address in her little address book—why, no one knows—and dated the entry.

"And then there was Harlan": with that phrase Anna set him apart from the usual run of her Fine Arts patrons. He was a difficult case, a stimulating challenge for a charming, sensitive, dedicated librarian who by the late 1930s was accustomed to having charming, sensitive patrons fall in love with her. In contrast with the others he was brusque and distant, and answers to the sorts of questions he asked were elusive. One day he asked her for information about the grounds, the canvas-priming substances, that pictures are painted on:

> I gave him some books on materials and techniques—evidently not what he wanted, for he soon left without saying a word. Another time he asked for anything on colors and what makes them permanent. Again he left unsatisfied, I felt sure. Much later I learned that he himself had been working for years on these aspects of painting—I had failed entirely to measure the depth of his questions. One day he asked me what the differ-

ence was between woodcuts and wood engravings. I answered him glibly from my recent reading, not realizing that here again was a field he'd been working in for years, and I had failed to go to the bottom of his question. He asked me if I could find any woodcuts of the old steamboats. This time I searched through all the old histories of river transportation and anything else I could think of, finding very few woodcuts but some drawings and a wealth of descriptive matter and history and wonderful old navigation charts of the rivers. Harlan barely glanced at it all, I thought. I felt I couldn't help this man, ever. There was something about him that I couldn't fathom.

Anna, married to Harlan for about ten years when she wrote these lines, had apparently learned that he was chronically hard to please and didn't try to appear otherwise. Far from resenting his attitude, she accorded him superior status as the deeper thinker. It seems to me, though, that Harlan's inquiries at the Fine Arts desk had less to do with painting than with the librarian. Else why keep stumping her with difficult research questions he had been pursuing himself for years? The library was a safe place for getting acquainted. There he was not a suitor risking rejection—he was a client, and every encounter was in his control. If he was perplexed and unsure of his next move, he could simply walk away. Eventually Harlan decided he wanted more of Anna's company, outside the library, but he was reluctant to ask her out. I think he feared that the relationship would collapse sooner or later, and he would learn for certain that he had been right—the love of woman was not for him; no woman would accept the kind of life he wanted to live.

From Anna's perspective, though, Harlan had several attractions as a would-be suitor. He came into the library "wearing a plaid woolen shirt and his stout hiking boots," Anna wrote, "and with the freshness of outdoors about him." Just the look of him took her back to summers on Michigan lakes. What's more, his intellectual curiosity was a match for hers. And he was a painter; he had the creativity she valued above all else and believed she was lacking. Still more attractions were gradually revealed.

Unaware of how good his chances were with Anna, Harlan dared only to drop cues—a mythic three cues. One day, probably in September 1940, he approached the librarian's desk—"with a shy smile" and with no book requests, Anna recalled—and informed her that he had just come back from a canoe trip down the Kentucky River. There is no knowing whether they had talked of canoeing before, but through either planning or luck, Harlan had hit upon one of Anna's great loves. Whatever she thought of Harlan himself at the time, with this cue he doubtless prompted Anna to begin speculating about his boat-handling skills and imagining being together with him in that canoe.

Four months later, in January 1941, Harlan worked up his courage to drop the second cue, the one that should have been irresistible. Leaving Fine Arts one evening, he paused at some distance from the librarian's desk. Anna asked what she could do for him, and he began talking about her piano playing. *He played the violin*, he said. "Oh, that's nice," Anna said, muffing her cue and going on about her business. Harlan left. About ten minutes passed while a courtship hung in the balance. Then, in an act of deep resolve or yearning or both, Harlan turned around and went back to the Fine Arts desk. Years later Anna admitted only to having thought, during those ten minutes he was gone, of how she had carelessly thrown away a chance to play music. But I suspect she spent the time weighing pros and cons, because when he stood before her again, she had a decisive greeting and a bold invitation ready for him. She was glad he had come back, she said, and she invited him to her apartment for the following Sunday, to play music. Harlan accepted.

Harlan arrived at Clifton Avenue on Sunday with the score of the César Franck Sonata in A under his arm. If he felt apprehensive, he had good reason. The late-nineteenth-century Franck sonata for piano and violin is a challenging masterwork, showy and feverish as well as dreamy and melodic. It could be embarrassing if the playing went badly, as it almost surely would, and he would probably make an awkward job of extricating himself. He didn't know that he could have counted on Anna's sensitivity as an accompanist. She adapted her playing to Harlan's and supported him, caring nothing about his failings.

In separate recollections Anna and Harlan recalled that day quite differently. Harlan said matter-of-factly, in his eighties, that the playing didn't go well. But for Anna, that was the day she began to know Harlan. It was in his playing, she wrote in her *Library Journal* drafts, "that I caught the first glimpse of what Harlan really is. His whole interest was centered in the music. He was not at all concerned with his playing, as such, so there was no exaggeration; no striving for effect, only his earnest attempt to convey the qualities of the music as he felt the beauty and the sweep of it." Anna thought it fitting that for their first real experience together they had not gone to a concert and heard others play, but had played a sonata themselves, experiencing the music directly. When they had finished playing, and he gave her a radiant smile, she felt that her failures to answer his questions at the Fine Arts desk had been eradicated. She felt she had finally given him what he most wanted of her: understanding.

Even so, Harlan still wasn't able to ask Anna out. As he was leaving her apartment that Sunday, he dropped the third cue: on Thursday, he said, he was going to the big international exhibition featuring Dutch and Flemish painters at the Cincinnati Art Museum. ("He didn't *ask*, you know," Anna said as she told this story years later.) There was no hesitation this time—Anna understood now what was necessary. She said she would like to go with him.

Harlan was waiting behind the wheel of his mother's Packard when Anna stepped out of the library at half past noon on Thursday, January 16. She thought he would take her to lunch at a nice downtown restaurant, such as the Colony, a favorite with the library staff. But instead he drove directly to Eden Park, to the art museum and past it, up to the high outer drive and the overlook. He parked at the curb and they got out. They walked a few paces over the winter-killed grass and sat down on the park bench in the clearing, facing the sweeping, sunny view down over the curve in the river that leads to Fort Thomas on the opposite bank. He produced lunch, a bag of baked goods, and when they had eaten, they drove back down to the museum and the exhibition. With a friend later, Anna laughed over the lunch at the Colony that was never to be.

With Anna's description of the rest of that day her autobiographical sketch comes to an end: "When we had enjoyed the exhibition for some hours . . . it was a relief to come out into the open air and sunshine again. 'It's still early,' Harlan said. 'We'd have time to go for a little drive before I have to take you home. Where would you like to go?' When I hesitated he said, 'If you leave it to me, you know where we'll end up—on the riverbank.'"

Harlan had a longtime dream of living in solitude, close to nature, painting the landscape of the Ohio River he loved, but his dream had been stymied by his perception of family duty. His two older brothers, Frank and Lucien, had left home and made successes of themselves, and Harlan, now aged forty-one, had stayed behind with his mother. She was determined that Harlan would not marry and leave her as her two older sons had done. Rose Swingle Hubbard was strong willed, respectable, and possessive, an austere woman with no capacity for small talk and no sense of humor. She was a churchgoing Protestant, though not particularly religious; in old age Harlan said he didn't remember his mother ever reading the Bible or uttering a word of prayer. Nor did he remember being shown any sign of love during his boyhood by either his mother or his father, who died when Harlan was seven years old.

Frank, twelve years older than Harlan, was a commercial artist in New York, and Lucien, ten years older than Harlan, was a Hollywood movie producer. Both of them, but especially Lucien, contributed to their mother's support and thus, indirectly, to Harlan's, an arrangement Harlan thought fair for having taken Rose off their hands. Their support of their mother made it possible for him to work only irregularly, at carpentry and bricklaying for a local home builder, and to spend much of his time rambling the river and the countryside, painting. Harlan and Rose had reached an understanding. Harlan maintained the house and yard, chauffeured Rose, and did her bidding, up to a point. Otherwise, he ignored her disapproval of his lack of interest in amounting to something and mostly did as he pleased. Still, the harness chafed.

Since boyhood, Harlan's guiding interests had been painting—he had had several seasons of art school after high school—and the writings of the nineteenth-century naturalist-philosopher Henry David Thoreau. Harlan had always been out of step with contemporary society; he wanted only to paint and be on or near the river. He wanted recognition for his painting, but not wealth or fame; he had no interest in being successful, in the world's terms. His most ambitious dream was to escape conventional living altogether and be, for a time, anyway, a shantyboater. He wanted to provide for himself with his own hands, free of the industrial system of division of labor that makes modern people totally dependent on one another and separates them from the earth. He had no theories to prove, no interest in developing a philosophy or converting anyone else to his way of thinking. He was driven solely by desire. To break into that life he longed for, Harlan needed, first, to be free of family responsibility and second, to find someone to believe in him, someone to give him courage and be his partner. Anna turned out to be that person.

Sometime in spring 1941 Anna introduced Harlan to her music-making friends and their "musical evenings" at a gathering at the home of Herschel Linstaedt, a widely known teacher of piano and organ in Greater Cincinnati. In particular, she introduced Harlan to Patricia and Warren Staebler. It was the founding of a friendship, and an informal string quartet, that would endure for forty-five years.

In 1936 Patricia Henderson—a freshman at the University of Missouri at Kansas City, Missouri—had fallen in love with her English composition teacher, Warren Staebler, and he with her. In summer 1937 Patricia visited Warren in his hometown, Cincinnati, where he had just begun graduate studies at the University of Cincinnati. One night Warren took Patricia to a musical evening at the home of Professor Boyce, a member of the UC English Department. Etta sang, and Anna accompanied her on the piano in songs of Schubert and Brahms. It was Patricia's introduction to *lieder* (German art songs), and to Anna. Though Patricia was only eighteen and (according to Patricia) "embryonic," Anna, nearly twice Patricia's age, "saw through to the person" and recognized her as a friend. That friendship was particularly important to Patricia, because her youth and her lack of background and education had earned her a cool reception from the women in Warren's family. Patricia and Warren married in late 1937 and moved back to Cincinnati in 1939. (In Indiana later, after having three children, Patricia earned bachelor's and master's degrees in music, taught college-level music, and was an arts writer for the local newspaper and *Arts Indiana* magazine.)

Soon after the 1941 evening at Herschel Linstaedt's house, the new foursome began meeting at Anna's apartment on Saturday mornings to play music. Starting with the Baroque trio sonatas for keyboard and two instruments by composers such as Bach, Corelli, Handel, and Vivaldi, they kept plugging away at each work in consecutive sessions until they could get through it without stumbling. Harlan and Warren played violin, and Anna and Patricia took turns at the piano part. Eventually Harlan gave Anna a cello. Even though she was experienced on bass viol, learning to play the cello was not easy for Anna; the cello player has to read off a different clef, and the tuning and the intervals are different. But Anna's experience with drawing a bow helped, and she was eager to learn, because the gift of the cello was a tremendous opening for the foursome: now they could move into the string quartet literature. At first Anna brought home from the library some simple things for the quartet to play, such as the Pogojeff *Quartetino*, and she wrote out some four-part transcriptions of easy

Bach chorales and keyboard preludes. Soon they were tackling anything and everything, completely undaunted by the technical difficulty
of the music. Someone, usually Patricia, had to count out loud constantly to keep them playing together.

The foursome continued playing through the years, on the shantyboat, in Payne Hollow, and in the Staeblers' eventual home in Richmond, Indiana. When the Staeblers' number began increasing in 1946
with Jonathan, followed by Mark and Mina (pronounced "My-nah"),
the adults learned to cope with the attendant distractions and played
on. In 1946 Warren began teaching at Earlham College in Richmond,
a convenient stopover for the Hubbards on the way to Grand Rapids.
Anna looked forward eagerly to those visits, for the friendship, the
good talk, and the music.

One such visit took place, not in Richmond, but in Foster, Ohio,
where the Staeblers were staying with friends before sailing to Italy to
join in doing relief work with the Quakers. It was July 1951; Anna
and Harlan returned to Fort Thomas from their shantyboating and set
out almost immediately for Foster, because this would be the last chance
at quartets with the Staeblers for two years. The foursome began playing a work by Hindemith, a group of five compositions that were not
all tonal—"contemporary" music, most people would call it. They
finished one and moved on to another. As usual, Patricia counted val-
iantly to keep everyone together, but in the end they fell to pieces.
Then it became apparent that not everyone had been playing the same
composition. Anna and Patricia began laughing uncontrollably, and
Harlan told them to pull themselves together.

Spring 1941 also brought day trips in Harlan's canoe. Because Anna
was president of the Staff Association at the library now, she was able
to change the work schedule for her own convenience. Instead of the
former half days, everyone now had whole days off. Anna spent hers
with Harlan, in a canoe or on the riverbank. Sometimes Harlan took
Anna to the place he called his camp, high on a Kentucky hill across
from the old river town New Richmond, Ohio, overlooking vistas far
up and down the river. It is difficult to imagine any greater contrast
with Paul Briol's "Camp" than Harlan's spartan lean-to, open on three
sides, little more to it than a roof and a stone fireplace. Likewise, the
contrast between the two men stood out in sharp relief. Harlan shunned
alcohol, tobacco, and social gatherings. He was the sort of man—
puritanical, he called himself—who would choose a mate and cleave

to her. Most important, he represented for Anna a route to direct experience of life. Both Paul and Harlan enjoyed listening to classical music, but Harlan, like Anna, preferred *making* music. Paul went to the river as a visitor or as a photographer—an observer. Harlan went to the river—canoed on it, camped along it, and painted it—as if his life depended on it.

In August, Anna vacationed in Michigan for two weeks with Barre. They stayed at Torch Lake on Grand Traverse Bay, near the top of mitten-shaped lower Michigan, and spent several evenings with Anna's former cello coach, Leo Cayvan, and his wife. Anna wrote to Harlan, and on the fourteenth she telephoned him. He wrote back immediately, only a few lines with no trace of sentimentality. He began, "Dearest Anna," thanked her for her letter and phone call, and wrote a few words about his mother's health. "Have a splendid time at the Lake," he closed. "Come back better for having been there. I can see it now, shining in the sun. Harlan." He enclosed a newspaper clipping, a photo of the paddlewheel towboat *J.D. Ayres.*

After a year of refining their canoeing kit and technique, and their relationship, Anna and Harlan were ready in spring 1942 for a longer trip. On Sunday, May 24, they loaded their gear into Barre's Plymouth and tied the canoe on top, and, beating the approaching wartime restrictions on pleasure driving by just a few months, Barre drove them 150 miles southeast into Kentucky, up the Licking River. A few miles past the town of West Liberty some country boys helped Anna and Harlan launch, and Barre took their picture as they set off.

For the next nine days they ate heartily on Harlan's camp cooking, walked through woods and across swinging footbridges, swam in swift water, and maneuvered the canoe through innumerable riffles. "I think the fast water is swell fun," Anna wrote in her log. They selected their campsite each evening with great care. The first one was at "the Leaning Beech Tree," Anna wrote, only a mile downriver from the launching spot. Sometime after Anna began writing about day two, she squeezed in a few more lines about day one, lines that were as close as Anna could come to recording a night of intimacy with Harlan: "All night the sound of the river. All night the whippoorwill. All night—."

By the afternoon of day three, the river was flowing through overhanging hemlock, rhododendron, mountain laurel, and Fraser magnolia; rivulet waterfalls streamed down over high rocky cliffs, and wildflowers grew in the mossy crevices. Wanting to prolong the day,

Anna rested and Harlan took over alone, with a double-bladed paddle. Anna leaned back against their mound of gear and began reading to Harlan from a book she called "Little Chronicle of Anna Magdalena Bach." Just before stopping, they heard a girl singing a mountain song. "The long notes echoed back from the cliffs," Anna wrote. "It was as perfect in its setting as the bird songs." With woods and the cliffs behind them, they camped that night in a clearing facing the river scene they had been reluctant to leave behind. "Bull frogs, lightning bugs, and again whippoorwills," Anna wrote. Inside their tent, with a gentle rain pattering overhead, they read a bit more by candlelight.

This "Little Chronicle," by Esther Meynell, published in 1925, was the first book Anna entered on her list of books she and Harlan read together. It is a small book, the fictional "diary" of Anna Magdalena Bach, the actual second wife of the great eighteenth-century composer Johann Sebastian Bach. Its theme is Bach's creative greatness and his wife's devotion to him and his art. When the opportunity for a walk through a beech wood arose on day five, Anna had another fine book ready, Marjorie Kinnan Rawlings's *Cross Creek*. But on day three—while Anna reclined in the canoe, facing Harlan, against the passing backdrop of waterfalls, mossy rocks, and lush junglelike vegetation, and while they lay close together in the tent by candlelight—the book Anna chose was *Little Chronicle*. It's unlikely that her choice was entirely random; Anna was sentimental about books. In her choice of a book to read at a certain time or to give to a certain person, she revealed a great deal about herself, because she saw emotional meanings beyond the mere meanings of the words on the page. Reading *Little Chronicle* to Harlan was a way for Anna to tell him what their playing music together meant to her, that through playing music together they revealed their souls. It was also a way of telling him, "I'm willing to support your creativity with all my energy, and through you I'll satisfy my own longing for creative self-expression."

Creativity was central to Anna's life. She liked to read good criticism of literature, art, and music: "At its best it can be illuminating, almost inspiring," she wrote Judy Moffett, "But can it ever be creative, I wonder." Shortly after Judy graduated from Hanover College in 1964, Anna wrote her that she and Harlan would be following Judy's literary criticism work and her teaching, but that they were even more interested in her creative writing. The following year Anna wrote Judy: "Harlan is always working at his painting. You will understand how much this means. Your writing means that to you. You understand that this creative activity is the very core of living."

But if creativity was the core of living, and since Anna believed she lacked the creative impulse herself, where did that leave Anna? What was *her* core of living? The answer is in her *Library Journal* drafts: the core of Anna's living was Harlan's creativity. "H[arlan]'s paintings and watercolors and woodcuts were the things I had known only indirectly through books," Anna wrote. That is, with Harlan she felt she now had *direct* experience of painting and writing. "His life—our life—was the stuff the paintings were made of—the paintings and the books." There was no judgment or criticism in Anna's reaction to Harlan's creative output. Most admirers of Harlan's paintings grant that some of them are better than others, but Anna admired all of them equally. When Harlan finished a painting he would hang it in the house for a while, and he and Anna would contemplate it and its meaning. "It was as if they'd had a child," Judy Moffett says, "as if Harlan had borne it, and Anna was the other parent—not too bad an analogy for the warm, possessive way she felt about it."

Anna's identification with Harlan's writing was just as strong. She liked to tell about the 1949 genesis of *Shantyboat* in the Natchez hospital. Harlan "couldn't just be in a hospital bed and doing nothing," she told a friend years later. In a voice of storytelling wonderment she added, "He started to write." During the creating of *Shantyboat*, Anna wrote in her *Library Journal* drafts, "we learned first of all what it means to write a book, to illustrate it, to see it through all the stages, to read the proofs, and finally to see it a completed thing facing the world in its brave gay jacket. This has brought us near to authors, given us a new understanding of a book as the direct expression of a man's best thought." As for Harlan's second book, *Payne Hollow: Life on the Fringe of Society*, Anna saw a dramatic tension in it that most others did not see: "I think you'll find there is a build-up," she wrote to Etta in October 1974. "The story gains an impetus, and increases in tension right up to the last sentence."

Harlan encouraged Anna to write. So did others; readers of Harlan's books wanted to know more about Anna. In the early days Harlan urged her to keep a journal; in the 1980s he suggested she write about her years in the Cincinnati Public Library. Friends encouraged Anna to write about her daily life at Payne Hollow, or at least a cookbook. She did write down some narrative-style recipes during the shantyboating years (see the appendix "Anna's Recipes"), but the en-

tries dwindled and stopped. Harlan may have been referring to the
recipes journal when he said in 1987 that Anna had tried to write a
few times, "but it didn't turn out to be much." Of course I know now
that Anna didn't consider herself capable of writing for publication. In
any case, she would have scrupulously avoided stepping into Harlan's
spotlight. Apparently she had no desire, either, to keep a private journal for the sake of self-expression, and so her writing was limited to
the letters that kept her connections with friends and loved ones alive—
and, after marrying Harlan, her feelings hidden.

In conversation with others Anna deferred to Harlan. On topics
that were his domain she was usually silent unless spoken to. She deferred to him not so much because he was the husband, I think, but
because he was creative. What's more, she considered him her intellectual superior even though she had more formal education than he. She
believed her role in the partnership was to understand and support
Harlan, not to criticize or try to change him. Steadfast in her role,
Anna overlooked Harlan's quirks and smoothed his way so that he
could paint and write with as little interference as possible.

Anna wrote me in October 1962 about another married couple
who were coming to Payne Hollow to play music. The wife said her
husband would bring his horn. "Does Bill just let her say he'll bring
his horn and play with us—without first consulting him?" Anna wrote.
"Imagine my promising Harlan would bring his violin! Imagine my
saying Harlan would do anything—without consulting him!"

It is said that a visitor was in the house with Anna one day when
Harlan came in the front door, wet and muddy head to foot. Without
a word, goes the story, he stalked through the house and out the back
door. When he was gone, the visitor asked Anna what had happened
to Harlan. Had he fallen into the river? "Oh, I could never ask him,"
Anna replied.

One day in the 1980s Paul Hassfurder, the young man who by
then was helping Harlan with chores, taped Anna and Harlan playing
music together. He played back the tape for them, and Harlan asked,
"What's that weird noise?" Paul answered: it was Harlan's sniffing.
"Why didn't anyone ever tell me?" Harlan asked. A reasonable question, but no doubt it was received as purely rhetorical. Anna would as
soon have asked him whether he'd fallen into the river.

A visiting friend once talked with Anna about Thoreau and his
going off to the woods alone to live simply. (Thoreau's writings remained prominent in Anna and Harlan's reading together.) The friend

asked Anna whether going off to the woods to live simply was different for a couple. Yes, Anna replied quietly, and she told this brief story she called "priceless": A young man visiting one day had asked Harlan's opinion about why Thoreau never married. Harlan said, "I suppose he couldn't find a girl who wouldn't interfere with what he wanted to do and the way he wanted to live." In relating this story, Anna summed up concisely her agreement with Harlan's reply: "Perfect answer," she said.

Reading *Little Chronicle* myself, I can substitute "painting" for "music," and "Harlan" for "Sebastian" and have no trouble imagining Anna speaking to me—and to Harlan—through the printed words:

> He was beginning to write that music with which his soul was
> full, and he needed a quiet existence and a wife to look after
> him in order that he might produce the gift God had bestowed
> upon him so abundantly.

> I do not think Sebastian was a very easy person to know—
> unless you loved him. . . . He was reserved in speech about
> deep things, he did not express himself in the words he said,
> but in what he was, and, of course, above all in his music.

> My one wish, my only object, was to please him and to make
> his home the place where he would be happiest in this world.

It was unlike Anna to misquote a book title, but she misquoted the title of *Little Chronicle* at least three times, twice in her log of the 1942 canoe trip and once on her reading list. Because the author customarily referred to Anna Magdalena in text as, simply, "Magdalena," the printed title of the book is *The Little Chronicle of Magdalena Bach*. But when Anna wrote down the title, she wrote "Little Chronicle of *Anna* Magdalena Bach," supplying the omitted "Anna." Maybe she merely wrote the complete name automatically; or maybe she wrote it purposely, irked by the title's incompleteness. Or maybe—and this is the interpretation I want to believe—Anna felt at some deep level that the book might have been about her and Harlan.

8

❧

Wedding Days

"Keep Mom happy if possible, but if it isn't possible go ahead and find your own happiness."

Anna to Nella Mae

The three Eikenhout girls were of different temperaments, but they did have these two things in common: they all threw off the religion of their parents and to varying degrees infuriated their mother with their marriages. The first down that path was Etta, the middle sister, five years younger than Anna and a near-total contrast. Anna was reserved, sentimental, and shy; Etta was outspoken, practical, and afraid of nothing. Etta was known in the family as the tough one of the three sisters. In time, her sisters and their mother all came to depend on her strength.

From Mam's point of view, Etta was the troublemaker, the daughter who would not be controlled and insisted on making her own decisions. In her teens Etta refused to join the Reformed Church with the rest of her age group. Years after Etta's graduation from high school in 1925, Mam wrote to Anna that Etta's wildness in high school had worried her, but at least Etta had never done anything that truly disgraced the family. After high school, Etta had a year at Albion College Conservatory of Music. Then money became scarce, and the family's contributions to her education ended. Mam later regretted that Etta had been shortchanged.

The resourceful Etta, only nineteen years old, went to Chicago and entered Western Union telegrapher school with the promise of a fifteen-dollar-a-week job at graduation. In fact, she snagged eighteen dollars a week by working nights in the Western Union office at the Chicago *Herald Examiner*. In Chicago, Etta was free to become an all-out flapper of the Roaring Twenties. She smoked, danced, rolled her stockings below the knee, and frequented speakeasies. She not only drank bathtub gin, she *made* it.

In December 1929, with the onset of the Great Depression, Western Union transferred Etta to New York. There, that same month, she married George William Price, a boyfriend from her Albion College days. He was born in East Tawas, Michigan, probably in 1904 (Etta was uncertain years later), and in 1929 he was a Wall Street accountant. He had designed sophisticated accounting systems for some of the large investment firms and was doing well. The marriage was a surprise to everyone, including—if you believe Etta's story—Etta. She and George (said Etta) were walking around the city one day when he took her into a license bureau. "Are you getting a dog?" Etta asked. "No, we're getting married," said Price. They were married at City Hall on December 21, 1929, and they lived at 19 Fifth Avenue, Greenwich Village, the New York City neighborhood infamous for the loose ways and entertainments of the Roaring Twenties.

No letter from Mam to Anna concerning Etta's marriage has survived, and it wasn't spoken of in the family at large. I found in Anna's written record just one pale reflection of Mam's displeasure: with chilly formality Anna entered her brother-in-law's name in her 1931 Christmas card list as "Mr. George Price." The marriage lasted nine years on paper, but only a year or so in fact. Price "went off to Buenos Aires on business," Etta wrote, "and that's the last I saw of him—until he wanted to marry his secretary years later." Etta divorced Price in Cincinnati at his request, and in later years she spoke of him rarely and bitterly. In Cincinnati she was known as Miss Etta Price.

The Great Depression deepened, and in 1932 Etta was laid off by Western Union. In February 1933, back in Grand Rapids to regroup, she was vocal soloist in the fiftieth-anniversary concert of the Schubert Club. John Eikenhout, who was prominent in the club during the 1930s as business manager and then president, was very proud of her. Perhaps the occasion redeemed Etta in her mother's eyes and helped offset her past. Once again Etta needed to get out of Grand Rapids and find a job. She asked Anna, who had been working in Cincinnati since 1928, whether work was available there. Yes, Anna assured her. With Cincinnati-based Procter and Gamble in mind, Anna encouraged Etta to make the move. "People always need soap," Anna said. But soap wasn't in the cards for Etta. She answered a newspaper ad and was employed immediately by the Cal Crim Detective Bureau, doing shadow and undercover work.

In 1936 Etta began a remarkable security career with Shillito's department store at Seventh and Race Streets. The shortage of men due to World War II led to her being named head of the "protection" department in 1944 and made responsible for safeguarding the store and its warehouses against fire and theft. By 1950 only one other woman in the country was in charge of a comparable department. During her fourteen and a half years at Shillito's, she made a total of about eight thousand arrests, an average of about eleven a week. Etta was the only woman deputy sheriff on active duty in Hamilton County. She handled all her own cases in court and filed more petty larceny warrants than any other private detective in Cincinnati, earning the nickname P.L. (Petty Larceny) Price.

Etta became well known around town and was a popular speaker with women's and civic groups. At the same time, having become notably *un*popular with the shoplifters she had put in jail, for her own protection she carried aluminum knuckles in her purse and kept a gun in the apartment. She knew jujitsu and demonstrated once by tossing Anna's friend Warren Staebler over her shoulder. Only when Etta had resigned did she allow her photograph to appear in the local newspapers.

Etta moved back to Grand Rapids in 1951 to take care of Mam. After Mam died of a cerebral hemorrhage in 1956, Etta returned to Cincinnati for five years and then moved to Florida, where in 1963 she married Ralph Crossley. The five years they had together before his death were the best years of her life, she said. She remained in Florida, living independently, until her death in 1991.

Etta was still working at Shillito's, and Anna was married and shantyboating with Harlan through the Louisiana bayous, when the last and worst of the wedding storms struck. At thirty-four, Nella Mae was still living at home with Mam. Nell was the youngest, the light-hearted, easygoing one of the three daughters, and a joy to her mother. In Mam's letters, Anna was "Nan"; Etta was "Tet"; but Nell might be "Bub," "Bubby," "the wee one," "honey girl," "little Nell," "my little pal," or "our wee lib'arian." Nell was particularly dear to Anna, too. Fourteen years older than baby Nell, Anna had cared for her and read to her, held her up at the piano keyboard and played for her before she was a year old, and coached her in her first steps. Anna was her ideal; she was twelve when Anna moved away and became a librarian. Nell attended Michigan State College of Agriculture and Applied Science, in East Lansing, from 1936 to 1938. Afterward she clerked in the

Grand Rapids library, then earned a bachelor's degree in library science in 1945 from Western Reserve University School of Library Science, in Cleveland, and returned home as a full-fledged librarian.

In early 1951 Nell accepted a diamond engagement ring from Stan Bartnick, who owned the garage where she serviced her car, and they were going to marry in June. Mam's third and last daughter was slipping out of her control. Her fury was monumental, because Stan was a Catholic, and her hatred of Catholics was of the virulent kind passed down through the generations, dating from the centuries-past persecution of Dutch Protestants by Catholic Spain. The sorry business engulfed Anna through letters. Nell wrote on February 16 that Mam was telling her "malicious stories about priests and nuns" and "old wives tales about the marriage 'duties' of a wife. . . ." "Your father would turn over in his grave," Mam told her; "you've disgraced me." But Nell would not "give up a good man for a principle of my Mother's." She recalled advice that Anna had given her during a period of relationship trouble some years before: "You said . . . 'Keep Mom happy if possible, but if it isn't possible go ahead and find your own happiness.'"

On March 10 Nell thanked Anna for a "wonderful letter. You said just the things I wanted someone to say to me. The sort of things a mother should say to her daughter." To escape the warfare with Mam, Nell had decided to move into a friend's apartment until the wedding. From March to May, Mam wrote Anna furious letters about Nell's disgrace, ingratitude, and betrayal. "I told both of them at the very outset to be friends only, and not to get serious, as it would only mean trouble for all of us," Mam wrote on March 8. Before the engagement she had telephoned Stan's family and told his sister that Nell and Stan were "getting too intimate, and I saw trouble ahead." Now Mam was making good on her predictions and creating as much trouble as possible.

When it became clear that Nell was going to marry Stan no matter what Mam thought, the tone of Mam's letters changed to self-pity. On March 19 she wrote: "I tell you Nan, she is expert at hurting me in every way she can, and I have to cry bitter tears every day. I am well aware I am a miserable misfit as a loving mother, but I have tried in practical ways to do my part. . . . they have utterly ignored my wishes. . . . Since he deceived me and kept on seeing her, I told him I don't want him in my house. So on Sat. she plans to move out into an apartment until she quits her job, little caring about the reflection which that will cause on my home and reputation."

Nell's moving out created a new problem for the family: Mam couldn't be left alone, "stewing herself into her grave," Etta wrote to Anna and Harlan on February 14. "Even I'm not that heartless, and I'm supposed to be the tough one in the lot." Etta—the daughter who had been considered the most likely to disgrace the family if anyone would, Mam's least favorite of the three—provided the solution. Acknowledging that she was logically the one to do so, she moved back home, claiming that the job at Shillito's had lost its allure and she wouldn't mind a rest anyway. Twenty-five years before, she would have found living alone with Mam impossible, "but now I'm sure I could take it."

The storm passed as quickly as it arose. Nell and Mam were reconciled as soon as the babies started coming. Nell gave birth to her first child, Lynda Susan, in 1952, and Lucian followed in 1953, Peter in 1954, and George in 1956. Etta became part of the little Bartnicks' everyday life, and after she moved to Florida in 1956, her return visits to Grand Rapids were great events for them. "Tetta" used earthy language. She took them shopping and pointed out the probable shoplifters. She told them Chicago tales of Al Capone and of men jumping from skyscraper windows to a gory death in the stock market crash of 1929. She was an exotic being from another world.

Nell eventually went back to work in the Grand Rapids library and continued working there until 1971, the beginning of eight years of living with cancer. She died in 1978 at age sixty-two.

Compared with Nella Mae's wedding storm, Anna's had been mild.

After the symphony concert at Music Hall on a certain winter night in early 1943, Harlan walked Anna to her streetcar stop as usual. The streetcar arrived, and on an impulse, as Anna took hold of the handrail and stepped up, Harlan declared that they must pass the coming spring together. Sometime later he told Anna he couldn't go through with the kind of wedding she probably had in mind, because he abhorred the typical church wedding ceremony, and so she let him do the arranging. On a rainy Tuesday, April 20, 1943, they went by train from Brent to Maysville, Kentucky, where they presented their Campbell County marriage license to a justice of the peace in the old courthouse. They were married, Harlan wrote, "with a ceremony as sincere and beautiful as that building. . . ."

Nearly forty years later Anna and Harlan told about the morning of their wedding day. They said they had agreed that if Anna wanted to go through with the marriage, she would take the early morning train from Cincinnati to meet Harlan at Brent, and if he wanted to go through with it, he would be there waiting for her. If both parties were present, they would ride on to Maysville together and be married.

I have imagined how the train trip began for Anna on that chill, windy morning. Entering Cincinnati's Union Terminal in the predawn dark, she had to pass under the huge banner that hung down in the center of the broad expanse of windows above the main entrance during the war. It read:

Strong in the strength of the Lord
we who fight in the people's cause
will never stop until that cause is won

In the great main concourse, relatively deserted at that hour, Anna may have heard the clicking of her heels reverberating from the marble floor to the ten-story half-dome rotunda of the magnificent terminal. The crowds would follow soon, and by the end of this average wartime day as many as thirty-four thousand people—more than twice the huge terminal's planned capacity—and 145 long, crowded passenger trains would have passed through. As Anna walked briskly to her departure track, she may have neglected to cast her customary glance at the two-story-high mosaic murals glorifying the rotunda walls. The thoughts occupying her mind that morning were hardly those of the average traveler, much less the average bride.

The Chesapeake and Ohio's eastbound No. 8, the local mail and passenger train called "the accommodation," pulled out at 7:10 A.M. with Anna on board. After crossing the Ohio River into Kentucky, the train meandered through Covington, Newport, Bellevue, and Dayton, the last stop before Brent. When No. 8 reached the Ohio River again, it picked up speed and turned south once more while keeping the river in sight. Anna waited and watched. As the little depot at Brent came into view—here Anna and Harlan's telling of the story resumes—the engineer, signaled by an apparition alongside the tracks, made the stop Anna had been waiting for. No. 8 didn't stop regularly at Brent, but Harlan had built a fire there and was waving a burning cardboard box aloft on a stout stick as a flare to flag down the train. Harlan boarded, and he and Anna rode together about fifty more miles along the Ohio, to the fine old river town of Maysville.

When they had been married for a year, Harlan wrote about their wedding day in the separate journal he kept from 1943 to 1950 for entries addressed to Anna on her birthday and their anniversary: "A year ago today," he wrote, "we walked down the river hill as day broke—a chill windy day. The sky was heavy, the earth wet with rains. Boarding No. 8 at Brent, we rode to Maysville, farther than we had ever gone before, on the little train."

Anna and Harlan walked down the river hill *together*? They boarded the train at Brent *together*? Then where did that grand tale about their rendezvous at the depot come from? Had Harlan simplified the details for his journal? Or, over the years, had Anna and Harlan confused the wedding-day train trip with some other one? The editor in me wants the facts nailed down, but the romantic says never mind. Anna and Harlan told the story with great delight, and that's how they remembered their wedding day—two independent people, each of them taking full responsibility for deciding whether there would be a marriage, and neither one having power over the other. Anna and Harlan put the essential truth into their myth.

After they had arrived at the Maysville station (Harlan wrote in the birthday-and-anniversary journal), Anna excused herself for a moment and left Harlan sitting on a bench, gazing at the river in the gray, wet weather. When she returned she offered him a chance to back out, and he declined: "You offered me a chance to withdraw from this enterprise, but that was far from my mind." After the ceremony they walked east along the railroad tracks through the hilly, picturesque town "and came to the country along the river, and finally to a damp hillside, with budding trees and wild flowers, and were alone and happy." Harlan made a little fire, and they had a snack. They walked on to Springdale and the country beyond. Back in Maysville that evening, waiting for the westbound No. 7, he made another fire to eat their supper by. A rain shower came up, and they took shelter alongside a coal car. At Brent they walked together up the hill to River Road and the streets of Fort Thomas that led to their first home, the studio.

Thirty-three years later, in a conversation preserved on tape, a friend asked Anna whether her family had had any reaction to her getting married and shantyboating down the river. Anna seemed caught off guard. With uncharacteristic hesitation she answered, in her carefully articulated way of speaking, "No-o-o, uh [pause], my mother's a [she paused again, searching for the right word] con*serv*ative person." Though the question had not been specifically about Anna's mother, Anna's thoughts had jumped directly to her. And though Nellie

Eikenhout had then been dead for twenty years, Anna did not say "my mother *was* a conservative person"; Anna seemed for that moment to be sensing her mother in the present. She explained that her mother had met Harlan before the marriage and liked him. "Mother was always very gracious about Harlan," she added, and then distractions in the room led the conversation in another direction.

Harlan, too, said in old age that Anna's mother had accepted him without a murmur. Mam had written to Anna on the eve of the wedding: "If you Ann, and Harlan, can be happy together, then I say, the sooner you two get married the better for all concerned. . . . You are both of mature age and are certainly entitled to whatever happiness you find together." There is no joyous endorsement in the message, but at least there is acceptance. According to Etta's telling, however, Mam had been shocked and disappointed at Anna's getting married, because she still expected Anna to come home and take care of her in her old age. And she tried to talk Anna and Harlan out of their shantyboating plan—perhaps she thought it wasn't respectable. Her effort "didn't work, at all, of course," wrote Etta years later; "sent them off entirely—probably more so than anything else could have done!"

The situation may have been aggravated by Anna's resigning, around that same time, from the family church. Though she had not attended any church for years, she now sent the Fifth Reformed Church of Grand Rapids a resignation letter. According to Etta, this unheard-of step "shook up the whole Consistory" (church council). Anna told Etta she was annoyed that the church was still asking her for money, but Etta thought the timing of the letter suggested that Anna resigned, "as she did so much more—to make H[arlan] happy." If the consistory was "shook up," the house at 1006 Madison must have rocked on its foundation.

Community opinion was of paramount importance to Nellie Eikenhout all her life, and she never completely stopped trying to control her daughters. All three of the wedding storms had passed, and Etta had been back in Grand Rapids for about a year when Mam wrote to Anna in September 1952 that she and Etta had attended church services together that morning: "Lots of folks remember Tet and I should think she would go [to church] more often. This being away from home has done things to my family which Daddy and I knew nothing about, and might have avoided, had we known!"

As for Anna's marrying, she did so against the opposition of more than one mother.

9

The True Direction

*It was our own boat we had built ourselves, it was our own
life we had chosen to live in this comparatively simple,
almost primitive way, and we brought to it every resource
we had. Far from leaving anything behind, we took with us
all that was most worthwhile out of our previous living.*

Anna, "Life in a Shantyboat,"
Library Journal, November 1, 1954

Harlan had tried to pacify his mother as long as possible. He had kept
her in the dark, the previous spring, about his having had a companion on the Licking River canoe trip: "Of course, Mom doesn't know
that Anna and I went together," he wrote his brother Frank. But now
Rose's efforts to hold on to Harlan had finally failed, and the peace
was broken. About two months after the wedding, Harlan assured
Frank that their mother was "coming around, and in her best mo-
ments even enjoys the new situation, and Anna's company. Anna is
doing her part wonderfully and is happy, I am sure. Very kind and
patient with Mom always." In his eighties, however, when he had out-
lived all the other participants, Harlan was more truthful: his mother
"didn't take to Anna, of course." No doubt Anna was kind and patient, but she must have suffered from Rose's hostility. Not long after
the wedding, the Hubbard-Staebler quartet was in session in the studio.
Patricia went up to the house and was subjected to Rose's unvarnished
views on Anna. "She got her hands on him through music," said Rose.
In Lucien Hubbard's family, oral tradition has it that Harlan's marriage
broke Rose's heart and that she accused Anna of poisoning her.

In those first months of marriage, Anna and Harlan went canoeing and camping as often as their jobs permitted. In late May they
took their small canoe to Brent, then paddled up Four Mile Creek and

had a swim. They left the canoe at Brent with Andy and Sadie Detisch, but first they passed a pleasant hour on the Detisches' shantyboat, eating lunch, watching the rain, and planning the houseboat they wanted to build someday.

Then in June, Rose became ill, and in July she had surgery. The doctor explained (Harlan wrote to Frank on July 19) that Rose "had a growth which he did not remove but by-passed the intestine around it, so she could function normally and have no pain." Harlan seemed to believe that his mother would recover. "I hope it works all right," he continued, "and she has no more trouble. . . . convalescence will of course be rather slow." On September 29 he wrote to Frank, "Mom isn't making any progress at present. In fact she seems weaker. . . . Of course this may be temporary, and she will soon begin to pick up." Rose continued weakening, however. Anna spent the month of October on paid vacation from the library and resigned effective October 31, but not, apparently, for the purpose of taking care of Rose; Harlan was doing that, with the aid of hired helpers. In later years Harlan said of Anna's resignation only that she wasn't meant for the daily grind.

Rose died in mid-November. Harlan had discharged his duty to his mother, and now he and Anna were free to begin their new life. A canoe trip on the Ohio in late November marked the beginning of a year of great changes for Anna and Harlan. Leaving the Packard at the Brent railway depot, they rode No. 8 to South Ripley, Kentucky, about forty-six miles upstream. There they took the ferry across to Ripley, Ohio, where Harlan had stored the canoe after a previous trip. In the next four days Anna and Harlan paddled upstream from Ripley thirty-four miles, by Harlan's calculations, stopping briefly in Maysville. He sketched. They read and hiked, camped in protected spots on the shore and on gravel bars, and bathed each night next to a roaring fire.

During this period, for perhaps the only time in their life together, Anna and Harlan were concerned about money. They feared that Harlan might have to get a job to support the house. A few weeks later, though, they ended their money worries by becoming landlords. Once they had rented the house, there was nothing else holding them in Fort Thomas.

Anna was "not a sharer of my beliefs about the way to live" at the time they married, Harlan wrote. But Anna adjusted—though she said years later that she had never felt she was making adjustments; she was simply spending more and more time with Harlan. On the canoe rides, then the camping trips, then in the studio, and then during their 1944 travels, Anna adjusted. Harlan grew restless in 1944. He and Anna made two adventurous hiking trips that year: through seven eastern states from February to April, and up the western lakeshore of lower Michigan and across the Upper Peninsula of Michigan to Lake Superior in August and September. By the end of the second trip they had made their decision. They would turn their backs on modern life and build the shantyboat they had talked about. They would take a drifting trip, eating what they could grow and gather themselves, and living intimately with the seasons and the river.

While that decision was brewing during the two hiking trips, Anna and Harlan both learned what Anna was made of. The going was often rugged in anyone's terms; for her it must have been very hard indeed. She had no history of epic adventures. Most of her canoeing had been done on mild little lakes. But now, in her forty-second year, she began hiking with Harlan through rain, wind, cold, snow, and ice, often ten, sometimes twenty miles a day. They climbed ravines and mountains. They hitchhiked in cars and trucks, and like the hoboes of the recent Depression, they even hopped freight trains. Now and then they had a night of luxury in a farmhouse, lodge, or hotel, but mostly they camped in their tent in the open or in rough shelters. Though they tempered the walking with bus and train rides and stretches of hitchhiking, still Anna's soft feet must have blistered. Sometimes she got wet through, and certainly she was often less clean and well pressed than she liked to be. Consideration kept Harlan from testing Anna beyond what he perceived as her limits—his pack weighed thirty-eight pounds, for instance, and hers only seven—but I believe she tested herself even harder, stretching her limits so as not to let Harlan down. Harlan said years later that a friend had scolded him for taking Anna out in such conditions. She didn't seem to mind, Harlan said.

The eastern trip began on February 22 at Union Terminal. Anna and Harlan took the night train—the C&O's crack train, the Fast Flying Virginian (the "F.F.V.")—to Washington, D.C., and arrived there at four o'clock the next morning. After eating their breakfast on a bench in the dark outside Washington's Union Station, they began a long walk around the Capitol and up Constitution Avenue as far as the White House. They stopped at the Corcoran Gallery and the National Gallery of Art on the way back and ate lunch on the same bench, then boarded another train at two o'clock for New York. Anna and Harlan stayed in New York three weeks, spending the weekends with

Frank and his wife, Frances, in Larchmont, and the rest of the time in Frank's one-room studio on Lexington Avenue in Manhattan. It was a convenient setup for visiting museums, art galleries, and concerts. They also visited Hilda and Bob Webber in nearby Bronxville.

On March 17 Anna and Harlan went by train to Catskill, New York, and, through the offices of Anna's Hope College friend Helen Van Ess, spent a couple of days at the Girl Scout campsite. On the ten-degree morning of March 19, Helen drove them to nearby Palenville, where they began several days of rugged hiking in the Catskills through rain, snow, and ice. Anna never forgot climbing, that first day, on an ice cone formed by a waterfall. She was afraid, and Harlan held her up from below and told her not to look down. On March 21 they took a bus to Saugerties, and by day's end on March 24 they reached Port Jervis, having hitchhiked in cars and trucks and walked a total of nearly fifty-seven miles. The last day was the hardest, twenty-one and a half miles of walking.

Next they went by bus to Pennsylvania and visited Patricia Staebler, who was working in a Quaker community called Pendle Hill, near Philadelphia. (Warren, a conscientious objector, was doing "alternative service" in Tennessee.) They reached Harper's Ferry, West Virginia, by train on Monday, March 27, and embarked the next day on the Appalachian Trail. Anna was "doing splendidly," Harlan wrote to Frank, implicit testimony that she was being tried severely. (I know of only two other times when Harlan accorded Anna that degree of praise. One was in 1949, when she worked relentlessly, sawing and splitting firewood and battling Nature in the shantyboat garden. The other was in 1986, when, desperately ill with renal cancer, she made an exhausting weekend trip to the last of Harlan's exhibition openings she would ever attend.) Snow, wind, and rain high up on the Appalachian Trail made the going so difficult that they descended into the Shenandoah Valley at Berryville, Virginia. From there they walked and hitched their way south on side roads, camping near the river at night. They took a bus from Staunton to Roanoke, where Harlan wrote Frank on April 3: "I feel that a real change has been made in regards to Fort Thomas. Up to now the old momentum was carrying us along. We will see what changes it means." The decision about building a shantyboat was simmering.

Arriving in Asheville, North Carolina, by bus on April 4 to begin the Great Smoky Mountains leg of the trip, they found winter still in residence. In snow flurries and a high wind they hitchhiked west to

Waynesville, bought supplies, and walked five miles north to Dellwood, where they spent the night with people named Campbell, "a hale old man and daughter Fanny," Harlan wrote in his log, who accommodated the travelers in a big upstairs room and gave them breakfast.

Their goal the next day was a town on the northeast corner of Great Smoky Mountains National Park called Mount Sterling, where they would be in position to rejoin the Appalachian Trail early the following morning. With the temperature at twenty degrees, and facing a strong wind, they set out for Mount Sterling along the eastern edge of the park. The going was "very rough," Harlan wrote to Frank, "a high wind and snow at times." Even so, they hitched only seven miles and walked twenty-one.

The following day, April 6, was warmer—thirty-five degrees. They obtained their fire permit at the Big Creek ranger station, then hiked to Davenport Gap, the easternmost point of the Appalachian Trail inside the park, and began what would be their most strenuous day of hiking in the Smokies. In their first three miles that day, they climbed steadily, about nineteen hundred feet—more than six hundred feet per mile, or more than twice the average degree of difficulty the National Park Service defines today as "strenuous." That night and the next they camped in shelters along the trail, and on the afternoon of April 8, their third day on the Appalachian Trail, they reached Newfound Gap. From this point on, the trip was almost luxurious.

They hitchhiked north on Newfound Gap Road, the narrow, winding, mountain ridge highway that bisects the park, to Gatlinburg, Tennessee. Warren Staebler was there, doing office work at Civilian Public Service Camp 108, previously a Civilian Conservation Corps camp, now (during World War II) being run by the Quakers for conscientious objectors. Anna and Harlan stayed two nights in the staff house for a dollar a night, enjoying the camp's cultural activities and, at last, spring in the mountains. Three more days of hiking and bus travel north through Tennessee and Kentucky, and they were home on April 13.

The next day was "a low day" for Harlan. He continued writing in his trip log: "There now seems no freshness to this country. It has worn grooves in my mind." He and Anna made a trip to Brent, but it didn't help. "I am wearied of that stretch from Brent downstream." During a three-month hiatus in the studio, Anna and Harlan read Thoreau's *Maine Woods*. They ate all their meals outdoors. They gathered wild berries. Harlan painted very little. The pending decision was nagging at them. After a hot, sticky day of house painting on June 14,

Anna and Harlan went to the river for a swim and watched a summer storm break. "There on the river shore," Harlan wrote in his journal, "old longings and plans were revived. We wondered at the delay, it was all so within reach." Four days later they broke another link with the modern world and sold the Packard.

Soon they were off again, on their Michigan trip. They spent the July 8 weekend with Nella Mae in Cleveland, where she was in library school, and then they had a long visit in Grand Rapids. Harlan had family to look up there too; his father had been born there. Barre wrote to Anna in Grand Rapids on July 17 from Florida, where she was living. She was enjoying the notion of Harlan "meeting the folks."

The trek began in earnest on August 9. Anna would not have to contend with ice or snow on this trip, but the sand was a nuisance. As they headed north along the Lake Michigan shore, they walked and slept in the stuff, and on windy days they ate some. The hard, wet sand at the water's edge was no problem for Harlan's callused feet, but Anna's were tender, and so she slogged through the deep, dry sand in moccasins and wool socks.

Harlan cajoled Anna into keeping her own log of the trip. Anna compared her thoughts and writing with Harlan's: "I hope that he will continue to write his own impressions, however, as his cryptic accounts are always so vivid, so very direct." When their route was interrupted by a channel, Harlan went looking for a means of crossing it, and Anna wrote, "Harlan's thinking goes deeper than mine—as is often the case—he is wondering whether (if there were no people here at all—if it were primitive wild country) we could make a raft of driftwood to put our things across, or would we have to walk all the way around this inland lake." The next day she added, "I should be happy to know more of what Harlan is thinking. His thoughts go far and deep."

All the while Anna went about sharing with Harlan her northern woods of pine, arbor vitae, and white birch, she was constantly reminded of the past. A "homely little lake at Arcadia" (north of Manistee) reminded her of the Diamond Lake of her childhood. At nearby Frankfort they camped at the entrance to Herring Lake, and Anna wrote in her log, "I could be homesick for a little lake like that— toute ma vie est là" (my whole life is there). August 13 and 14 they spent near the Interlochen music camp, going to the students' chorus and orchestra rehearsals and talking with them at Sunday night supper at the hotel. Next they spent two nights with Leo Cayvan and his wife at Torch Lake, the same Torch Lake where Anna and Barre had taken their last vacation together three years before. There's a melancholy tone to Anna's log entry about the visit, only four lines in the small notebook, written on August 17, the day after she and Harlan left: "Torch Lake, where we stayed from Monday afternoon until Wednesday noon, with the Cayvans, seems far away."

On August 20 Anna and Harlan reached the northernmost point of the "mitten" and were about to cross the Straits of Mackinac by ferry to the Upper Peninsula. Anna had been eager to see this part of her Michigan for the first time. Harlan recorded the sights they saw and the adventures they had while traveling west across the peninsula—the Straits, Mackinac Island, Fort Mackinac, abandoned mines, Tahquamenon Falls, sharing their campfire with a hobo, riding all day in an empty box car, the first sight of Lake Superior at Au Train Bay, lumber camps, virgin forests—but through it all, Anna wrote nothing. The log entry she made on August 19 at Sturgeon Bay was her last for ten days.

From August 20 to 29 Anna felt too "low down" to write in her log. When she took it up again, she wrote: "This morning I seem to feel as fresh as I did when we were beginning this hike. For the first time in several days I feel like writing in my log." She implied that the low feelings had been familiar: "I don't know—I really don't—why I should be down—and pretty low down—sometimes and then, the next morning, up again. But I'm mighty glad it's up this morning." When I first read this part of Anna's log I wondered whether her puzzlement was genuine. What if this low mood had had something to do with Harlan? Since Anna shared her journal with Harlan (I reasoned), of course she wouldn't record anything negative about him. But that suspicion is unworthy of Anna; more likely, she would suppress any thoughts or feelings that might be disloyal to Harlan. I think Anna truly did not know what caused her low moods.

I've tried to imagine why Anna might have been feeling so "low down" this particular time. Perhaps her thoughts were dwelling on Barre—thoughts of their vacation together at Torch Lake; of the general delivery letter from Barre that she knew would be waiting for her in the Mackinaw City post office; of the trip to the Upper Peninsula she and Barre had once planned but had been unable to take. Thoughts, perhaps, of the contrast between Harlan and Barre as traveling companions: quiet, serious Harlan, sketching, writing in his log, focusing his attention on the landscape; fanciful Barre, joking and laughing, sharing all her observations, talking for the sheer joy of connecting.

But there was at least one thought of Barre that Anna would have been unable to face: the thought that intense emotional intimacy, such as she had known with Barre, had gone out of her life for good.

On August 21 Anna received the letter she had been waiting for. There is an undercurrent of sadness in it. "Don't worry about getting letters off to me," Barre had written on August 17; "a card like the last one is quite enough to let me know that you don't forget me." Anna's depression lifted on August 30, at Skanee, at the western end of the Upper Peninsula. On a rainy, cold September 4, Labor Day, at the northernmost tip of the Upper Peninsula jutting out into Lake Superior, Anna and Harlan waited for the bus that would be the start of their journey home. Anna was thinking of summers gone by: it was just the sort of day "we girls have had so often, at the lake," she wrote in her log, "for breaking up camp and going back to town."

The following day they took the train to Green Bay, Wisconsin, to visit Lee and Art Thiele. In Lee's eyes the Hubbards, in clothes rumpled from their packs, made a sorry appearance. Lee was amazed at Anna's wearing slacks; she didn't wear them herself and knew no other women who did. She was surprised, too, by the way of life Anna had chosen after her refined upbringing. (I wonder whether Anna told Lee she had hitchhiked and hopped freight trains.) On September 8 they left Green Bay for Chicago, where Harlan had family, and two days later they took a night train for home. That train ride on September 10, 1944, was the climax of the year of great changes. "We were returning home," Harlan wrote, "and all missions were completed. Anna said, 'Now is the time to build the shantyboat we have talked of for so long.'"

Set free by Anna's words, Harlan began work immediately. In two stages, on October 5 and 6, with the help of a friend and his pickup truck, Harlan moved his carefully selected salvaged lumber from a demolished building in Covington to the construction site he had chosen near the Detisches' shantyboat at Brent. On October 6 he wrote in his journal: "This is the day we begin a new venture, facing now the true direction." That night Anna and Harlan camped in their tent near the lumber, and the next day Harlan built a shack for housing until the boat took form. It was no ordinary squatters' shack—Harlan's inventiveness and Anna's homemaking standards set it apart. It was fourteen feet wide, because its floor was to become the shantyboat floor, and those boards mustn't be cut. To rest evenly on the sloping riverbank it had to be shallow from front to back, but it was tall enough to sit in comfortably, and it held everything Anna and Harlan needed. It was covered with canvas that could be rolled up and down, and at the front, in the middle of the wide view of the river, on a platform of stones, rested a fireplace Harlan had fashioned from salvaged junk.

Anna gave the shack the same degree of attention she gave every place she ever called home. Harlan marveled that she could stay so neat and clean on the riverbank, and he admired her way of "setting the rude table with camp tinware as carefully as if it were fine china and silver upon a linen cloth." Sitting inside the shack before the fire on rainy days, Anna and Harlan were as snug and cozy as they could have wished. Before long they were telling time by the passing of the trains on the C&O railroad tracks just a few yards above. In late November the move onto the shantyboat was nearing. Harlan called the installation of the little cookstove on November 23 "an event, for I have pictured this stove on a shantyboat for years." (My uncle, Dan McTamney, happened by that day while Harlan was marking a hole in the roof for the stovepipe, and he had in his car a compass saw, the very tool Harlan needed to carry out the job.)

One day about two weeks later, a friendly little black-and-white terrier appeared at the campsite. From then on she was under foot, and whenever Harlan returned from a jaunt or an errand, she was there to welcome him home. During the night of December 11, Anna and Harlan's first night sleeping aboard the shantyboat, the little dog sealed her adoption by making her bed at their feet. Two days later the volunteer had a name, Skipper, and Harlan could no longer remember the place without her. He wrote about how it was, coming home to the dark, rough hillside and seeing the boat on the shore. At his whistle the door opened, loosing a flood of lamplight and the sweet greetings of Anna's voice and Skipper's fierce barking. The preceding scene is just as real to me: Anna alone on the shantyboat, writing letters, sewing, lighting the lamps, and setting everything to rights. She gives the stew a stir, and then, hearing Harlan's whistle, she opens the door to him while Skipper barks a welcome.

The shantyboat was afloat by the end of the year, and the outfit was completed in February by the construction of a johnboat. There was no hurry about departing; Anna and Harlan spent two years on the shantyboat at Brent and learned the ways of the river. Summers were disrupted somewhat by the commotion at Coney Island amusement park, across the river from their mooring, but there were compensations in the fireworks displays, and in the sounds of the deep whistle and pounding wheel of the steamboat *Island Queen* coming and going with her Cincinnati passengers. By far the greatest good Harlan found in Coney Island, though, was its dump, a reliable scavenging ground for useful junk.

From Brent on May 8, 1945, Anna and Harlan heard Cincinnati tumultuously celebrating Allied victory. The following year—on December 22, 1946, to be precise—while other Americans were buying tract houses and filling them with all the labor-saving appliances the booming postwar economy could produce, Anna and Harlan cast off in the shantyboat and joined with the timeless river. The events of the world ceased to intrude on them. They had no plan that day, not for the shantyboat trip or the rest of their lives. "We just thought we'd build a boat and take a trip down the river," Anna said years later. "We didn't think for a minute that we'd live on that boat for seven years."

Eventually the drifting part of the journey extended to three and a half years, four winters, and fourteen hundred miles down the Ohio and Mississippi Rivers to New Orleans. Each of the Hubbards' three long layovers at Payne Hollow, Bizzle's Bluff, and Natchez lasted seven to nine months; they did their drifting in winter, when the river is high and swift. Sometimes Harlan had to tow the shantyboat from the johnboat while Anna stood on the main deck and pulled a long pair of oars called sweeps, but usually the boat was powered only by the current. They might tie up for a night or a week in each new place, depending on weather and whim. Anna said much later that they hadn't told anyone the really frightening things that happened during the shantyboat years. The constant possibility of danger from snags, ice, wind, and larger boats intensified the pleasure of putting in to safe harbor, playing some music, bathing before the fire, reading a chapter, and falling asleep to the lapping of waves against the hull.

When they reached New Orleans in early 1950 they considered what to do next. Harlan wanted to stay on the boat another year to finish writing *Shantyboat*, though he said later that they would have invented some other reason if they'd had to. And so they extended their shantyboating with the trip through the bayous. When they ended their journey a year later, they considered how to get their books, tools, paintings, three musical instruments, and two dogs back to Kentucky. They dismissed prosaic thoughts of station wagons and pickup trucks, and then—inspiration! With the proceeds from selling the shantyboat Harlan bought a ten- by four-foot steel-pipe trailer chassis at a welder's shop and built a boxy wood body to fit. The purchase of a ten-year-old dark-blue Dodge sedan to pull the trailer made the gypsy caravan complete. Anna and Harlan were rightly proud of the trailer, which ranks high among Harlan's marvelous contraptions.

Anna and Harlan still had no firm plans. Why settle down now, with a gypsy caravan at their disposal? After a round of visits in the Midwest they headed for the Pacific. Anna thought the gypsy life was great fun: "As usual, we just started out and made it up as we went along." Harlan sketched and made watercolors. They played music and read every day, as they had on the shantyboat. Anna was thrilled by the Rockies, and so they camped at the foot of the mountains for a week before starting across. Later they camped for a whole month in the southwestern desert.

Eventually Anna and Harlan reached California for a visit with Harlan's brother Lucien and his wife, Alice. As a movie producer, Lucien had worked with early filmmakers Jesse Lasky, Irving Thalberg, Louis B. Mayer, and Darryl F. Zanuck, and with most of the major studios—MGM, Paramount, Twentieth Century Fox, Universal, and Warner Brothers. Among his many productions were *Wings* (the first "best picture" Oscar winner, 1929); *42nd Street*, the 1933 musical comedy with Ruby Keeler and Dick Powell; and the first of the Hardy Family films (1937), with Mickey Rooney and Lionel Barrymore. Anna and Harlan could have met all the movie stars in Hollywood, but instead they sat for hours at the edge of Lucien's tennis court, up against the ivy-covered fence, working together on the *Shantyboat* manuscript.

On April 30, 1952, after nine months of camping, the trailer and the dogs and Anna and Harlan came home to Fort Thomas again, but it wasn't home for them any longer. In the studio they now thought of as only a base camp, Anna and Harlan again considered what to do next. At first they thought living in the studio might do for a while, but no, it was too great a letdown. It was time to look for a permanent home. They wanted a few quiet acres where they could provide for themselves by foraging, fishing, and gardening, without electricity and other modern contrivances. A peaceful place, far enough from the noise of towns and automobiles, yet near enough to libraries and concerts, where Harlan could build a simple house of wood and stone. This homestead on the "fringe of society" would be the culmination of Harlan's dream, now shared by Anna.

Weeks of searching followed. The stretch of the Ohio between Brent and Maysville that Harlan had once been partial to had changed for the worse during their shantyboating years; he was discouraged.

The shantyboat and johnboat moored on Gilmore Creek, below Milton, Kentucky, 1947. "We pull into the backwater where we are safe from wind, current, and floating drift. There, gently swaying between the trees, we enjoy the new outlook and the excitement of the fast-flowing river outside our harbor" (*Shantyboat*, 39). (Courtesy Don Wallis)

(Top) The Hubbard house in Fort Thomas, Kentucky, built by Harlan in 1923 to his own design, after a farmhouse he considered pure Kentucky (courtesy Betty Hubbard Heasley). (Middle) Harlan painted in the small bedroom below the skylight for a time, and slept on the unheated enclosed porch on the living-room end (here, the right-hand end) of the house. Mia (at left) was four or five when Dan snapped this from in front of the studio (D. James McTamney photo). (Bottom) The studio. When the Hubbards left Fort Thomas, Harlan stored his paintings of the 1930s here, and thirty years later he found they were better than he remembered (D. James McTamney photo).

(Right) Dan McTamney and niece Mia, 1945, as they looked when they visited the shantyboat at Brent (J. Anthony Bill photo). (Below) Rose, Mia, and Harry, their first Christmas in Fort Thomas, 1946. Hanging above is one of Dan's paintings by Harlan, probably of the steamboat *Courier* (D. James McTamney photo).

Anna and Harlan in the backyard of
the studio, the stonework grill and the
hedge of lilacs in the background,
1944. (Courtesy George Bartnick)

North light pours through the window as Anna reads in the studio,
early 1940s. The raised fireplace is in the right-hand corner.
(Courtesy Don Wallis)

Harlan and Sambo in the johnboat, June 1954. (Photo by the author)

Harlan, folded like an accordion, gutting and cleaning a catfish, June 1954. (Photo by the author)

Inside the Payne Hollow cabin. Above Sambo is the vanity cabinet. *Let's Cook It Right* is on the middle bookshelf, the reading table is in the foreground. The fireplace was later replaced by a storage cabinet and drawers. (Ran Cochran photo, Cincinnati *Pictorial Enquirer*, October 23, 1955, reproduced with permission of Randy Cochran)

The vanity cabinet and pull-down drawer. (Ran Cochran photo, Cincinnati *Pictorial Enquirer*, October 23, 1955, reproduced with permission of Randy Cochran)

(Below) Anna making up the bed in the one-room cabin. (Ran Cochran photo, Cincinnati *Pictorial Enquirer*, October 23, 1955, reproduced with permission of Randy Cochran)

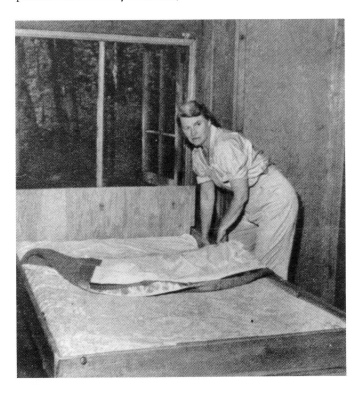

(Above) Anna in her pink sunbonnet, June 1954. (Below) Harlan and the giant sunflowers lining the path through the lower garden, August 1954. (Photos by the author)

(Right) The desert cooler in the breezeway behind the cabin (Ran Cochran photo, Cincinnati *Pictorial Enquirer*, October 23, 1955, reproduced with permission of Randy Cochran). (Below) Anna showing some young visitors her cupboard of flours and herbs in the 1970s (courtesy Don Wallis).

Harlan took this picture of Mia and Anna, dressed for an expedition to Madison and Hanover, July 1956.

Anna ornamented her new fireplace-cookstove with her Old Country brass things. Here she's putting something into the oven. (Allan Kain photo, Cincinnati *Pictorial Enquirer*, August 24, 1958)

(Above) Sliding the bed into its spot between the wall and the bookcase was an acquired skill. (Below) The Steinway end of the lower room. Snapper under the piano, and Curly in foreground. (H. Harold Davis photos, © *The Courier-Journal*, January 19, 1964, reprinted with permission)

The Henry Eikenhout family, about 1891. Rear:
Effie, who died in the influenza epidemic of 1918,
and John. Front: Henry Eikenhout's mother; Henry
holding Roy; Henry's wife, Anna, holding Bill; and
Mattie. Two other Eikenhout boys had died in 1882,
and Henry Jr. was yet to be born, in 1894. (Courtesy
George Bartnick)

Ancestors of Anna Wonder Eikenhout

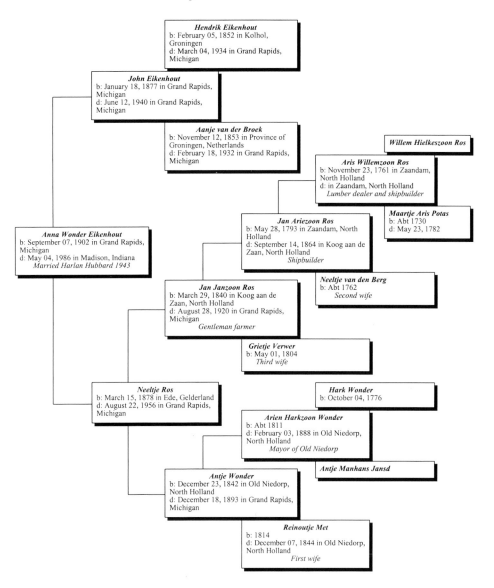

Hendrik Eikenhout
b: February 05, 1852 in Kolhol, Groningen
d: March 04, 1934 in Grand Rapids, Michigan

John Eikenhout
b: January 18, 1877 in Grand Rapids, Michigan
d: June 12, 1940 in Grand Rapids, Michigan

Aanje van der Broek
b: November 12, 1853 in Province of Groningen, Netherlands
d: February 18, 1932 in Grand Rapids, Michigan

Willem Hielkeszoon Ros

Aris Willemzoon Ros
b: November 23, 1761 in Zaandam, North Holland
d: in Zaandam, North Holland
Lumber dealer and shipbuilder

Maartje Aris Potas
b: Abt 1730
d: May 23, 1782

Jan Ariezoon Ros
b: May 28, 1793 in Zaandam, North Holland
d: September 14, 1864 in Koog aan de Zaan, North Holland
Shipbuilder

Anna Wonder Eikenhout
b: September 07, 1902 in Grand Rapids, Michigan
d: May 04, 1986 in Madison, Indiana
Married Harlan Hubbard 1943

Neeltje van den Berg
b: Abt 1762
Second wife

Jan Janzoon Ros
b: March 29, 1840 in Koog aan de Zaan, North Holland
d: August 28, 1920 in Grand Rapids, Michigan
Gentleman farmer

Grietje Verwer
b: May 01, 1804
Third wife

Neeltje Ros
b: March 15, 1878 in Ede, Gelderland
d: August 22, 1956 in Grand Rapids, Michigan

Hark Wonder
b: October 04, 1776

Arien Harkzoon Wonder
b: Abt 1811
d: February 03, 1888 in Old Niedorp, North Holland
Mayor of Old Niedorp

Antje Manhans Jansd

Antje Wonder
b: December 23, 1842 in Old Niedorp, North Holland
d: December 18, 1893 in Grand Rapids, Michigan

Reinoutje Met
b: 1814
d: December 07, 1844 in Old Niedorp, North Holland
First wife

Anna's family tree, researched mostly by Anna and put into family-tree computer software by the author.

(Above) The house in Old Niedorp, North Holland, where Anna Wonder Ross (Anna's maternal grandmother) was born. The couple on the balcony may be her brother, Dirk, and his wife. (Below, left) Jan Ross (1840–1920), Anna's maternal grandfather. (Below, right) Anna Wonder Ross (1842–1893), Anna's maternal grandmother. (Photos courtesy Patricia Magaw Fuhs)

(Above) Nellie and John Eikenhout, probably their wedding portrait, 1900.
(Below) Anna (left) and Etta, about 1910. (Photos courtesy George
Bartnick)

From left: Anna, Etta, their cousin Lucille, and Nella Mae, 1918. (Courtesy George Bartnick)

The Eikenhout family home, 1006 Madison SE, Grand Rapids. (Courtesy George Bartnick)

Anna at high school graduation. (Courtesy
George Bartnick)

(Above) Hilda Bell, Anna, and Charles Bell, about 1920 (courtesy Robert Webber). (Below) Postcard from Diamond Lake, where the Eikenhout family spent the earliest of their summer vacations (courtesy George Bartnick).

Anna at the lake, June 1921. (Courtesy George
Bartnick)

(Above) Lee Holden. (Below) Anna. Canoeing on the lake, mid-1920s. (Photos courtesy George Bartnick)

Cincinnati's new public library in 1874—in the words of *Harper's Weekly*, "the largest, best-arranged, and only fire-proof public library building in the country," with "the largest and best collection of books west of the Alleghanies" (March 21 issue, 1874).

Barre Pritchett, 1933. (Courtesy George
Bartnick)

(Right) From left: Nella Mae, Etta, and Anna in Cincinnati, 1935. (Below) At Pickerel Lake, Michigan, 1933. From left: Barre, Anna, Nella Mae, Etta, and Etta's friend Fran Bailey. (Photos courtesy George Bartnick)

(Left) Paul Briol, 1926, ten years before he and Anna met. (Below) Paul Briol's "Camp," Foster, Ohio, April 2, 1939. From left, standing: unidentified, Paul Briol, Saradel Emerson Sadler; seated: Joe Austin, Dorothy Austin, Mary Briol, Forest Frank (executive director, City Charter Committee of Cincinnati). (Photos courtesy Jan Briol Chinnock McLean)

(Above) Anna in the Fine Arts department of the old Cincinnati Public Library, 1940 (courtesy Thomas Moorman). (Below) The Ohio River overlook, Eden Park, Cincinnati, where Anna and Harlan had their first picnic lunch together (photo by the author, 1996).

Portrait by Harlan of his mother, Rose Swingle
Hubbard, about 1941. (© Bill Caddell, reproduced
with permission)

The Hubbard brothers, from left, Frank, Lucien, and
Harlan, at Payne Hollow, June 1956. (Courtesy
George Bartnick)

Barre (right) drove Anna and Harlan to West Liberty, Kentucky, to begin their Licking River canoe trip in May 1942. (Courtesy Don Wallis)

Anna and Harlan launch their canoe, and their lives together, on the Licking River. Barre took their picture and saw them off. (Courtesy Don Wallis)

Anna on the prow of Harlan's canoe during the August 1942 continuation of their May trip. (Courtesy Helen Thiele Buran)

The fourth campsite on the Licking: "Gravel bar to land on, rushing water just out there, a clear little creek running into the river just above, a big hill beyond the bend ahead, and back beyond this immediate bank, a wide valley with three farms visible, and the high hills beyond" (Anna's trip log). (Courtesy Don Wallis)

Brent, Kentucky—the bend in the Ohio River where the shantyboat (left) was built. The I–275 bridge passes over the spot today. (Courtesy George Bartnick)

Perhaps February 19, 1945, the first washday at the shantyboat. "To see [the clothes] out on a line on the riverbank made us truly live here. . . . Where now are your electric washing machines?" (*Shantyboat Journal*, 36). (Courtesy George Bartnick)

"The heavy, slow-moving tows made no disturbance as they went by, but there were some fast diesels that often came down with a few empty oil barges, tearing up the river" (*Shantyboat*, 31). (Courtesy Helen Thiele Buran)

"Though we went no more to the beloved country upriver, we were reminded of it each morning by the passing of Number Eight. It blew for Brent with a soft-toned whistle that meant river almost as much as the steamboat whistles" (*Shantyboat*, 80). (Courtesy George Bartnick)

Anna in shorts, and Harlan with a catfish, on the Cumberland River, 1948. The now-fully-realized shantyboat is festooned with laundry and fish nets. The eight-foot windows and the large main deck flouted shantyboat conventions, and the ten-by-sixteen cabin held both a wood-burning stove and a fireplace. When guests were aboard, the Hubbards slept in the pop-up compartment they called the "texas." (Courtesy George Bartnick)

Camping in the desert, December 1951, in the camping trailer, a flat box with a lid that could be propped up to sitting height. The snug sleeping compartment held the rubber air-mattress bed from the shantyboat. Anna praised the handy lift-up panels, convenient lift-out cupboards, and pleasing color combination of the natural oiled wood and the blue car. (Courtesy George Bartnick)

And now Anna made another of her quiet suggestions, one that perhaps she had been holding onto a long time, waiting for the right moment. Why not visit their old friends in Payne Hollow? Anna said.

They put aside the disappointing search and in mid-June went back to Payne Hollow. They camped on the ridge that first night, and then their old friend Owen Hammond offered to haul their trailer down the hill with his tractor. The hollow had been ideal for the summering-over in the shantyboat in 1947, and it was ideal still. It had a creek, a spring, and of course the river. It had good bottomland, which had already furnished the Hubbards one fine garden.

What's more, the place offered Harlan a recycling opportunity on a grand scale. Growing in abandoned uphill fields were all the berries they could pick; the processed surplus could be stored in the abandoned root cellar. Still standing there in the hollow were the stone foundation and the stone chimney marking the sites of two abandoned farmhouses washed away in the 1937 flood. There was even an abandoned steamboat landing. The hollow was neglected and wild, a cast-off waiting for someone to scrape away its rough surface and make it useful again.

One thing led to another, and they decided to stay. Owen Hammond sold them about seven acres (later they bought about fifty more), and that fall Harlan began building. In November they moved into their twelve-by-sixteen cabin on the wooded bluff overlooking the river. They made of it a smooth passage, a natural progression, from the drifting shantyboat life to a rooted life in Payne Hollow. In leaving the shantyboat behind, they had once again taken with them from their previous living all that was most worthwhile.

10

The Art of Living

Every time we come back, we realize again how fortunate we are to have this for our home. The river, the hills, the quiet, and time for the things we want to do—and then a blazing fire on our hearth.

Anna to Patricia and Warren Staebler,
December 30, 1953

On a winter day when the Hubbards had lived at Payne Hollow for twenty-five years, Harlan wrote that the river was "just as beautiful as it has been since creation. Today, windless with fog, the earth covered with snow to the water's edge, the world ceases to exist." Anna's young nephew George Bartnick once commented to Anna and Harlan that while driving through Louisville on the way to Payne Hollow he had been struck by the contrast between the modern city and the river flowing alongside. "There's a timelessness to the river," he said, adding offhandedly, as kids do, "d'you know what I mean?" In unison they erupted, "Yes!"

Anna and Harlan both had a sense of their life as an entity distinct from themselves, to be planned and shaped in such a way as to yield the greatest possible satisfaction. Even in those heady winter days of early 1945, as Harlan was finishing the interior of the shantyboat cabin— "We had so much fun at all this that we sometimes felt like children playing at keeping house"—he realized that sometimes they had to stop working and keep some leisure time "for other activities and for just living, or we will miss our way." When they withdrew from work, "time became as smooth and even as the current outside our windows, and we began to realize our true aims in coming to the river."

In his seventies Harlan wrote that they were "still tinkering" with their life at Payne Hollow "to make it smoother and more productive, more significant." The significance was in the simplicity; making the life smoother and more productive was a matter of efficiency. Anna's systems became too fixed, Harlan thought; she wasn't "alert enough for new possibilities." Harlan was always refining his systems, making a game of increasing his efficiency to keep his routine work from becoming boring. Harlan did the fishing, gardening, wood cutting, carpentry, goat tending, beekeeping, and grain grinding. Anna cooked, baked, canned, made cheese and yogurt, sewed, ironed, and cleaned. They did the washing together. Their competence and skill made simple living look easy.

Harlan described, in his fifties, what "living simply" meant to him and Anna: he hoped that a lifetime of doing the same "simple acts" and enjoying the same "plain sensations" over and over would make them happy and contented. He listed his own simple acts: "To arise in the frosty morning at the point of daybreak, climb the hill and cut wood, while the sky lightens above the soaring trees; to eat this wholesome, sweet food, to use my body, hands and mind at the endless work I have to do; to read by the firelight, to sleep warm and snug; all this shared and enjoyed by my loving partner—what manner of a man originated this idea of a happier life beyond death?"

In her own sphere, Anna too made an art of simple living. Although she gave herself no credit for creativity, the life she made in the house at Payne Hollow for herself and Harlan every day was her creation. Giving careful attention to her daily work, she made it important and by so doing, increased her own dignity. Setting a beautiful table, preparing varied and delectable meals, ornamenting the house with Old Country treasures, transplanting wildflowers to the dooryard, arranging flowering branches for the table, preserving the reading and music times inviolate, keeping an orderly house where all those things could be fully enjoyed—these were her gifts for artful living. She made the ordinary sacred and transformed what otherwise might have been only a rustic life into an artful one.

Another of Anna's ways of making the ordinary sacred was by celebrating holidays. At Halloween one year she motivated Harlan to write a one-act play; he set the scene in Andy and Sadie's shantyboat at Brent. Another year each of them carved a jack-o'-lantern. Anna made a squash pudding for supper and wore black slacks with an orange-and-black blouse. And Harlan's costume? He wrote with no emphasis or comment, as if this sort of thing happened all the time at Payne Hollow, "tonight I am dressed like a scarecrow."

Anna's favorite holiday was Christmas, an echo of her childhood. At Payne Hollow, as on the shantyboat, Harlan would cut a tabletop-size cedar tree from the woods. He and Anna would decorate it with strings of popcorn and their old ornaments, and with the "little old-timey clips" that Harlan still had from "when he was a tiny boy," Anna said, they would attach little candles they had hand-dipped themselves. Then on Christmas Eve, with a great fire blazing in the fireplace, they lighted the candles and watched them burn.

In the peace of Payne Hollow, Anna and Harlan focused on the fundamental. "We're always trying to go a little beyond, a little deeper, a little closer to the fundamental things," Anna wrote in the *Library Journal* drafts. Among the "fundamental things" of Payne Hollow she mentioned the growing and gathering of their own food and the making of bread from grains they ground by hand. Anna wrote to Judy Moffett in 1969 about a collection of modern poems she and Harlan were reading: "Am I wrong in feeling that there is too much emphasis on the very things that modern readers already have filling all their waking hours? Surely the eternal things—the things that Harlan and I love and live with here— . . . have a greater meaning than anything in the man-made culture of our cities. I am reading this latest collection of poems hoping to find there an awareness of these great deep natural truths."

In their daily activities Anna and Harlan lived a centered, inwardly attentive life, Harlan in his painting, writing, and manual work, and Anna in her music and reading, her involvement in Harlan's creativity, her letter writing, and, drudgery excepted, her homemaking. She had always understood what things were the most important in life. That deep knowledge is what Robert Basye had recognized in her as "native sincerity." It was what Barre Pritchett had meant when she wrote in March 1937 of Anna's "feeling for real things"; "you are so blessedly real," wrote Barre.

Anna's centeredness, her grace, shone in her calm demeanor and careful listening. George Bartnick recalls Anna's deep listening in early January 1986, Anna's last winter. In front of the fire with her at Payne Hollow, George was singing Christmas carols and accompanying himself on guitar. "She listened meditatively, drinking in the songs," George says. With a glowing smile Anna said wistfully, "It's so nice to hear the old carols."

From the moment George had begun singing, he was joined by the Hubbards' dog, Ranger. The calf-size redbone coonhound, known as the biggest dog in Trimble County, had adopted the Hubbards in winter 1977, when the river froze. Harlan put food out for the pathetically skinny red dog, and when he missed making the regular food delivery one day, the dog came to the door and joined the family. Since none of the Kentucky neighbors knew anything about him, the Hubbards assumed he'd crossed the ice from the Indiana side and been stranded when the river thawed—stranded permanently, as it happened, because landlubber Ranger wouldn't even go out with Harlan in the johnboat. Of all the canine hunters in recorded Payne Hollow history, Ranger was top dog. At peak form he once caught forty groundhogs in a single summer. On the terrace one day, Anna and Harlan heard Ranger barking. "He's got another groundhog," Harlan said with a smile. "Oh dear," Anna sighed, "we haven't used up the last one yet." Another time, on a winter night, they heard Ranger barking at the door. He came charging inside, Anna wrote Etta, "<u>all wet</u> from head to tail!" and wanted out again right away. They saw he had caught a raccoon and left it on the doorstep, "and <u>it</u> was soaking wet too!"

In accompaniment to George's carols Ranger raised an amazing din—a hunting hound with a huge skull case, baying inside the small house. Yet neither Anna nor Harlan, who was listening from the upper room, reacted in the least or said a word to the dog. Anna continued listening deeply to the carols. Finally, as George and Ranger paused for breath, Anna turned to Ranger and said ever so quietly, "Can't you stop just for a minute, boy?"

The Payne Hollow life did not include parenthood. I see it as fortunate for both Anna and Harlan that because of Anna's hysterectomy in 1939, parenthood wasn't a possibility they had to deal with. To deliver for the first time in her forties, in the medical conditions of the 1940s, would have been risky for Anna. And Harlan's vision of his life on the fringe of society had never included the raising of children. Anna's being unable to conceive only added to her suitability as Harlan's partner. Not only was it great good fortune that Anna and Harlan found each other in middle age, it was providential that they did not do so earlier.

Many years after Anna's hysterectomy, down-to-earth Etta wrote: "I had a minimum of family and kids inclination, myself. . . . I don't think Anne cared a lot about it, either." (It is indicative of Anna's hiddenness that Etta only *thought* she knew how Anna felt about having children.) Indifference toward being a parent herself could partly explain Anna's reaction to Patricia Staebler's news of her first pregnancy. The Staeblers and the Hubbards were together at Brent for a quartets session on the shantyboat when Patricia told her. Anna understood instantly that the arrival of children might put an end to the quartet. She answered, "I always imagined it would be just the four of us."

Harlan volunteered a comment on the subject of children when he and Anna were interviewed on tape in 1985 by Christy Canida, then in third grade. Christy asked what their greatest compromise had been. After they both answered that they would have liked more time for doing the things they enjoyed, there was a long pause. Then Harlan added that it would have been nice to have some children like Christy and her brother, Ben, to grow up at Payne Hollow and see what they would turn out to be. I take Harlan's statement as nothing more than well-meaning condescension to his young interviewer. Though Anna and Harlan delighted in bright, imaginative, mannerly children such as Christy and Ben Canida—and though Anna frequently remarked to friends on the importance of parenthood—I think they saw their life together as entire. Their marriage, with a mutual support system at its center instead of children, suited their temperaments and their life goals. Anna added nothing to Harlan's remark, and I have listened hard for the thoughts behind her silence. Any other wife might have felt insulted or provoked by the hypocrisy, but Anna's understanding of Harlan was complete and nonjudgmental. I hear her thinking, "Oh, well, that's just Harlan."

Anna said she had not given up anything in marrying Harlan and choosing to live the rustic, isolated life he wanted. That life, in fact, seems to have offered her many advantages. On the fringe of society her shyness was no handicap. With the peace and quiet she had much more as well: A man to love and be loved by. A home of her own. Someone to play music with every day. Through Harlan's painting and writing, the experiencing of creativity. And through their reading, large daily doses of the literature and the fine arts subjects that had been her forte in the library. What's more, life with Harlan was adventure and fun. "I have a wonderful time with Harlan," she wrote in her *Library Journal* drafts, "doing things I'd never dreamed of doing, things I could not do alone." The latest in the cavalcade of earnest feature stories published about the Hubbards over the years had just appeared in one of the newspapers when Anna said to Patricia Staebler, "Nobody seems to realize what fun we have."

She was happy with her choice, and Payne Hollow was her idea of heaven on earth. She loved the house itself. "Like the river rat in the fine old story 'The Wind in the Willows,'" Anna wrote, "we are fond of our 'bijou riverside residence.' . . . It has a hand-crafted look and a unique beauty. . . . No one in the world but Harlan could have built this house." She loved the hollow and the river, too. Coming home was always a great pleasure and a relief, whether she had been away for weeks in Grand Rapids or a day in Madison. "Every time we come back," she wrote, "we realize again how fortunate we are to have this for our home. The river, the hills, the quiet, and time for the things we want to do—and then a blazing fire on our hearth."

At Thanksgiving 1954 Anna and Harlan were away for three weeks visiting the Grand Rapids family and the Staeblers. "Can you imagine how it would be, coming home to Payne Hollow after being away three weeks?" Anna wrote me. They found the johnboat just as they had left it on the Indiana shore. The river was the same, too, neither higher nor lower, but now they could see their cabin across the river through the bare trees; they had come home to a winter landscape. It took many trips to and from the car to load all the musical instruments, suitcases, boxes, baskets, and groceries into the johnboat. A cold drizzle started up, and the wind raised waves and kept tearing loose the poncho covering the cargo. Harlan rowed at an angle to keep water from splashing in. A fast diesel with a big tow passed them in mid-river, and they rode high and low in its wake. While Harlan unloaded the johnboat Anna bustled around, putting things away and finding mouse nests: "I couldn't help smiling as I remembered the Beatrix Potter 'Tale of Johnny Town Mouse' and his country friend Timmy Willie. . . . Do you know Timmy Willie, Mia?" Soon they were settled, home again: "But you know without my mentioning it that Harlan had built a big jolly fire in the fireplace, first thing. My, but it was good to see a real blaze on a real hearth again and to warm ourselves spiritually as well as physically by its glow."

Much as Anna loved the hollow, the house, and the things in it, what she loved most was the idea of home. "Weren't you afraid when your husband sometimes left you alone on the boat?" a city librarian asked her during the shantyboat journey. "Mercy, no!" Anna answered. "That tiny cabin was my home, after all." "Home," for her, was wherever Harlan was. Anna once told Patricia Staebler about an acquaintance who, when her husband of many years died, left her longtime house and friends for a city apartment convenient to concerts and the library. That, Anna said, was what she would do, too. She put it another way when, recently returned from a visit to Grand Rapids, she was asked whether she missed the conveniences there, and what she would do if left alone at Payne Hollow: "I'm just here with Harlan," Anna replied.

Loving Harlan as she did, Anna adapted to his way of life and to Harlan himself. Harlan had an artist's self-absorption, the Swingle family determination from his mother's side, and bachelor habits of forty-three years. Having lived with his mother until middle age, he was experienced in evading the influence of women. He had firm ideas about how things should be done, and when crossed, he could be petulant and sharp tongued. I was embarrassed once or twice, hearing Harlan speak sharply to Anna. I recall the hurt look on her face and the filling of her eyes, yet her control was such that no tears spilled over. The Hubbards' young friend Bill Caddell, a Hanover College student of the 1960s, was one of the few persons who heard Anna be sharp with Harlan—if, for example, he hadn't washed properly or had brought the wrong thing from the garden or had asked unexpected guests to stay for a meal when she didn't want them to. But if Anna ever returned Harlan's fire, I know of no one who heard her do so.

Only rarely did she complain about him. In the early 1980s Anna once consulted the Hubbards' friend Dr. Marcella Modisett about a nosebleed. Anna's blood pressure was high, and Marcella asked her whether she was worried about something. Anna said no, but she was upset with Harlan. On the trip to Madison that day, Anna explained, she had wanted Harlan to wait until they had crossed the river and reached the car before putting on his good shoes, but he would not, and so he got them muddy.

In certain of their everyday habits, however, they were much alike. For example, Anna's thriftiness meshed with Harlan's genius for recycling the castoffs he found on the riverbank and in trash dumps. He framed his paintings with driftwood. He split a utility pole he found on the shore and made a footbridge out of it. For years he and Anna wrote letters on fine paper snipped from a huge, tightly wrapped roll that had washed up on the riverbank undamaged inside. One of his finest scavenging triumphs was achieved during the 1955–56 construction of the new room. Harlan came down from the ridge one day with a big old black can, a piece of trash from a farmer's dump. Anna turned her nose up at it until he scratched it with his knife to show her it was copper. Harlan transformed that piece of junk into the new room's focal point, the hammered-copper fireplace hood.

Between them they used it up, wore it out, made it do, or did without, uninterested in the balance in their savings account. Their income was small but sufficient for many years from Anna's social security, library pension, and insurance policy, and from the rental income on the house in Fort Thomas—from 1943 to 1974 a steady, unchanging eighty dollars a month. In 1974 the house sold for nineteen thousand. With that and the one thousand they already had in the bank, Anna and Harlan obtained a certificate of deposit. "Harlan's eyes were wide," says the Hubbards' friend Jonathan Greene, "when he said he was earning more in interest than he had earned in rent." If Harlan were to receive a windfall (asked another friend that same year), such as a huge check from a publisher, would it make a difference in his life? None, Harlan answered. "In fact, we don't know what to do with the money we have now." In the 1980s, as the buyer of one of Harlan's paintings was writing a check for two hundred dollars, Harlan commented that he and Anna could live on that for about six months.

Both Anna and Harlan were indifferent to money, but not in the same degree. It was Anna who paid the bills, completed the tax returns, and managed the certificates of deposit. I can easily see her as the family financial manager, exercising her penchants for recordkeeping and thrift. She wrote Etta in November 1983 that Harlan's paintings were making "a good deal of money right along. We just put it in the bank where it earns interest. Living here as we do we don't need much money. Maybe some day, if Harlan can't keep up this place any more, we'll have to make other arrangements—which will no doubt cost more. We don't worry about that in advance. We'll make out, when the time comes."

Harlan, on the other hand, felt burdened by money. The bequest of $5,000 he received from Frank's estate in 1985 only annoyed him. When Anna had been dead for seven months, Harlan became temporarily confused about his finances. He thought Etta might already have inherited the accumulated principal; he had forgotten that she was to receive only the interest, and not until after his death. He was excited by the prospect of being a poor man and by the challenge to his resourcefulness that poverty would present. Though the hoped-for poverty eluded Harlan, he continued living simply. When he died in January 1988 he had approximately $310,000 in the Milton bank.

Harlan appreciated the cleanliness, order, and grace Anna had brought into his life, but he couldn't maintain her standards on his own. I think he was only half joking when he said, after she died, that he was still trying to keep the house clean "because I am afraid of her, I guess." The blend of Anna's homemaking sensibilities with Harlan's way of life had been no accident—she asserted herself and her needs. Right from the beginning, in the studio and at Brent, the blend produced remarkable results. As for the shantyboat, doubtless no other such shantyboat was ever seen on the midwestern rivers as the Hubbards', with its large windows, its potbellied stove and its fireplace, its tidiness and simplicity, and the cello in the built-in storage spot. In the 1950s, as Harlan constructed the Payne Hollow settlement, Anna continued seeing to it that her needs were met.

Anna denied having had any role in designing the house. Yet Harlan provided central heat, niches for her Old Country treasures, running water in the kitchen, and a splendid, fine-tuned cookstove with an oven, and to hold these comforts and conveniences he built a larger, finer house—big enough for a Steinway baby grand—and more outbuildings than he had ever envisioned building for himself. All this, from a man who had once dreamed of "a wild existence on the riverbank" in "a dark, smoky cavern with an earth floor, like the habitations of the pioneers." Harlan's dream of simple living had been sidetracked by marriage. In April 1962 Anna went to Cincinnati for a day, and in rare solitude Harlan wrote in his journal: "I see Anna now as from a distance, a loving thoughtful person. She is not me, however; her desires and ideas influence our living more than mine do, in all kindness she tries to put my desires and ideas into practice, but the result is only her conception of what I am aiming at, joined with the realization of her own personality."

In the mid-1970s Harlan was still holding on to his vision of a simple life. He told a friend he doubted he would ever break out of his way of life at Payne Hollow, because "you establish a pattern. It's a prison, almost. Especially Anna gets set here. She isn't as adaptable, doesn't need or desire change as much as I do. I can think of a lot of things I can do." What would he do? the friend asked. "This is almost it," Harlan answered; he wanted to "just go a little farther, live simpler, more within your own abilities, depend less on the outside."

A few years later Harlan indicated that his thinking had changed, mollified by the comforts of life with Anna. "I wanted to go all out," Harlan said in the 1981 videotape *Life on the Fringe of Society*, and live "a more primitive life than this, much simpler and more withdrawn from society, but several factors made it very difficult to do. One of them was Anna. I think she was not as far out as I was, ever, and I think she might have had the right idea anyway, because if you want to live in a place for twenty-eight years, you do want to be comfortable, and warm in the wintertime."

After Anna died, however, Harlan's ideal of simple living came back in its old forms. For the first time, at the age of eighty-six, he was free to arrange his daily life without taking into consideration the views of either his mother or Anna. In his journal he wrote about getting rid of the "superfluous and conventional," about freeing himself from "the bondage to Anna's desires and mental quirks." His statements were inconsistent: He might like to live in a cave. A barn might do, something like his studio-workshop, maybe. Or he might move down into the cellar. He thought about moving to some new place, but he didn't want to waste any precious time looking for it or modifying it. In the end he conceded that caves lack light and ventilation, and said he was content after all, with his wood floor, glass windows, and efficient heating. He consolidated his living and painting space in the upper room of the house, closed it off, and called it his apartment.

Nowhere else is Anna's gift for living more evident than at the end of her life, in the way she met death from cancer in 1986. When Patricia and Warren Staebler saw Anna in the Madison hospital shortly before she died, she was pale and weak. Anna murmured something about food, and Patricia thought she was asking for some custard, but Anna shook her head, righted herself, and whispered, "Hospitality." Patricia realized that Anna was thinking about offering food because she had callers in her room. Soon she wilted back down into the bed. When the Staeblers were leaving, Anna raised herself up again and motioned to Patricia. She whispered, "Freundschaft" (friendship) and some more German words that Harlan and Warren recognized as the lyric of a Schubert song.

Anna died on the morning of May 4, 1986. After cremation, Harlan took the plain can of ashes back to Payne Hollow and set it on the table in front of the window wall facing the river. He startled people by saying Anna's ashes were good company for him. On June 13 he held a burial service at Payne Hollow with a limited number of invited guests present. In addition to Harlan and Etta were Paul Hassfurder;

Marcella Modisett; Louis and Mary Ellen Munier and their son, Ray; Helen Spry; Patricia and Warren Staebler; Carol and Richard Strimple; and Nita and Dan Webster.

Harlan had picked the gravesite and designed the composition of gravestone boulders and gravel carefully, esthetically. The site is just below and in front of the house, shaded by trees near the path to the river and overlooking the garden, facing a wide view of the river and hills. Two boulders are in the composition: a sandstone boulder in front—"truly a work of nature," he wrote—and behind it, "a wide flat stone surfaced with small fossils. White stone, broken into small bits by the action of current and waves, lay on the ground about the stones." Everyone gathered on the slope around the stones while Paul, Richard, and Ray dug a hole with a post-hole digger, about thirty inches deep. Harlan made some remarks and lowered the can into place, and Paul, Richard, and Ray filled in the hole. Later in the summer Harlan sketched his frontispiece design from *Payne Hollow* on the front stone, and his sculptor friend Mike Skop, of Fort Thomas, carved it. The design shows the names "Harlan" and "Anna," in their respective handwriting, written in a sideways heart, as if carved in a tree by a pair of lovers.

When the burial was completed, everyone went to the terrace and began conversing. After a time, Harlan asked Patricia Staebler into the house to play something with him. Patricia suggested one of the serious but joyous Handel sonatas, but Harlan said, "No, let's play this," a song titled "Bist du bei mir" (If thou art with me) from the *Notenbüchlein für Anna Magdalena Bach* (Little notebook for Anna Magdalena Bach), a collection of simple keyboard pieces composed for Anna Magdalena by her husband and sons. Patricia played the piano accompaniment, and Harlan played the vocal line on the violin. I wonder whether Harlan was remembering *The Little Chronicle of Magdalena Bach*. This is the translation of "Bist du bei mir" in *Little Chronicle*:

> If thou art with me, I would gladly go
> To death and to my rest.
> Ah, how contented would be my end
> If thy tender hands would close
> My faithful eyes.

When Anna was gone Harlan talked more openly. He told more than one person that the doctors had expected Anna to recover sufficiently to go home, but, badly upset by the colostomy that had been made necessary by the spread of the cancer, she refused food and lost ground quickly. Rather than linger impaired, she made what Harlan called "a clean and decisive break with life."

If I could talk openly with Anna just once, I would ask her about the loves of her life. I wonder how it was for her, being married to a man so much her emotional opposite. Harlan was constrained by the emotional reticence he called a Hubbard trait. Anna thrived on sentiment; Harlan scorned it. He praised the music of Bach because—a finer distinction than I'm capable of—it "can be sweet and tender without a trace of the passionate, sentimental or romantic. It is never weak, it is always masculine." Emotional reticence stands out in the birthday-and-anniversary journal Harlan kept briefly for Anna. Throughout seven years' worth of biannual entries, his best efforts to write warm, intimate, loving words to Anna reveal his emotional limitations. The first entry, written when they had been married five months, is typical of the rest:

Sept. 7, 1943

This birthday of yours was different from any in the past, the first in what I hope will be a long series of happy years. Circumstances will never be the same. Another time we may not make elderberry jelly, have a cake quite like this one, or such a salad for lunch. This cloud [his mother's illness and hostility, probably] will pass, there will be others, perhaps darker. But I will be with you always, and will try to keep you as happy as you are now.

Don't mind this. I know this book is not for sentimentalities, but this is your birthday.

Not only was Harlan emotionally reticent; he had been unable to shake the memory of his first love. He had been in his early thirties, and she was about four years older than he, and married. In August 1933 Harlan addressed himself to her in his journal: "I am surprised at the intensity of my feeling toward you. It all looks hopeless, when I consider how steadfast and determined we both are, and how different our ambitions and desires. . . . I confess, to myself, that I am unhappy when I think I have given you up or lost you." But she was not his intellectual equal: "Yet when it seems that nothing stands between us, I am overcome by the feeling that you are impossible and undesirable, that the whole affair is unthinkable." Fifty years later Harlan wrote about her in one of the commentaries he added to his early journals for publication. The published commentary was much shortened and toned down from the draft, in which he wrote the following:

> Even in this first love of woman, I was not aggressive, and eventually, before matters got out of hand, I was able to extricate myself, assisted by her reluctance to sacrifice affluence to a poor artist, even if she loved him. I was not heart broken, for my deep consciousness had told me from the first that enduring happiness was not to be hoped for. . . . I still mourn my loss.
>
> After this experience I was never the same. Yet I enjoyed a decade almost free from sexual torment. . . .

In his last summer Harlan said she had seduced him and that the period had been one of the happiest and most miserable times of his life. She was very affected and hadn't much education, and her piano playing was elementary, he said; there was no possibility of real intimacy between them. Still, he had carried the memory of first love all his life—was "never the same"—and remembered the feeling of being swept away in a strong current until he caught hold of a piece of driftwood and pulled himself out.

The month after marrying Anna, Harlan described their courtship and marriage as "something growing into ripeness, or a flowing together of water"; it was a marriage of mature equals, but it was not the raging torrent of first love. The absence of passion in Harlan's writing about Anna, coupled with their emotional reserve in the presence of others, led some onlookers to speculate whether the Hubbards' marriage was an exclusively spiritual union. Apparently it was not. As might be expected, there is nothing explicit on the record from either of them about physical intimacy, but there is Anna's "All night the sound of the river. All night the whippoorwill. All night—" in her log of the Licking River camping trip in 1942. And Susan recalls something Etta once said: Anna had asked Etta (in the 1970s, Susan thinks it was) whether men ever lose interest in sex. The implication was that Anna wished Harlan would.

Near the end of his life Harlan told an interviewer that his relations with women had always been "pretty slapdash" and that he had been trying lately to make some improvement in that regard. Perhaps that explains why, in his eighties, he had become an enthusiastic kisser, a development that startled several of the Hubbards' women friends. (One of them described his on-the-lips technique as smacking and unsexy, but practiced.) Despite good motives, Harlan sometimes showed a stunning insensitivity by kissing those women friends in front of Anna.

Someday, some other writer may try to follow Anna and Harlan into the bedroom, but as for me, I can go no farther than the piano and my recollection of an old advertisement picturing a pair of nineteenth-century musicians, a man and a woman. The violinist has just taken his violin from under his chin and is still holding it high, in his left hand, and the pianist is being swept up from her piano bench in the violinist's right-armed embrace. I can see Anna with Harlan like that. They would not have been so different from many another pair in which the woman is interested mostly in the embrace and the romance surrounding it, and the man is interested mostly in what comes next. I have trouble imagining a shy Dutch woman's Victorian restraint evaporating in sexual abandon. Anna could not have cleared up the matter for me. Love and sex—two of the fundamentals closest to the human essence and most unthinkable as topics of conversation with Anna.

Some will suppose that Harlan expressed privately to Anna the feelings he wouldn't express in front of others or in his writings. To me the supposition seems unrealistic. I'm told Anna and Harlan sometimes rode together in the car or moved about in the house together for hours without speaking; some say the silence was silent communion. It strikes me, rather, as Harlan's having nothing to say and Anna's being accommodating. Others will say the bond between Anna and Harlan was so deep and secure that ordinary expressions of reassurance were unnecessary. The bond was deep and secure, yes, but most women want that reassurance, and Anna needed it. Several years ago I wrote down a sentence from a manuscript I was editing. With thanks to the now-forgotten author, here it is: "Marriage has a hidden purpose—the healing of childhood wounds." Anna needed in marriage the expressions of love she hadn't received in childhood, but as many grown-up wounded children do, she chose an emotionally limited mate. Anna accepted Harlan's emotional reticence early in the relationship. Anna was a great observer of people—she would study faces in snapshots—and she had been a student of Harlan's personality since the days when he was her library patron. Instead of love letters, Harlan sent her newspaper clippings about steamboats. One of Anna

Magdalena Bach's fictional diary entries comes to mind again: "I do not think Sebastian [Harlan] was a very easy person to know—unless you loved him. . . . He was reserved in speech about deep things, he did not express himself in the words he said, but in what he was, and, of course, above all in his music [his painting]." Anna knew that a great deal of Harlan's love belonged to nature and the river. "Harlan is wedded to the river," she once told a friend. Another great portion of his love belonged to himself: he meant above all else to find joy through living close to nature and to express himself as fully as possible through his art. Anna accepted these things and learned to compensate for Harlan's emotional limitations. One of her ways of compensating was through music.

Playing music with the Hubbards was primarily, as one of their former music partners put it, a "social experience." I heard Harlan play the violin often in the 1950s and later on tape, and I heard only squawking and scraping. His technique had little chance of improving, with age and manual labor turning his hands ever knobbier and more gnarled. Anna's technical skill on the piano was greater than Harlan's on the violin, but the piano was out of tune much of the time in humid Payne Hollow. Yet these drawbacks did not seem to diminish Anna's pleasure. A Hubbard friend who had never heard Harlan play asked Anna once, in the 1970s, "Is he good?" and Anna answered, without qualification, "Yes. He's good." At one time I thought Anna's great loves for Harlan and for music had deceived her ears. Later I came to believe she heard the truth, but love and loyalty had made her exceptionally tolerant. Now I think the explanation is more complicated. Anna expressed herself through music, and she needed to believe that when she played music with Harlan they were communicating in perfect emotional accord. She took his playing, however flawed technically, as emotional output and made of it what she needed. She did not let the physical realities interfere.

Anna's compensating for Harlan's emotional shortcomings shows plainly in the rare surviving letters she wrote him. They were parted for a time in January 1946, when they had been married about three years and Anna went home to Grand Rapids to help nurse her mother through a respiratory infection. Harlan accompanied her, then returned to the dogs and the shantyboat at Brent. Anna missed him badly. "I'm just sick without you," she wrote in the last of the four undated letters. "But all this will be over soon, I hope. I didn't know myself it would be so awful—alone." In her answer to Harlan's first letter, Anna said Harlan had written her all the details she had been wondering about: "what time you got in, how you found the boat and the dogs, how everything had stood the cold, the stage of the river, and the direction of the wind. Yes, and what you found to eat for breakfast!" Anna interpreted Harlan's recital of these mundane facts as an expression of love: "You knew I would want to know all those little homely things," she wrote. In her fourth letter she did more of the same. "Oh Darling, Darling!" she began; "Your precious letters! Bless you for writing to me so often. Bless you for writing about Jupiter and the ring net and fresh eggs specially delivered across the icy gang plank—and all those things that mean home to us."

She was content to see meaning in the frequency of the letters and the evoking of their shantyboat home, and she didn't seem to regret the absence of burning words of love. She originated her own: *I love you so, and I need you so, Darling. . . . I am thinking of you every minute. . . . I want so terribly to be with you. . . . I do love you so for everything that you are. . . . You know my whole heart is there with you. . . .* One day Anna talked and talked to her mother about Harlan— *how splendid you are, how wonderful you are to me, how happy we are together—and it is good to be able to tell someone about these things that otherwise I keep locked in my secret heart.*

Nearly thirty years later Anna was in Grand Rapids again, visiting Nella Mae. The everyday activities of Anna and Harlan's life still formed the vocabulary of their shared language, and she was still thinking of him every minute:

> If the weather is nice, Stan and Nell and I will go out to the cottage this weekend. I'll be thinking of you, hoping you have some quiet time for yourself. I'm thinking of you every minute anyway. I think of you out in your workshop, hammering, and working in the garden, and bringing in a bucket of vegetables which you will cook all together in one pot, no doubt. And taking care of the milk, perhaps making cheese, but reading too, and playing music. All good things.
> I'll be there again in a few days to share it all with you.
> Oh, Harlan!
> I do love you so!
>
> Your Annie

When I think of the lovers Anna and Harlan, I think of this story told to me by their friend Helen Spry about Harlan's hospitalization for snakebite in 1983, when the Hubbards were in their early eighties. Hospital food didn't satisfy Harlan, and so Anna would take him home-grown provisions. Anna had not routinely hiked up to the ridge for many years, but now, typically carrying four shopping bags full of food, she would start up the steep hill from Payne Hollow to meet Helen halfway—she always outfoxed Helen with this maneuver—and together they would walk the rest of the way up to Helen's car. On Harlan's first good day of recovery, Anna dropped her shopping bags on the hospital room floor the moment she saw him, rushed to his bed, and flung herself across him with embraces and kisses, which Harlan enthusiastically returned. Helen, who had never seen them display any affection before, nearly fell over a housekeeper in her haste to get out and leave them alone.

Harlan's love for Anna was deep and quiet. He would have had no elegance or grace in his life without her, he said; from the primitive shelter he built, she had made a beautiful home. And he probably would never have built the shantyboat if she hadn't encouraged him to go ahead and do it. She was responsible for his writing *Shantyboat,* too. "She's my courage," Harlan said. I've already quoted Harlan's journal from that day in April 1962 when Anna was away and Harlan was glad of the solitude—"Her desires and ideas influence our living more than mine do," he wrote. The entry concludes in abrupt contrast: "This afternoon, I reworked the sink as a surprise to Anna and because it could be done now with no interference of her routine." The love and deep consideration are unspoken: Harlan had used his rare solitude to prepare a surprise for Anna.

In their thirty-four years together at Payne Hollow, the solitude Anna had welcomed as a part of her life with Harlan grew steadily scarcer. In her seventies Anna reminisced about the uninterrupted solitude of the shantyboat days, when "there would be weeks on end when we saw no one, and it was wonderful. Now it's rare when we have a day alone, to ourselves." In her last letters to Etta, the shantyboat days were much on her mind.

In 1971 Anna showed how much she needed solitude. That was the year Harlan's young friend Gene Akers briefly became the linchpin in Harlan's plan for keeping the Payne Hollow life going as he and Anna grew old. Gene Akers lived in the country near Terre Haute, in west-central Indiana. He loved rivers and steamboats, and after reading *Shantyboat* in the mid-1950s he had gone looking for author Harlan

Hubbard, and they became good friends. Several times a year Gene visited Payne Hollow with his wife, Lu, and their three children. In about 1965, with Harlan's approval, Gene began slowly building a cabin on the Hubbards' property on the opposite side of the creek as a camping place for himself and his family. In 1971 Gene asked Harlan's permission to live there with Lu year-round after his retirement, which was coming up soon, at age forty-three, from his job as a radio operator with the Indiana State Police. Harlan was agreeable, but Anna objected. Harlan wrote Gene in September that he had "never been averse to the idea of another family living here, and nobody would be more welcome than you folks, but Anna is still against having close neighbors." Thinking Anna might come around eventually, Harlan suggested that Gene and Lu continue using the cabin for camping and make gradually longer stays before committing to it. Meanwhile he and Anna could get used to their presence. "I am sure it will all work out if we do not try to force the issue."

But the plan didn't work out. Later that month Gene was riding his bicycle home late at night as usual after working the 4-P.M.-to-midnight shift and was struck and killed by a drunk driver. The following spring Lu turned the cabin over to Harlan, and Harlan responded with a check "to pay Gene," he wrote Lu, for the materials. A few years later Harlan praised Gene to a friend. With his mechanical skills Gene could have handled the Payne Hollow "transportation division," Harlan said, and he was "a good man," whom Harlan had trusted to take care of everything at Payne Hollow as he trusted himself.

Harlan began simplifying. He stopped keeping goats, butchering the last one in 1978. Around the same time, he began accepting offers of help, first with woodcutting. Bob Canida and Paul Kelly, two young Hubbard friends from Madison, began bringing six- to eight-man teams to Payne Hollow to cut with chain saws, in a single day, the Hubbards' entire winter supply of wood. In 1980 Harlan arranged with Paul Hassfurder of Hanover for regular help with chores. About two years later Richard Strimple of Cincinnati became Harlan's supplier of outboard motors and began helping him with other heavy work as well. These energy-saving compromises prolonged the Hubbards' independent living at Payne Hollow without sacrificing solitude—the solitude that now was more important to Anna than to Harlan.

Each time Anna said good-bye to a group of visitors and was left in peace again, washing dishes at the kitchen window, what did she think of, I wonder: Playing trios with Hilda and Charles? Talking for hours with Barre? A Japanese-style cottage on the Little Miami River? Mountain laurel and rhododendron overhanging a mountain stream? . . . To me and to many others, Anna was the energetic, gracious mistress of Payne Hollow. Few of us had any notion of the other Anna, the vulnerable woman who lived at a high emotional pitch through music, art, literature, and relationships—the hidden Anna.

11

~

Hidden

The last letter . . . had so much of you in it! The you that
sometimes goes so far away—away even from yourself.

Barre Pritchett to Anna, June 30, 1938

Anna had the Dutch and Victorian preference for keeping her sorrows
private. No one I interviewed about her, no matter how long they had
known her, claimed to have been close to her in the sense of knowing
her sorrows or the story of her life. At age ten, when I arrived at Payne
Hollow for my first visit and found Sambo standing alone on the dock,
I thought it odd that Anna hadn't written me that Skipper had died. I
understand now that though Anna must have been doubly grieved by
the loss of a well-loved dog that also had been a living symbol of the
earliest, sweetest, shantyboat days of her marriage, she preferred not
to say so. It follows, of course, that Anna could not share the pain of
losing her beloved sister Nella Mae. When Nella Mae died in 1978,
Anna didn't tell her Madison and Hanover friends; they found out
later, when Anna spoke of the pity of such a beautiful girl dying much
too soon.

Surviving letters from Hilda and Lee show that Anna wrote to
them about her losses and sorrows until the mid-1930s, when she
learned that Paul Briol was married. The character of their letters to
her changed then, as if Anna had begun guarding her privacy more
closely. Hilda and Lee seem to have known little about Anna's heartaches during the late 1930s. Certainly by the time Anna married, the
door marked Private was firmly closed. She and Harlan read aloud to
each other the letters they received, and she signed most of her outgoing letters "Harlan and Anna." She had ceased treating her correspondence as her own, and letters were no longer an outlet for her hidden
feelings.

Maybe Etta, who died four years before I began writing about

Anna, had been the exception, I thought; maybe she had been Anna's lifelong confidante. But I decided otherwise when I discovered how drastically Anna's letters to Etta deviated from the facts surrounding three life-and-death incidents during Anna's last years. One of the three incidents involved music. (To call music a life-and-death matter for Anna is a forgivable exaggeration.) In July 1985 the Hubbards' friend Don Wallis dropped in at Payne Hollow one day with a friend named Cynthia Mapes, a trained singer. Cynthia saw Anna's book of songs by Brahms on the piano and said she knew some of them. While Don and Harlan listened on the terrace, Anna accompanied Cynthia's singing. The music stopped, and Anna came out to Harlan in tears. She couldn't see the notes on the page, she told him. Harlan had no comfort to give her. He awkwardly offered her his glasses, which were of no use, and still in tears she hurried back into the house. The incident was over in a moment.

Anna was worried about her eyesight that summer. Failing eyesight was a threat to her continued playing, because she was dependent on reading the notes. The vision was particularly blurred in her right eye, and she had not had an eye examination in years. (Two months later she did have an eye examination and was found to have cataracts. The one on the right eye was removed on September 17.) In addition, the room was dim as she accompanied Cynthia that afternoon. Frustration tinged with fear had pushed her to tears, but there was no hint of any such emotions in the letter she wrote to Etta the next day. The singer had a powerful voice and good command of German, Anna wrote, and it "wasn't a bad performance at all." In passing, Anna complimented Etta's singing in the old days. It was as if Anna's distress had never existed.

The second incident involved Harlan's prostate cancer, the cancer he died of in 1988. In June 1980 Harlan sought medical attention because he had noticed his pulse skipping a beat now and then. No evidence of heart disease was found. He was diagnosed as having a condition called irritable myocardium, and the doctor concluded that the treatment would be more troublesome for Harlan than the condition itself. However, the physical examination revealed a hardening of Harlan's prostate gland; there was a possibility of prostate cancer. He was referred to a urologist but stopped seeing him when the symptoms improved.

When Harlan was next examined, while hospitalized for snakebite in September 1983, he had advanced prostate cancer. It had spread to his bones and was incurable. On September 21 Harlan underwent a bilateral orchiectomy (surgical removal of the testicles). It was hoped that in the absence of testosterone, the growth-promoting hormone produced by the testicles, the prostate tumor would shrink and stop squeezing the urethra (the tube that leads from the bladder) and that Harlan's difficulty voiding would be alleviated. Harlan was released from the hospital on September 24. The bilateral orchiectomy didn't have the desired effect, and a second operation became necessary: transurethral resection of the prostate, in which the ingrown cancerous tissue was reamed out from around the urethra. The resection was done on October 6, and Harlan went home a second time on October 11.

Anna's letter to Etta on October 7 diverged widely from the story told by the medical records. She painted Harlan's condition as routine prostate enlargement, a "complication" following the snakebite. She said nothing about cancer or about the first operation, the bilateral orchiectomy, which she characterized casually as "some other treatment" that hadn't given Harlan any relief. The second operation, the resection, she called "minor surgery" and "nothing unusual," and she suggested Etta not even bother telling the Grand Rapids family about it. "This time, we're going to have Harlan on the road to recovery," she concluded. The Harlan whom Anna portrayed to Etta as recovering from routine treatments was a man with incurable cancer.

The third incident is the story of Anna's own last illness, which also involved Harlan's bout with colon cancer. A year of heavy stress began for Anna in late January 1985, when Harlan's appetite left him and he began growing weak. Nevertheless, he and Anna made a strenuous trip on February 20 to the Kentucky state capitol in Frankfort, where he and other painters from around the state were exhibiting. To meet the friend who was to drive them there, they had a rough climb up the hill to the ridge through snow and ice. Thawing and refreezing made the downhill return in the dark, one treacherous step at a time, even rougher; each of them fell once.

A few days later Harlan had a friend take him to the hospital. He had lost weight and was anemic, and on March 4 he had surgery to remove a large tumor from the left side of his colon. (The medical records indicate that the colon cancer was probably unrelated to the prostate cancer—a cause for concern because, of the two types, colon cancer is the faster growing.) The doctors wanted Harlan to stay in town to regain his strength and be nearby for chemotherapy. Friends Louis and Mary Ellen Munier offered the Hubbards indefinite use of a modern, furnished riverfront cottage about five miles upriver from Madison on Route 56. Anna and Harlan lived there for about fifteen weeks from mid-March to early July. For Harlan the cottage period was an exciting opening for new possibilities in living and in his art. Free from the never-ending work at Payne Hollow, he made a bright corner of the main room into an unobtrusive studio and turned out many paintings that pleased him.

Anna, on the other hand, stoically endured much worry and exertion that spring and summer. Living in two places put great demands on her psychological flexibility. Her routines were disrupted; she was deprived of the tranquillity of Payne Hollow; and her contribution to the partnership with Harlan, the artful life she re-created daily at Payne Hollow, was diminished. Only at Payne Hollow was she most truly herself. Early in Harlan's recovery Anna made several arduous trips back to Payne Hollow. Helen Spry would drive Anna to the top of the ridge, and they would walk down the hill together. They would move all the furniture and Anna would wet-mop the floors with cold water. When the work was done, they walked back up the steep hill, carrying bags full of things Anna and Harlan needed at the cottage. When Harlan was stronger, he and Anna went to Payne Hollow together about twice a week.

On the electric range in the cottage Anna had to relearn cooking, and she burned a good deal of food before getting the hang of the fast burners. At first there was a chemotherapy appointment in town every day. The constant bustle was hard on her, and she was worried about Harlan. Her worries about his health she kept to herself; to Etta she wrote only that she feared Harlan's time for painting would be reduced again when they returned to Payne Hollow. In June, Anna wrote to Etta that she couldn't quite imagine living at Payne Hollow again: "It seems so far away, and impossible. But Harlan is planning on going back there." In fact, Harlan suggested they move to a small house on the ridge, but Anna said no, she wanted to stay at Payne Hollow. They went home in the first week of July. By then Harlan's chemotherapy was weekly.

On August 1 Anna wrote to Etta that a scan had revealed another small tumor in the same general area, one that was inoperable. Rather than advance to more aggressive chemotherapy, Anna and Harlan took their doctors' recommendation and chose to continue with the current course of treatment. Through the summer and fall, as they waited to find out whether Harlan's colon cancer was remaining in check, the tiring weekly trips to Madison continued. After Harlan's treatment they would spend the night in the cottage and return to Payne Hollow the next day. This schedule continued until mid-October, when another scan showed there had been no further tumor growth, and chemotherapy was cut back to every other week. During the weeks of anticipating that scan, Anna and Harlan hadn't talked about Harlan's illness. "Of course this has all been a terrific strain, you can imagine," Anna wrote Etta when the waiting was over.

Meanwhile Anna's own illness had begun affecting her, and she said nothing to anyone about that, either. The stresses climaxed in early 1986 with two major receptions and exhibition openings marking Harlan's donations of several of his prized old paintings. The first, at Hanover College, took place on February 2. The second followed in mid-March at the Behringer-Crawford Museum in Covington, less than two months before Anna died of renal cancer. On Friday, March 14, Paul Hassfurder drove the Hubbards up to Covington in their car. They spent Friday night with a friend, and the opening took place on Saturday night. Looking tired and withdrawn, Anna stayed seated most of the time and spoke in little more than a whisper. The opening was followed by a testimonial dinner. After spending a second night in Covington, the Hubbards returned to Payne Hollow on Sunday, March 16. When Anna was admitted to the hospital in Madison nine days later, she said she had been aware of the mass over her kidney for some time; she wasn't sure how long. She reported loss of appetite, weight loss of about twenty pounds, and extreme weakness since the previous summer. But she had said nothing to anyone, not even Harlan. He hadn't noticed the ebbing of her strength, weight, and spirits until February. And then, having noticed it, he "let" her make the Covington trip and praised her stoic performance: "Anna has held up wonderfully," he wrote a friend from Covington. "She was splendid."

My modern biases interfere with understanding this part of Anna and Harlan's story. For me, nothing else is more important than taking care of oneself, and devoted partners do whatever is necessary to keep each other attentive to their health. But for Anna and Harlan, apparently, one's health was a private matter, inviolable even within marriage. How much of Harlan's attitude toward Anna's physical welfare may have been due, in addition, to denial or self-absorption or lack of concern with worldly realities, I can't say. As for Anna, I doubt she even considered missing the Behringer-Crawford opening. Harlan's achievements were her great pride, and this opening of a permanent exhibition of his work was a signal event. To attend the Frankfort exhibition the previous year, Harlan had disregarded his own fatigue and weight loss and endured a difficult trip, and just twelve days later he underwent surgery. Now Anna matched Harlan's effort and accompanied him to Covington. I suppose Anna must be given credit for surpassing Harlan in stoicism. He had voluntarily sought medical help more than once, but Anna would not admit to being ill. Was avoidance the reason? Determination, more likely. I can easily imagine Anna making up her mind to ignore her condition and not to endure long-term treatment.

After the Hubbards returned to Payne Hollow on March 16, Anna went to bed exhausted. Retired doctor Marcella Modisett learned from Paul that Anna was staying in bed, and on March 24 she and Helen Spry (a retired registered nurse) went to Payne Hollow together. Marcella questioned Anna, and Anna complained only of tiredness, not pain. Yet when Marcella touched the area over Anna's left kidney, Anna admitted she had been hurting there. Anna agreed to be seen at the hospital, and arrangements were made for an ambulance to come for her the next day, March 25. Before the appointed time to cross the river and meet the ambulance, Anna got up, bathed, dressed nicely as always, and wrote letters to Susan and Etta. She walked down to the river with some help, sat up in the johnboat as she was ferried across, and refused to be placed on a gurney on the other side; she walked up the steep, muddy riverbank from the johnboat to the ambulance unassisted.

The cancer was too far advanced for treatment; the abdominal wall, the left renal vein, and the liver had been invaded. One of the physicians recorded that surgical removal, "the only good treatment" for kidney cancer, was "not indicated" (that is, useless) in Anna's case. Nevertheless, when Anna and Harlan were presented with the choice between no treatment and attempted surgical removal, they chose surgery. When Helen Spry visited Anna on the eve of the surgery, Anna wanted girl talk. "Come and talk to me," she said. "Sit here on the side of the bed." Nurses were coming in to do things for her, and Helen tried to break away. It hurt her to see Anna feeling so bad. "Anna, I've talked to you about everything I know," Helen said. "Just tell me everything you did today," Anna coaxed.

Anna underwent surgery on April 3 for removal of the left kidney. A portion of the sigmoid colon also was removed, necessitating a colostomy. The spleen was lacerated during surgery, and it too was removed. Anna did well at first, but she refused food and continued weakening. The Hubbards' friends Carol and Richard Strimple were visiting, and Carol asked Anna whether she wanted Etta to come. Anna replied that she had already said her good-byes to Etta. Anna probably was referring to her last letter to Etta, the one she wrote the day she left Payne Hollow for the hospital. To see a good-bye in that letter, Etta would have had to know Anna very well—and perhaps she did. The letter contains nothing about going to the hospital; it's almost entirely chatty as usual, beginning with a report on the success of the Behringer-Crawford opening and how pleased Anna and Harlan were with the museum itself. Anna reported on the severe weather in Covington, praised her hostess, and added that Paul's driving "helped to make the trip pleasant"—the arduous trip she had rightly dreaded, the trip that had exhausted her. Then, at the end of the letter, Anna uncharacteristically admitted to being tired:

> And now that is all over. And I am very tired. Harlan is perfectly splendid. He takes over the housekeeping and the meals, and lets me rest.
> It is spring here. The wildflowers are coming out. Harlan and Paul are getting the garden started. It is beautiful weather, day after day.
> So that is the picture, to date. Good to have your letter, Et. I count on your letters. I'll be looking forward to the next one.
> So much love to you always!
>
> Harlan and Nan

Anna's painful feelings were hidden not only from others but from herself as well. Perhaps no one ever really knew her. When Anna was gone and Harlan was alone, he said he knew things about her that no one else knew, but even so, he didn't claim to have understood her. Anna had been dead four months when Harlan addressed this journal entry to her: "You seem very close to me, and I know you better and love you more than when you were living. You have become a different person, a more true image, I think, because I see into you deeper, and see you starkly, almost as a stranger; for you kept your true self not only from me, but from yourself and the world in which you moved, going way back. You have had a tragic life. I think now I should have tried to understand you. I did, dimly, try. I accepted the figure you put forth for the world to see, and went no farther." The paragraph startles with its bluntness. It would discourage further investigation—who can understand her better, after her death, than Harlan did while she lived?—had Harlan not been a better observer of landscape than of people.

Anna had episodes of melancholy, sadness, sad longing—terms that in the modern era have been replaced by "depression." The record of those times goes back as far as 1938, in that summer when she recovered from her temporary loss of interest in music and Mam wrote, "These moody people, as we seem to be, are not always the happiest." A few days afterward, Barre wrote that Anna's last letter "had so much of you in it! The you that sometimes goes so far away—away even from yourself." Perhaps depression was tormenting Anna during much of the late 1930s, when she had many good reasons, so to speak, for being depressed. These times, the psychologists tell us, were when the feelings she was keeping down threatened to break the surface.

The ten-day silence in her log of the Upper Peninsula hiking trip with Harlan in 1944 was one of those times. Harlan made a few oblique references to others while Anna was living: "A bad day for Anna," he wrote in his journal in 1947; and in 1948, "a left handed day, with Anna lying in bed for the first time in these five years." When she was gone, he said openly that during their life together she had had periods of depression that lasted several days. She didn't talk to him about them, and he went on as if nothing was wrong. Late in Anna's life, several others saw signs of depression in her too: sometimes she appeared mentally and emotionally absent, not even interested in Harlan's current project, and sometimes she was snappish.

Perhaps I haven't learned all the secrets about Anna that Harlan said he knew, but of the ones I have learned, I believe the weightiest was that she hadn't received the love she wanted from her mother. I believe too that behind her sad times lay a four-generation mother-daughter story: The story of Reinoutje, who died in 1844, when her daughter, Anna, was only two. Of Anna, whose married life was full of never-ending nineteenth-century homemaking chores and who, by the time her daughter Nellie was born in 1878, had six other children to see to, half of them younger than six. Of Nellie, uprooted and taken to a foreign country when she was fifteen, and left motherless six months later. Of Nellie's first daughter, Anna, who inherited this legacy.

Harlan had the self-confidence to say openly, in old age, that his sole relation to his mother had been that of respect and duty, but Anna was unable to say how she really felt about her mother. Those feelings were closed off, because in childhood her mind had distorted reality:

each time Anna's mother sent her out of the kitchen and back to the piano was another confirmation that something was wrong, not with Mother, but with *her*. The vulnerability her family had observed in the young Anna evolved into a certain guardedness noticed later in her life by some of her Payne Hollow friends—a carefulness about what she said when conversation began moving out of the realm she was comfortable in and began to touch on sensitive topics such as family. Part of Anna seemed blocked off, something sad. She could be warm without being open, and she conveyed a sense of being afraid someone might say something she would have to ignore. She seemed very much the grownup child who had been mentally defending herself against hurts all her life and could no longer hear, or tell, any painful truths. Much of her energy was drained by avoiding those truths: that her mother had objected to her marrying, for example, or that Harlan had faults, that the work of Payne Hollow was hard on her, that her eyesight might be failing, that Harlan had incurable cancer, that she was too ill to travel to a distant exhibition opening.

I resisted Harlan's use of the word "tragic" in connection with Anna. I could not, would not, see Anna-of-the-artful-life, the mistress of Payne Hollow, as a tragic figure. Harlan's calling her life tragic must have been an overstatement, I thought, like others in his later journals, where he referred to a wren caught in a mouse trap and a black snake killing baby rabbits as tragedies. But another time Harlan used another form of the word in a way that seems more apt in relation to Anna: "The tragedy is—not to express yourself fully. . . ."

Harlan and the shantyboat-and-Payne-Hollow life offered Anna what she wanted. Harlan wrote to Etta in May 1987: "No one [but Etta] knows Anna so well, no one knows our devotion to one another, which enabled us to set up a way of life that satisfied both of us. I had my longed-for life on the river and life in the 'wilderness,' but at the same time Anna could realize her own personal desires. It is really an amazing achievement. . . ." There was much happiness in Anna's life. She loved Harlan and took pride in his writing and painting. She loved the fun and adventures they had together. She loved the natural beauty, the reading, and the music. She achieved an artful life worthy of being admired and emulated. As Harlan said, the blend of those two personalities in a harmonious, significant life was amazing. Only Anna knows whether her life, on balance, was happy or tragic, but I have no doubt which way her opinion lay. And so if there was any tragedy, in Harlan's terms, in Anna's life on the fringe of society, it was that by living in those protected surroundings with the emotionally reticent Harlan and continuing to work hard, unconsciously, to keep her pain hidden, she kept much of her personality unexpressed.

I can't help wondering about the ways Anna's life might have been different if so much of her emotional energy had not gone to covering up her fears and sorrows. The notion of psychotherapy was far removed from Anna's world. Still, I wish Anna could have tried closing her eyes and imagining herself, as the grown woman she was at that moment, walking up the steps of her house in Grand Rapids and into the living room. I wish she could have imagined sitting down next to little Anna on the piano bench and putting her arm around her as tight as she once held that dolly of hers. I wish she could have imagined saying to little Anna all the things she might have wanted to hear: *I love you more than anything else in the world. You are good at everything you do. Tell me a story of your own. Draw me a picture. Come and help me in my kitchen. Here, take my hand and come with me. We don't have to stay in this house anymore. . . .*

12

Anna Always with Me

Your letters! I have treasured them, every one of them, all these years.

Anna to Mia, April 11, 1972

Anna's friends respected her reserve, and friendships with her developed to the extent she permitted; there was much about Anna to be enjoyed in a formal friendship. But the relationship between Anna and me, her child-friend, deteriorated. By the time I was in eighth grade Anna and I had had our best years. We became stuck in the past, in the time when she had been so taken with "little Mia" and when she and Payne Hollow had been so much a part of my childhood.

I should never have tired of going to Payne Hollow. I loved its coziness and self-containment, its storybook desert-island atmosphere. It was the best summer camp any little girl ever had, and Anna, the head counselor, gave me the praise I thrived on. But my emerging self couldn't measure up to her fixed, intense interests in books, French, and music. My desire to please her began fighting with my guilt over wanting to be free of her expectations, and, too young to make allowances for her, I began pulling away. Our letters had dropped off to two a year by the time I graduated from high school, and though we would continue corresponding for seventeen more years, we had already exchanged almost three-quarters of all the letters we would ever write.

In high school my popularity with my classmates increased, but around boys I was still a wallflower. In the middle of my first year Anna asked about "the recent dances and other out-and-out social affairs." She wanted for me what her youthful shyness had deprived her of: "I can imagine you've been enjoying everything . . . and looking as pretty as a picture in the new dresses provided for each occasion. I wouldn't be a bit surprised, either, to learn that other people find you not only pretty, but very attractive." Around this time I became aware that the "best self" I had been giving Anna in letters could bear improving. I wrote to her that I was in a sorority, but I didn't tell her it was a source of nagging anxiety to me—it was only a front organization for more dances, every one of which I avoided. I wrote her about participating in the city-wide high school freshman debates and, according to Anna, made it sound like "a lively social affair." Naturally, I couldn't tell her my partner and I were woefully unprepared and that debating against boys paralyzed me with embarrassment. And I wrote her about my new piano teacher, a less demanding one who let me get away with not practicing. In fact the new freedom was fine with me, but I couldn't make any such confession to Anna, so I reported to her with semitragic overtones. Of course Anna's response was genuine; I think of it as her intellectual credo:

> Mia, dear, I was so concerned when you wrote that your music lessons are not as inspiring as they used to be. It's a shame! When you had such a fine start! But you have sized up the situation very well, and even realized that it is up to you to carry on, by yourself, as your former teacher would want you to do. Actually, you have run into a situation which everyone has to face sooner or later. The time comes, inevitably, when you have to carry on your own education independently. Some people go on learning and growing intellectually all their lives. Others stop learning the minute the stimulus of a formal education set-up is removed.
>
> I think you have the intelligence to go on with your piano study, trying to learn to play each piece as well as if you had your favorite teacher to encourage you. It is a challenge. You must never be satisfied with less than your best. After all, you know better than anyone whether you are playing the piece well or not. You hear all the mistakes. Casals once said the most important thing was for a musician to hear himself. So try to hear yourself—and then keep working at the difficulties until you have conquered them and you hear that it sounds right.
>
> A young woman who was studying 'cello with another great 'cellist, Feuermann, told how Feuermann had said to her, "The difference between you and me is that you don't care about that G flat, but I do." You must care about every smallest detail and do your best to make it perfect. Yes, it takes practice, and that takes time. But you can do this—when you practice, make your time count for as much as possible. That means give your best

attention to what you are doing. Use every ounce of your
intelligence every minute you are practicing. You can do it!

This was Anna to the core, carrying on her own education independently. Twice she named for me in letters her four main interests in
life: her music and reading with Harlan, and Harlan's painting and
writing. (Both times, in letters five years apart, she named the music
first.) She never stopped learning. In August 1985, in her eighty-third
year and the last summer of her life, she was waiting along with Harlan
to learn whether his colon cancer was under control, and she was
feeling ill herself. She wrote then to Etta that they were expecting a
German visitor and she had picked up a German reader at the Hanover
College library—"because we have to brush up on our German."

Between ninth and tenth grades I visited Payne Hollow for just a day;
my big trip that summer was to visit Uncle Dan in Atlantic City. Tenth
grade was almost over when Anna wrote: "Each year I think, 'Mia
will be too grown up to want to come here and float on her inner tube
and play with Curly and Snapper.'" In June: "I was hoping there would
be a letter from you in the next mail, telling us when you would arrive.
Perhaps there is a letter waiting in the box this very minute." In July:
"If you can come to see us in August that will be fine! . . . If you <u>can</u>
come, let us know, and then <u>come on</u>." I kept putting Anna off, and
she tried to entice me back to Payne Hollow by recalling memories.
"There's always the river to dunk in, and the goats to enjoy, and the
piano to play. I saw a most beautiful big yellow butterfly yesterday!
There are four eggs in the phoebe's nest over the front door. Plenty to
do and to see." But I wanted nothing to do with the muddy river now,
I had never forgiven the goats, and playing the piano meant more
trios. I was too young to be lured by memories. I didn't go to Payne
Hollow at all that summer, and I didn't receive another letter from
Anna until May of the following year. Its tone was elegiac, and it ended
with only "fondest greetings":

May 24, 1960

Dear Mia,
    It will be summer very soon now. This glorious sunshine
today is making me think of such summery things as going
swimming and having our friends come to spend part of their
vacation with us. I'm wondering if you can come to see us this

year. We'd love to have you. Your visits with us in previous summers are precious memories now. I know you will probably be making plans for something exciting, and worthwhile, too, like your art course last vacation. In what direction are your thoughts turning this year? . . . Do write and tell us what is going on. . . . No doubt you are very busy with school activities just now. But perhaps when this rush has subsided you can find a minute to write to us. . . .

So many things—and such a variety of things—make me think of you, Mia. The other evening, when some Hanover students were visiting here, a great moth flew against the window screen where the lamp was hanging. It was a beauty. Suddenly I thought of you and how you used to make pets of the butterflies! . . .

Mia, I've just had a thought. If you would like to bring any of your friends to visit here with you, we'd be pleased to have them. You could bring them for a longer or a shorter time, as it suits you best. We are hoping you'll come some way, alone, with friends, with Uncle Dan, with your father and mother— any way, but some way.

Snapper and Curly are the same wonderful playfellows you remember them to be. We all send you fondest greetings, especially

Harlan and Anna

That July I spent a week at Payne Hollow for the last time.

After high school I was ready to quit being shy. In September 1961 I went off to Marquette University, a large coeducational Jesuit university in downtown Milwaukee, and made a busy social and quasi-professional life for myself in the College of Journalism. Inspired by Anna, I took two years of German. And on pianos in dormitory lobbies and basements I continued playing my familiar music. I knew Anna was waiting, hoping, to hear about my advancing self-education in literature and music, and I felt guilty. I wasn't reading anything she would consider worthwhile, and I hadn't learned any new music since high school.

August 6, 1962

Dear Mia,

You were in my thoughts especially this morning. We were canning tomatoes. I say "we" advisedly, since Harlan was helping me with the scalding and peeling. I was thinking of the many times you have been my right-hand man with some canning job, tomatoes, or beans, or beets, or berries. You've had a taste of almost every kind, I think. Often, when I refer to some previous year's record, I find the entry in your handwriting. It was fun having you come for a visit each summer. Those were happy times.

I'm wondering what you are busy with this vacation. And how was the second half of your school year? . . . And do tell me whether you have any chance to play music at school. I really can't imagine there would be much time for it in your full schedule. There would be time if you cared enough to <u>make</u> the time.

I must tell you something else that has kept you in my mind lately. I've been reading the whole series of Laura Ingalls Wilder books which I got to send our niece and nephews. Didn't you think "Farmer Boy" was splendid! But "The Long Winter" is still my very favorite. It will soon be time to think what books I can give those youngsters for Christmas. Have you any extra good ideas? Pass them on to me, if you do.

What are you reading for your own pleasure? Harlan and I are reading Emerson's "Journals" and finding them most rewarding. We're also embarked on the project of reading Thayer's "Life of Beethoven," and again finding it very worthwhile. <u>Reading</u> is hardly the word for Erwin Bodky's "The Interpretation of Bach's Keyboard Works." We're <u>studying</u> that one with the scores right at our elbow for reference. Then for "reading." "Felix Holt," and "Dear Theo," and Turgenev's "A Hunter's Sketches." And of course we'd have some like "Zebulon Pike Southwestern Expeditions" and William Lewis Manly's "Death Valley in '49." Our French reading at the moment is J.J. Rousseau's "Confessions."

In the music department, we're concentrating on Beethoven's Violin Sonatas. And of course there's always Bach. Are you studying some new music this summer?

Mia, I feel I haven't seen you in so long. . . . We'd be ever so pleased if you'd come down to the riverbank and ring the bell to be ferried across. You'd find everything much the same here, Snapper and Curly, and the goats, and a big garden. But do come, if it appeals to you at all. We'd love to see you.

Another long letter came from Anna later that year, touching on many of her Payne Hollow themes:

October 26, 1962

Dear Mia,

This morning after breakfast and after Harlan had read a few more pages in our current book of adventure—John Steele's account of gold mining in California in 1851—Harlan was standing with his back to the fireplace fire, soaking up a little extra warmth before going out to chop wood, and he asked, "Is there anything you want me to do for you?" I couldn't think of a thing! So many times during the day, when Harlan is out somewhere, I think of something I want him to do for me. But when he actually confronted me with his question this morning, my mind was a complete blank. So I missed a wonderful chance.

As I sat by the fire a minute after Harlan had gone out I wondered just what I would do myself in these morning hours between 7:30 and 10 o'clock, when I'd have to begin preparing dinner. Yes, ten o'clock would be plenty early to begin operations. I want to bake a brown bread while the dinner fire heats the oven. I have the ingredients, molasses, raisins, wheat flour, walnuts (I picked those out last night by the evening fire), soy flour (I heard Harlan grinding that early this morning while I half dozed again after he'd got out of bed). For dinner, lima beans (in a bucket in the cellar; I can shell them out in half an hour), butternut squash (I must cook an extra number, to have some left over for squash pies tomorrow), stewed tomatoes (in the cellar), apple salad (apples, celery, walnuts—yes, I have everything, even honey), a can of our meat.

Well, what am I going to do then until ten o'clock? I could sew on that wool-lined comforter I'm refacing. One more morning's work will finish that repair job. Why in the world did I start that, anyway? It is wool and warm; you can't buy wool batting anymore. I tried. And there are times when the down [comforter] is too hot. But no, I don't think I want to sew this morning, after all. I could houseclean another cupboard. Oh, not this morning!

I could practice my part of the Brahms Horn Trio. I missed an awful lot of notes when Harlan and I played our two parts together yesterday afternoon, especially in the second movement, the Scherzo. I do want to be able to play it all well when Bill Sloane comes to play it with us again. We made such a mess of it when we tried it with him about a year ago. It's a wonder he'd come again! . . .

Isn't it cold this morning! My hands are stiff. I'll wait until

later in the day to practice. It froze last night, for the first
time. . . . The sweet basil left in the garden is turned black now,
frozen. The hedge of poke bushes that has been such a lovely
colorful touch along the edge of the garden is wilted and black
this morning. The canvases over the banked-up celery and over
the patches of lettuce are white with frost. Harlan says in this
climate we can expect our first frost by the middle of October.
We've had ten extra days of garden this year, you might say.
Harlan has continued to swim in the river every day until this
week. That's a record.

I know what I'll do this morning—I'll write to Mia! I was
going to write yesterday, but somehow I didn't. Oh yes, it was
the lost goat. I had that goat on my mind and I couldn't seem
to start thinking of a letter. . . . I kept worrying about that lone
goat out in all the bad weather. At dinner time I asked Harlan if
the herd was still in. He said he'd driven them out an hour ago.
And sure enough, a few hours later they all came back, all <u>ten</u>
of them. . . .

Well, thank goodness my mind is at ease about the goats
now. So this is my chance to write a letter to Mia. But would
you believe it—it's ten o'clock! Time to start dinner! Where has
this morning gone!

I'll have to answer her fine letter another time. She's such a
dear to write to me, when she's so busy, too. But I'm so glad
she wants to. I <u>have</u> missed her letters. She's a wonderful girl.
There's no one quite like her! How pleased I was to see her
when she and Harry came this summer! It was so jolly being
together and chatting about this and that, just as we always
used to do, while we did the dishes. And Mia remembered
where everything was!

It was good to talk to her about the children's books. She
appreciates them and loves them as I do myself, and as Nell
does, too.

And then to have her play the piano! I'm glad she's not
neglecting her music. She does play so well. . . . Ten o'clock!
Here it is ten fifteen! No letter writing today!

Just—Much love from Harlan and Anna

At the end of the letter, Anna had linked me in her thoughts again
with Nella Mae. Now I see what Anna wanted to believe—that an
interest in children's books was something she still shared with both
Nell and Mia. She needed that link with the past. There had been a lot
of book chatter between us in letters when I was ten and eleven, but

my interest in children's books waned. For years, to please Anna, I trotted out my reminiscences about the particular books I had loved when I was a child, but my interest was specific and nostalgic, not a living thing. This 1962 letter was the last one in which Anna mentioned children's books to me.

While my college experience was taking me farther and farther away from Payne Hollow, Anna had other young people coming into her life from Hanover College. With no childhood history to bias their outlook, they saw Anna and Harlan and their life more clearly than I could, and they were drawn irresistibly. One such young person—a special one, for Anna—was Celia Mitchell. The second time Celia went to Payne Hollow she felt as if she had come home. She felt "a sense of wonder, of having discovered, finally, a serene loveliness which made sense." Anna opened her arms wide to Celia and hugged her. In the spring Anna showed Celia the wildflowers coming up in the woods. Celia asked Anna about how she organized her life and about her homemaking systems. Anna told Celia about the musical evenings in Cincinnati and her feelings about music. And in Celia, Anna had someone to talk with about children's books.

For dessert one day when Celia was visiting, Anna spooned some of her home-canned pears and raspberries into her grandmother's crystal sherbet glasses, the stemmed, wide-mouthed glasses hand etched with a twining grapevine pattern. "Sunlight streamed through the window," Celia wrote years later, "turning the pears to iridescent opals and the raspberries to live coals. [Anna] studied them a moment and put her hand on my shoulder; we smiled. So lovely the fruit and the absence of words."

"We expect you will achieve much in your chosen field of journalism," Anna wrote shortly before my graduation. "We can look for a branching out into other fields now, too, I think. . . . You may even do something really creative. The greatest success of all may be in the field of relationships. This is exactly where I feel you have already distinguished yourself." Anna had stopped asking me what new music I was learning and what I was reading. Now her hopes were focused on my future, and at the same time she seemed to be registering approval of my intention to marry. Jim Cunningham (I call him Jamie, as his family does), of Detroit, had graduated two years before me, and we had reached an understanding that we would marry after I finished school. He moved to Washington, D.C., and began his career as a security officer in the Central Intelligence Agency.

I was proud to be allied with a Cold Warrior. Minoring in political science at Marquette, I had been taught that Communism was evil and that the Soviets' goal was to take over the world. I had no reason for doubting, since the keynotes of my college years had been the construction of the Berlin Wall—it began on my eighteenth birthday, August 13, 1961—and the Cuban Missile Crisis, those two weeks in October 1962 when Americans believed nuclear war might actually happen. Of course, these concerns were irrelevant at Payne Hollow. When Jamie met Anna and Harlan in 1964 I had my first inkling that a gulf was opening between my life and Anna's. Jamie drove out to Fort Thomas and met my parents, and it seemed natural to take him down to Payne Hollow. (Anna liked him and wrote me later that she thought it a great thing that I had chosen "a Michigan boy.") Full of pride in his new profession, Jamie told Anna he worked for the CIA, and Anna asked, "What's that?"

After graduation in June 1965 I moved to Washington to share an apartment with another female Marquette graduate and take a job as an editorial assistant with a trade association of weekly newspaper publishers. Soon I reported to Anna that Jamie had given me a diamond ring, and she answered: "What a wonderfully happy time this is for both of you! There will never be anything quite like it. . . . Oh, I keep thinking of all the different kinds of happiness in store for you." Later that year I wrote Anna that my wedding date was set for the following April, and she responded by telling me about Harlan's marriage proposal. I know now how rare it was for Anna to reveal so personal a memory: "April was the month Harlan and I decided on, too, years ago. I can't help thinking back to the time when we were enjoying a winter season of symphony concerts together, as you and Jamie are doing now. It was after one of the concerts, when Harlan was saying good night to me; quite abruptly he said, 'We must be together this spring.' And so we were." (Anna's description of the proposal left my imagination free to picture the scene taking place at the door of her apartment and dissolving into a long, romantic kiss. But now, knowing that the proposal took place at the door of a departing streetcar instead, I suppose Anna scarcely had time to recover from her surprise before she was pulled away. How like Harlan, that his instinct for avoiding emotional scenes served him well even at the adrenalin-charged moment of proposing marriage. And how like Anna, to fix upon the sentimental kernel of Harlan's proposal and dismiss the rest.)

Anna's infrequent letters in the late 1960s, keeping pace with mine, were still nostalgic and filled with news about Payne Hollow.

July 6, 1968

Dear Mia and Jamie,

You have been in my mind so much lately. We are expecting my young niece, Susan, to come and spend a couple of weeks with us, and I have been thinking of all the good times Harlan and I have had when little Mia was our house guest. That was our great pleasure and privilege for many years. Now I am looking forward to Susan's visit, hoping it will be something like your visits of years ago, Mia. . . .

The news you wrote at Christmas time, that you were to have a piano to play on, made me happy indeed. Often I have thought of the fun you must be having with it. Harlan and I play together almost every day. Once in a great while some friend comes and plays with us, a cellist from Louisville, a violist from Bloomington, a pianist from Cincinnati. . . .

We still manage to get to Louisville for a concert now and then. Mia, do you remember the time we dashed off to Louisville with you, the very evening you arrived here, to attend that quartet recital outdoors at Garden Court. And how hungry you were! With only some bananas for supper, bought at a grocery store on the way!

Everything here is pretty much as you remember it. Snapper and Curly look as always, Snapper's one ear not quite as straight as the other. They are great favorites with everyone who comes. They still love to go out in the boat when Harlan baits up his fish line.

The fishing has been good. Several times the catches have been large enough to warrant smoking a batch. The garden had a setback in June. For the first time since we've been here the river came up high enough in June to cover the lower garden with six feet of water. . . . In the meantime, we've had an abundance of early vegetables on the upper level, spinach, peas, potatoes, well, everything. Even cherries this year! And raspberries!

The goat herd numbers ten now. One of the does surprised us by having twins in June. . . . You just know how cute they are. . . .

Does all this sound familiar?

One thing more. Since you have been on my mind, I have remembered you enjoyed "Anna and the King of Siam." I think that will be our next Christmas gift to Susan.

I haven't said anything about Harlan's painting. He goes on quietly painting pictures, some boats, some landscapes. He has exhibitions regularly. The show of boat and river paintings—fifty of them—at the American Commercial Lines new offices in Jeffersonville was <u>very</u> fine. Then last February the exhibition at Hanover College was mostly landscapes—and that was very well received, too. . . .

All these sheets are really only to tell you we love you very much—as always.

Harlan and Anna

One sunny September day in 1970, while visiting in Fort Thomas, Jamie and I drove down to Milton and out onto the ridge, where the fences were decorated with the purple of ironweed and the yellow of little roadside sunflowers. We left the car and walked down the hill to Payne Hollow the easy way, by the old roadbed. Anna's hair was white now, pinned up in curls on the top of her head. As we talked indoors, Anna sat attentively with her hands in her lap and smiled fondly at us. I played some Chopin for her. Jamie and I went with Harlan to his studio, where he showed us the old paintings, the ones he eventually donated to Hanover College and the Behringer-Crawford Museum. While I was photographing them, Harlan stepped to the open door and gazed up at the hillside. As he looked and listened, he stood with his knees slightly bent as always, like a riverman balancing himself on a shifting deck. Anna served us a fine meal, and afterward she and I gossiped while she washed the blue-and-white dishes and I dried them with a linen dish towel.

A short letter followed in December, and then, for what would prove to be the last time, I heard Anna's familiar voice in her next letter:

April 11, 1972

Dear Mia and Jamie,

You have been in my thoughts especially these last weeks. Perhaps it is the wild flowers. . . . There's another reason why you have been in my thoughts, Mia particularly. If I go around here, about my work, with a smile on my face and a special look in my eye, that's because I'm thinking of little Mia who used to come and stay with us for a while each summer. This May, in just a few more weeks, Harlan and I are expecting to

have a girl come from Principia School in Missouri to spend a
week with us. She's a senior there and will be a freshman at
Hanover College next fall. She has heard about us and this
place and she has asked to visit us. . . . You can imagine how I
am wondering how the whole thing will turn out. And you can
understand that I am remembering those times when Mia came
to be with us. But nothing can ever come up to those visits of
Mia's! They were altogether special.

It was so very good to see you and Jamie last fall, Mia. And
then your letter at Christmas time brought you very near. Your
letters! I have treasured them, every one of them, all these
years. Well, my dear—our love to you both!

Harlan and Anna

In early 1973 Jamie was assigned to Tehran, Iran, as assistant security
officer in the American embassy, responsible for protecting the American ambassador. There were many good things during the four years
we were there, but the city was ugly and dirty, and the possibility of
terrorist attacks on Americans was an everyday reality. Westerners
were welcomed by the shah and his government, but not by the Is-
lamic fundamentalist mullahs and their followers, who took over the
country by revolution a few years after we had left. I became accustomed to having weapons around the house and to Jamie's going to
work armed. Terrorists couldn't breach the security program Jamie
had mounted around the ambassador, but they did succeed in killing
six other Americans while we were there.

I kept busy doing low-level administrative work for U.S. government agencies and spending every cent of my modest paycheck on the
city's exotic goods. With my thoughts bouncing from covetous dreams
of fabulous Persian carpets to nightmares of terrorist ambushes, I was
a long way from Payne Hollow. Writing the truth to Anna and Harlan
would only disturb the equilibrium and alienate me from them, and so
in my letters I steered a middle course between the two extremes of my
life, materialism and violence.

I had been in Tehran about a year and a half when, in late August
1974, my parents' health collapsed. My emergency visit home stretched
into five months, during which my mother died and my father recovered and moved to a retirement home in Virginia. When the time came
to empty the Fort Thomas house, I passed a message to Harlan. He
came as soon as he could, and together, on a sunny fall day, we went

into the studio for the last time. The years had intensified the smell of damp wood smoke. As Harlan poked around, I thought of the days when Anna and I had been so happy there, playing house together in her honeymoon cottage. He took some last odds and ends back to Payne Hollow and had an old Fort Thomas friend in real estate sell the property.

For Jamie and me there were no more personal crises during our second two years in Tehran. Home again in spring 1977, we adopted the suburban lifestyle of Northern Virginia and merged into the pace of Greater Washington. Afire with belated career ambitions, I became a freelance editor. The two letters from Anna that followed my settling in Virginia, and the three that had preceded them, were nothing like her letters of the old days. All were brief. None contained any reminiscences, or anything of Anna herself or of life at Payne Hollow. They were *polite* and, to my ear, empty. During the last months of 1976, as Jamie and I were preparing to leave Tehran and make a round of homecoming visits to our relatives, I had written Anna that we wanted to visit Payne Hollow. In her reply she mentioned that she had been hearing news of Daddy from a mutual acquaintance, Nora (not her real name). This would be the theme of her last three letters.

"Ever since your good letter arrived," Anna wrote, "we have been cheered by the thought that you will be coming to see us early in the new year. . . . We have had good reports about Harry from [Nora]. More than once she has written to tell us some special news from Harry." It was more of the same in Anna's Christmas letter of 1977: "It was wonderful seeing you again. That was last March. [Nora] gave us your address in June. [Nora] writes to us now and then, always telling us how happy and busy Harry is." A year later I sent flowers to the December 1978 opening of Harlan's exhibition at the Carnegie Arts Center in Covington. Johnny-on-the-spot was Nora, and once again Anna reminded me that Nora had been reporting on Daddy: "[Nora], you know, writes to us and tells us the latest news she has of Harry. [Nora's] most recent note contained three pictures of Harry."

Three short letters in three years, each one reminding me that Anna was getting the news about my father from Nora instead of from me. It was a new refrain to replace the old ones: *We will want you to play your piece for us when you come. . . . You will have it perfectly in hand and completely memorized, no doubt. . . . Be sure to bring duets for us to play. . . . You may be sure we'll keep you busy playing trios. . . . Do*

*you ever read any French stories outside of class for your own amuse-
ment? . . . There would be time* [for playing piano at college] *if you
cared enough to* make *the time. . . . We can look for a branching out
into other fields now.*

Somewhere inside my chest a pressure valve flew open and I declared, *Enough! I can never please her, and I'm through with feeling
guilty! If all we have left to write about is news of Daddy, and Nora is
such a fine reporter, then what's the point of writing!* The following
Christmas neither of us wrote. For another year or two I thought sometimes, "I should write to Anna," but after a while the "should" went
away. When I heard about Anna's death, nearly eight years after our
last exchange of letters, I dismissed as sentimentality the feelings of
regret and sorrow that threatened to spring up. I believed then that
Anna and Payne Hollow no longer had anything to do with me.

When Anna was gone, Harlan wanted to "cut down everything to the
bone," he said, to simplify his life and eliminate chores for his eventual survivors. He brought Anna's trunks of Old Country treasures
down from the attic where they had rested for thirty years, and Susan
took them back to Grand Rapids. Many of the everyday household
things he set out in his studio for friends to take as they pleased—his
flea market, he called it.

Harlan was equally troubled by the large accumulation of papers
at Payne Hollow and was relieved when the University of Louisville
Archives agreed to establish a "Harlan and Anna Hubbard" collection. On October 30, 1986, William Morison, director of the University of Louisville Archives, visited Payne Hollow and, Harlan wrote
Etta the next day, accepted "14 or 15 loaded boxes" of papers. Harlan
archived many of Anna's papers and letters. In writing to Etta, however, Harlan showed where his thoughts were concentrated when he
wrote, not of the Harlan *and Anna* Hubbard collection, but of "a
Harlan Hubbard collection of my manuscripts, journals, letters, photographs, water colors, wood block prints, sketches, etc." He reported
to Etta that Morison had told him not to throw anything away, and he
added, "Think of all that stuff we burned when you were here!" He
was referring to Etta's visit the previous June, when, after the burial
service for Anna, Etta had helped Harlan go through Anna's things.

Anna's sense of the sacredness of letters and objects was alien to
Harlan and Etta, and together they had destroyed a lot of material.
There's no telling how much of it had been damaged by mice or mil-

dew and how much was simply deemed unimportant. Harlan did more burning in September and noted it in his journal, addressing himself to Anna. The only letters he specifically mentioned burning were mine:

> The mass of printed or written-on paper that you left behind, stuffed into every possible unused space, must be removed and looked over, the valuable and useful must be stored in a suitable place, the rest ruthlessly destroyed by fire, as your cast-off body was reduced to ashes. . . . Yet so much of you went into some of those papers—your correspondence with Mia M. when she was a little girl, for instance. Her precisely written letters to you are like yours to her, though I suppose most of the latter have been destroyed—I wonder if Mia still has them. Her ardent and innocent love for you may have died in the long course of years.

Five months after Morison's visit, Harlan was still destroying things of Anna's. On April 5, 1987, he wrote to Etta that he was sorting through the twelve large drawers he had built for Anna in his workshop. "You can imagine what I find—old letters and Christmas cards, unwanted clothing, materials, books. Occasionally a treasure, but not much of it worth keeping." The loss of this unknown amount of information about Anna is a pity. I particularly regret the loss of my letters to her, of course, not only because they could have told me so much about my childhood self but also because Anna had treasured them. I understand Harlan's wanting to clean house and simplify his daily living. And I know he didn't feel emotionally attached to "things" (except his own paintings) and had no intuitive understanding of people who did. Still, it saddens me that Harlan held my letters in his hands, paused to think how much of Anna was in them, and then rated them not valuable. Over a period of twenty-eight years he had heard Anna read every one of my letters aloud and apparently had registered some notion of the pleasure they gave her, and still, in the end, he didn't find them worth keeping.

Harlan gave the Steinway to Ted Wadl, according to Anna's wishes. Ted was a viola player retired from the Cincinnati Symphony Orchestra who had been coming to Payne Hollow for years to play trios and tune the Steinway. Ted offered to sell the piano for Harlan, but Harlan preferred to make it a gift. On Sunday, November 9, 1986, with Richard Strimple taking the lead, a crew of eight strong Hubbard friends took Anna's Steinway out of Payne Hollow. Down the stone steps from the house they carried it, minus the massive legs, a few paces at a time. Down the steep path into the lower garden and across, down into the creek bed, up over the other side of the creek, and into Bob Gosman's tractor-hauled farm wagon, a distance of about two hundred yards. Bob, the Hubbards' nearest neighbor at the top of the hill, drove the tractor up while the others rode behind in the wagon with the piano. It had been thirty years, to the month, since the piano had come down the hill the same way. Without Harlan's knowledge beforehand, Ted sold the piano to a Cincinnati piano dealer, who had the insides rebuilt and then resold it.

In Louisville on December 11, 1986, at the Kentucky Center for the Arts, the governor of Kentucky presented Harlan with the Artist Award for Lifetime Achievement. In accepting the award, Harlan spoke of a new period of his life beginning, and of his hope that his work would now rise to a higher level. Of the eight persons and three organizations honored that night, only Harlan received a standing ovation.

Harlan felt well in August 1987—he had been on monthly chemotherapy for a year and a half, and a scare about his liver had been disproved—but a swelling on the left side of his neck was found to be prostatic cancer in the lymph nodes. In the house on the night of November 20 he fell, striking his face and upper body against the dropleaf chest. His left cheekbone and two or three ribs were fractured. When Harlan had been in the hospital for six days, his young friends Bob and Charlotte Canida took him to their riverside home in Madison, near the bridge. They brought in a hospital bed and gave over their living room to him, with its peaceful picture-window view of lawn, trees, the river, and the Kentucky hills. There Harlan spent the last weeks of his life, cared for by several of his friends and visited by many more. He was unconscious the last three days, and with Marcella Modisett and Don Wallis at his side, he died on the night of January 16, 1988.

Seven and a half years later, in July 1995, I set out to write about Anna, lugging with me a burden of guilt for all the ways I had disappointed her. In one hope after another—trios, children's literature, solo piano, intellectual reading—I had let her down. I hadn't branched out into other fields or advanced my self-education; I had become thoroughly worldly; and then I had broken off our friendship on the basis of a petty resentment. Smart as I had always thought I was, I had committed one of humankind's most common mistakes: I had failed to realize the value of Anna's friendship until she was gone.

Still true, all of it, but now I know that a good many others also felt inadequate in relation to Anna. Hubbard friends who comprehended the fullness of the Payne Hollow life told me they had asked themselves, "What could *I* possibly offer the Hubbards?" and spoke of their own regrets. Some feel they let the Hubbards down in various ways. Others are apologetic about owning modern gadgets and otherwise falling short of the Payne Hollow ideal. Anna and Harlan are icons for many of us, and it seems we still want their approval.

I learned also that the tapering-off of Anna's interest in our correspondence during the 1970s may have had less to do with me and my failings than I supposed. Nella Mae's cancer was a lightning strike in 1971. The cancer was widespread; she had surgeries, aggressive radiation treatment, and then-experimental chemotherapy. Seven years of remissions and further onslaughts followed, until Nell died in 1978 on the day after Thanksgiving. At the funeral Anna was stricken. She wept silently, her face contorted and her body bent over in grief. Nell's death marked the true beginning of Anna's old age. She told none of her friends about her loss, and scant weeks later she hid her grief at the Carnegie Arts Center exhibition opening. She sent a round of gracious thank-you letters, including the one to me. But 1978 was the first year since the Hubbards' marriage that they did not produce a wood-block Christmas card, and it was the year Anna stopped keeping her list of books she had read with Harlan. Nell's death was a blow to Anna's vitality.

Above all, I learned there had been much neediness in the friendship between Anna and me, and that we had stopped fulfilling each other's needs. The more involved I became in the world, the less I needed Anna and Payne Hollow. The more young friends visited Payne Hollow and shared Anna's interests with her, the less Anna needed little Mia. Neither of us knew how to find a different way to "be" with each other. It seems we had both been playing out chapters in our own mother-daughter stories. I had found with Anna the action and involvement my mother couldn't give me, and Anna, by praising and encouraging me, had been trying to set right, in the next generation, her relationship with her own, unpleasable, mother. I interpreted her praise as pressure to be perfect, and the absence of praise as disapproval, and Anna's mother-daughter story ultimately repeated itself. When it appeared from her last few letters that she saw nothing left in me to praise, I had to get out, as Anna and Etta got out of Grand

Rapids. I didn't have to move hundreds of miles away, though; I only had to stop writing letters. The day the pressure valve blew, I stopped trying to be what Anna wanted me to be. Over the years, mostly by what she left unsaid, Anna had taught me not to tell her what I really thought and felt. But at the same time, in those letters full of praise, she had contributed enormously to my store of self-confidence. Perhaps it was her contributions that expanded my self-confidence to the bursting point and made it possible, even necessary, for me to break away from her.

Anna was more interested in little Mia, the bright child full of promise, than in the person I became. Knowing that, I still want more from Anna than she was capable of giving, more than I myself knew I would want someday. I want Anna to have been the older-woman friend I've never had, who would talk to me about living. I want us to have become friends on a more equal footing and exchanged confidences—girl talk, but *intimate*, as defined by my generation, not hers. I want to ask Anna whether it truly was shyness that made her quit teaching; at what point in her relationship with Paul she found out he was married; what words she used in telling Robert about Harlan; what Anna wrote to Hilda and Lee about Harlan during their courtship, and what happened to her 1940–44 letters from Hilda and Lee; what her mother said about her marrying Harlan; how much she missed Barre. . . . But of course Anna could not have answered these kinds of questions.

I know now that I had in Anna's letters the best of what she was able to give me. Because of the letters, I know more about her influence on me than I know about my mother's. Yet I've only begun to recall everything that happened between Anna and me, and to recognize all the ways I was affected by the gift of childhood time alone with Anna in the studio and at Payne Hollow. I still love books and music—not as Anna did, but in my own way. I'm organized; I need system, ritual, efficiency, and tidiness, and I keep records and journals of various kinds. I want things done in the house *my* way. Year by year I grow more sentimental and need more peace and quiet. It was a search for Payne Hollow in the suburbs, I suppose, that led me to this house with Jamie after the chaos of Tehran; beyond the backyard a patch of county-owned forest mutes the roar of nearby highway traffic and harbors a creek, and woodland plants and creatures. I look at the woodsy view from my kitchen window while I'm washing the dishes by hand, and for drying them I have a drawer full of linen dish towels. I'm fond of cozy cabins, sweet basil, feeding wild birds, expeditions, and wildflowers by the door.

Anna and Harlan are much on my mind now. Though I have no dreams of homesteading, I carry Payne Hollow around with me as the ideal of interior peace. The peace of home is my escape from technology, materialism, overcrowding, incivility, popular culture, and all the rest. I don't need self-help books on how to live a centered life—I have Harlan's books, Anna's letters, and my memories of Payne Hollow. Like Harlan, I know and love Anna better now than I ever could have while she was living. I feel about her as she assured her nephew George he could feel about his mother, Nella Mae: "All your life, George, you can feel that Nell is there, very close, loving you and understanding you." Anna's love for little Mia is always with me.

Chronology

ᦁ

1877	Anna's father, John Eikenhout, is born in Grand Rapids, Mich.
1878	Anna's mother, Nellie Ross, is born in Ede, province of Gelderland, the Netherlands.
1893	Nellie Ross emigrates to the United States with her parents.
1900	January 4—Harlan Hubbard is born in Bellevue, Ky.
	August 2—John Eikenhout and Nellie Ross marry in Grand Rapids.
1902	September 7—Anna Wonder Eikenhout is born.
1907	November 3—Henrietta (Etta) Eikenhout is born.
1916	May 16—Nella Mae Eikenhout is born.
1920	Anna graduates from South High School.
1920–22	Attends Grand Rapids Juneior College.
1922–25	Earns a B.A. with high distinction and a B.S. in education from Ohio State University; graduates Phi Beta Kappa.
1925–27	Teaches French at Hope College, Holland, Mich.
1928	July—moves with Kay Learned to Cincinnati.
	September—begins library training at the Cincinnati Public Library.
1929	April—is appointed an assistant librarian in the Fine Arts department.
1939	Puts Harlan's name and address in her little address book.
1940	June. 12—John Eikenhout dies.
1941	January 12 (?)—Harlan visits Anna's apartment to play music.
	January 16 (?)—Anna and Harlan go to the international exhibition at the Cincinnati Art Museum.
1942	May 24—they begin a nine-day canoe trip on the Licking River.

1943	April 20—they marry in Maysville, Ky.
	November 16—Harlan's mother dies.
1944	February 22—Anna and Harlan begin a seven-week hiking trip through seven eastern states.
	July 8—they begin a nine-week hiking trip through Michigan.
	September 10—Anna tells Harlan it's time to build the shantyboat.
	October 5—the lumber for the shantyboat arrives at Brent.
	December 11—the first night of sleeping on board.
	December 27—the shantyboat is afloat.
1946	July 13—the McTamneys move into the Hubbards' house in Fort Thomas.
	December 22—the shantyboat voyage begins.
1947	January 27—the Hubbards tie up at Madison, Ind., for a week.
	February17 to November 29—at Payne Hollow.
1948	April 1 to November 5—at Bizzle's Bluff on the Cumberland River (Kentucky).
1949	March 1 to December 6—at Bisland Bayou, six miles above Natchez, Miss.
	May 10—Harlan has surgery for a ruptured appendix.
1950	April 7—the shantyboat leaves the Mississippi River at Harvey Canal.
	May 2—enters the bayous on the Intracoastal Waterway.
1951	July 1—is sold.
	September—the Hubbards begin their driving and camping trip through the West.
1952	April 30—they return to Fort Thomas.
	June 18—move their camping trailer down into Payne Hollow.
	November 12—occupy their newly built cabin.
1956	With the addition of a larger, lower room, the cabin becomes a house.
	August 22—Nellie Eikenhout dies.
1974	December—the house in Fort Thomas is sold.
1978	November—Nella Mae dies on the day after Thanksgiving.
1983	September 10—Harlan is bitten by a copperhead.
	September 21—has first prostate operation.
	October 6—has second prostate operation.

1985 March 4—has colon surgery.
    March 19 to July 1 (?)—Anna and Harlan live in a
     friend's cottage five miles upriver from Madison.

1986 March 15—exhibition of Harlan's donated paintings
     opens at the Behringer-Crawford Museum,
     Covington, Ky.
    March 25—Anna is admitted to the hospital.
    April 3—has surgery.
    May 4—dies.
    June 13—memorial service at Payne Hollow.
    December 11—Harlan receives the Artist Award for
     Lifetime Achievement from the governor of Kentucky.

1987 November 21—Harlan is taken to the hospital.
    November 27—to Bob and Charlotte Canida's house.

1988 January 16—Harlan dies.

1991 January 1—Etta dies.

"Books Harlan and I Have Read Together"

೭

Anna's reading list, which she titled "Books Harlan and I have read together," begins in 1942 with *The Little Chronicle of Magdalena Bach*—a book the Hubbards read on their Licking River canoe trip the year before they were married—and it continues until 1978. The original is in the Harlan and Anna Hubbard Papers, University of Louisville Archives, box 18, folder 44. This is an alphabetical version of Anna's chronological list.

After typing Anna's list, I searched for each entry on the online catalog of the Library of Congress. When that search failed or turned up multiple possibilities, I went to the online catalogs of the Cincinnati Public Library, Hanover College, and (as a fallback) the Washington, D.C., Research Library Consortium. Where Anna's entries and the results of the catalog search were unambiguous, I supplied full names of authors and full titles of the works. Where Anna's entries were vague or incomplete, or the results of the catalog search were not definitive, I put my best guess into an endnote (the endnotes appear at the end of the list). Extraneous notations are omitted, such as those about who had loaned the Hubbards the book and when they returned it.

Anna's chronological list is an intriguing and enlightening look into the daily life of the Hubbards. Some harmless and possibly even beneficial papers might be written in future on the subject of what books the Hubbards were reading as they were drifting down the Mississippi, as they were settling Payne Hollow, and so on. The advantage of presenting the list alphabetically, however, is that the scope of titles and authors read by the Hubbards is more easily grasped. In addition, alphabetical presentation permits the eliminating of duplicate entries, of which there are more than thirty in Anna's list. Any title that the Hubbards returned to, whatever their motive, carries some additional weight, which I have represented by placing an asterisk after entries that appear in Anna's list more than once, and more than a page or two apart—an indication that some years passed in between readings.

Adams, Henry, *The Education of Henry Adams, an Autobiography* *
Aeschylus, *Agamemnon*
———, *Prometheus Bound*
———, *Seven against Thebes*
———, *Suppliant Maidens*
Agee, James, *Letters of James Agee to Father Flye*
Akinari, Ueda, *Tales of the Spring Rain (Harusame monogatari)*
Akiyama, Terukazu, *Japanese Painting*[1]
Alcott, Amos Bronson, *Journals*
———, *Table-Talk*
Anderson, Charles Roberts (ed.), *Thoreau's World: Miniatures from His Journal*
Andrews, Roy Chapman, *Across Mongolian Plains*
Angier, Bradford, *Living Off the Country: How to Stay Alive in the Woods*
Anson's Cruise around the World[2]
Artists on Art[3]
Atkinson, Brooks, *Once around the Sun*
Auchincloss, Louis, *The Rector of Justin*
Aulich, Bruno, and Ernst Heimeran (tr. D. Millar Craig), *The Well-tempered String Quartet: A Book of Counsel and Entertainment.* . . .
Aurelius, Marcus, *Meditations*
Austen, Jane, *Emma*
———, *Mansfield Park* *
———, *Persuasion* *
———, *Pride and Prejudice* *
Balzac, Honoré de, *Cousin Pons*
———, *Le curé de Tours*
———, *Eugénie Grandet*
———, *Père Goriot*
Bartram, William (ed. Frances Harper), *TheTravels of William Bartram* *
Basch, Victor, *Schumann, a Life of Suffering*
Bates, Marston, *The Forest and the Sea: A Look at the Economy of Nature and the Ecology of Man*
Bates, Marston, and Donald Abbott, *Coral Island: Portrait of an Atoll*
Bauer, Marion, *Twentieth Century Music: How It Developed, How to Listen to It*
Beaglehole, John Cawte, *The Exploration of the Pacific*
Beam, Philip C., *Winslow Homer*
Bell, Quentin, *Victorian Artists*
Benesch, Otto, *Rembrandt*
Benét, Stephen Vincent, *John Brown's Body*
Benoit, Pierre, *The Casino of Barbazan*

Benson, Arthur Christopher, *From a College Window*
Berenson, Bernard, *Essays in Appreciation*
Berlioz, Hector, Memoirs[4]
Bernicot, Captain Louis, The Voyage of Anahita Single-handed round the World *[5]
Beston, Henry, *The Outermost House: A Year of Life on the Great Beach of Cape Cod*
Beyreuther, Erich, *Nikolaus Ludwig von Zinzendorf in Selbstzeugnissen und Bilddokumenten*
Binyon, Laurence, *The Flight of the Dragon . . . Art in China and Japan. . . .* *
———, Painting in the Near East[6]
Bird, Isabella L., *A Lady's Life in the Rocky Mountains*[7]
Birren, Faber, *History of Color in Painting*
Bishop, Charles, *The Journals and Letters of Captain Charles Bishop on the North-west Coast of America . . . 1794–1799*
Bishop, Isabella Lucy (Bird), *The Yangtze Valley and Beyond: An Account of Journeys in China. . . .*
Blackmore, R.D., *Lorna Doone*
Bode, Carl, and Walter Roy Harding (eds.), The Correspondence of H.D. Thoreau[8]
Bodky, Erwin, *The Interpretation of Bach's Keyboard Works*
Born, Wolfgang, *American Landscape Painting, an Interpretation*
Borrow, George Henry, *Lavengro: The Scholar—The Gipsy—The Priest*
Boswell, James, *Boswell on the Grand Tour: Germany and Switzerland, 1764*
———, *The Journal of a Tour to the Hebrides with Samuel Johnson*
———, *Life of Johnson* *
Bowie, Henry P., *On the Laws of Japanese Painting. . . .*
Bradbury, John, *Travels in the Interior of America*
Brahms-Clara Schumann letters, vols. 1 and 2[9]
Brion, Marcel, *La peinture moderne, de l'impressionnisme à l'art abstrait*
Brody, Elaine, and Robert Fowkes, *The German Lied and Its Poetry*
Brontë, Anne, *Agnes Grey*
Brontë, Charlotte, *Jane Eyre*
———, *The Professor*
———, *Shirley*
———, *Villette*
Brontë, Emily, *Wuthering Heights*
Brooks, Van Wyck, *The Confident Years: 1885–1915*
———, *The Flowering of New England*
———, *New England: Indian Summer*
———, *The World of Washington Irving*
Brown, Maurice J.E., *Schubert: A Critical Biography*
Browne, Sir Thomas, *Religio medici*
Browning, Robert, *German Poetry: A Critical Anthology*

Buck, Pearl, *My Several Worlds, a Personal Record*
——— (tr.), *All Men Are Brothers (Shui hu chuan)* *10
Bukofzer, Manfred F., *Music in the Baroque Era, from Monteverdi to Bach*
Bullen, Frank Thomas, *The Cruise of the Cachalot*
Burling, Judith, and Arthur Hart, *Chinese Art*
Burney, Fanny, *Diary and Letters of Madame d'Arblay*
Burroughs, John, *Fresh Fields*
Burton, Sir Richard Francis, *Arabian Nights' Entertainments: Or, The Book of a Thousand Nights and a Night*
Cahill, James, *Scholar Painters of Japan: The Nange School*
Camus, Albert, *L'été*
Canaday, John, *Embattled Critic: Views on Modern Art*
Canby, Henry Seidel, *Thoreau*
Candlin, Clara M. (tr.), *The Herald Wind: Translations of Sung Dynasty Poems, Lyrics, and Songs*
Capell, Richard, *Schubert's Songs* *
Capote, Truman, *Other Voices, Other Rooms*
Carlyle, Thomas, *Critical and Miscellaneous Essays*
———, *Journey to Germany, Autumn 1858*
———, *Reminiscences*
Carrel, Alexis, *Man the Unknown*
Carson, Rachel, *The Sea around Us*
Carson, Rachel L., *Under the Sea Wind*
Carter, Hodding, *Lower Mississippi*
Cary, Joyce, *The Horse's Mouth*
———, *Mister Johnson*
Castiglione, Baldassarre, *The Book of the Courtier*
Cather, Willa, *One of Ours*
——— (ed.), *The Best Stories of Sara Orne Jewett*
Cervantes, *Don Quixote*
Channing, William Ellery, *Thoreau, the Poet Naturalist*
Chapman, R.W., *Jane Austen*
Chateaubriand, François-René, vicomte de, *Itinéraire de Paris à Jérusalem*
———, *Les Natchez*
———, *Voyage en Amérique*
———, *Voyage en Italie*
Chaucer, *Canterbury Tales* *11
Chekhov, Anton, Stories12
Chiappusso, Jan, *Bach's World*
Chichester, Sir Francis, *Gipsy Moth Circles the World*
Chubb, Mary, *Nefertiti Lived Here*
Church, Peggy Pond, *The House at Otowi Bridge: The Story of Edith Warner and Los Alamos*
Cobbett, William, *Rural Rides* *
———, *A Year's Residence in America*

Coffin, Charles Monroe, John Donne[13]
Coffin, Robert P. Tristam, *Kennebec, Cradle of Americans*
————, *Selected Poems*
Coffin, Robert P. Tristam, and Alexander M. Witherspoon (eds.), *Seventeenth Century Prose and Poetry*
Coleridge, Samuel Taylor, *Biographia Literaria*
Coles, K. Adlard, *In Broken Water . . . Adventures of a Six-Tonner through Holland and among the Frisian and Danish Islands*
Colette, Sidonie Gabrielle, *Sept dialogues de bêtes* *
Collins, Wilkie, *The Moonstone*
Congreve, William, *The Way of the World*
Conrad[14]
Constantin-Weyer, Maurice, *Un homme se penche sur son passé*
Cook, James (ed. Christopher Lloyd), *The Voyages of Captain James Cook round the World*
Corneille, Pierre, *Le Cid*
Cottman, Evans W., *Out-Island Doctor*
Cousteau, Jacques-Yves, *The Silent World*
Cranach, Lucas, *Cranach*
Crawford, F. Marion, *A Roman Singer*
Crespelle, Jean Paul, *The Fauves*
Cuming, Fortescue, *Sketches of a Tour to the Western Country. . . .* [15]
Damrosch, Walter, *My Musical Life*
Dana, Richard Henry, *Two Years before the Mast*
Danielsson, Bengt, *From Raft to Raft*
Darling, F. Fraser, *Wild Country: A Highland Naturalist's Notes and Pictures*
Dart, Thurston, *The Interpretation of Music*
Darwin, Charles, *Charles Darwin's "Beagle" Diary*
————, *The Origin of Species*
————, *The Voyage of the Beagle*
Daudet, Alphonse, Contes[16]
————, *Tartarin de Tarascon*
David, Hans, and Arthur Mendel (eds.), *The Bach Reader: A Life of Johann Sebastian Bach in Letters and Documents*
de Bisschop, Eric, *Kaimiloa: d'Honolulu à Cannes par l'Australie et le Cap, à bord d'une double pirogue polynésienne*
DeCannes, L., Baudelaire[17]
de Charlevoix, Pierre-François-Xavier, *Journal of a Voyage to North America*
de Crèvecoeur, J. Hector St. John, *Letters from an American Farmer and Sketches of Eighteenth-Century America*
Defoe, Daniel, *Memoirs of a Cavalier, or, A Military Journal of the Wars in Germany and . . . England*
————, *Robinson Crusoe*
de Hartog, Jan, *Waters of the New World Houston to Nantucket*

Delacroix, Eugène (tr. Walter Pach), *The Journal of Eugène Delacroix* *
de Maupassant, Guy, *Boule de suif*
de Montaigne, Michel, *Essais*
————, *Montaigne par lui-même (Images et textes présentés par Francis Jeanson)*
————, *Tros Essais, I-39, II-1, III-2, expliqués par Georges Gougenheim et Pierre-Maxime Schuhl*
———— (ed. Donald M. Frame), *Selected Works*. French Masterworks Series.
de Montherlant, Henry, *Port-Royal*
de Montulé, Édouard (tr. Edward Seeber), *Travels in America, 1816–1817*
Denecke, Gerhard, *Eine Kindheit in Dresden*
de Nerval, Gérard, *Voyage en orient*
De Quincey, Thomas, *Confessions of an English Opium-Eater*
————, *Reminiscences of the English Lake Poets*
de Rouvroy, duc de Saint-Simon, Louis, *Mémoires sur le règne de Louis XIV. . . .*
de Tocqueville, Alexis (ed. R. Clyde Ford), *De Tocqueville's Voyage en Amérique*
de Vaca, Alvar Nuñez Cabeza, *The Journey of Alvar Nuñez Cabeza de Vaca*
de Voto, Bernard (ed.), *Journals of Lewis and Clark*
Dewey, John, *Art as Experience*
————, *A Common Faith*
Dickens, Charles, *Bleak House*
————, *Dombey and Son*
————, *Hard Times*
Diderot, Denis, *Diderot par lui-même: images et textes présentés par Charly Guyot*
————, *Oeuvres*
Dinesen, Isak, *Out of Africa*
————, *Seven Gothic Tales*
Doughty, Charles, *Travels in Arabia Deserta* *
Drake, Daniel, *Pioneer Life in Kentucky*
Drews, Wolfgang, *Gotthold Ephraim Lessing in Selbstzeugnissen und Bilddokumenten*
Du Maurier, George, *Trilby*
Duhamel, Georges, *Le combat contre les ombres; roman*
————, *Le Notaire du Havre*
————, *La nuit d'orage*
————, *Vue de la terre promise, roman*
Dumas, Alexandre, *Voyage en Russie*
Duthuit, Georges, *The Fauvist Painters*
Eckstein, Gustav, *Hokusai: Play in Fourteen Scenes*
Edwards, Tudor, *The Lion of Arles: A Portrait of Mistral and His Circle*
Eichendorff, Joseph, *Aus dem Leben eines Taugenichts*
Eifert, Virginia, *River World: Wildlife of the Mississippi*

Einstein, Albert, *The World as I See It*
Einstein, Alfred, *Essays on Music*
Elbin, Günther, *Holland ist eine Reise wert*
Eliot, George, *Adam Bede*
———, *Felix Holt, the Radical*
———, *Middlemarch*
———, *The Mill on the Floss*
Emerson, Ralph Waldo, *Essays*[18]
———, *Thoreau*[19]
——— (ed. Bliss Perry), *The Heart of Emerson's Journals*
Erasmus, Desiderius, *Colloquies* *[20]
———, *The Praise of Folly*
Euripides, *Medea*
Evelyn, John, *Diary*
Ewen, David, *Musical Vienna*
Falcon-Barker, Ted, *1600 Years under the Sea*
Fanby, Eric, *Delius as I Knew Him*
Fay, Amy, *Music-Study in Germany*
Fellows, Madrigals[21]
Fellows, Otis, and Norman Torrey (eds.), *The Age of Enlightenment: An Anthology of Eighteenth Century French Literature*
Ferrari, Enrique Lafuente (tr. James Emmons), *Velasquez: Biographical and Critical Study*
Fielding, Henry, *The History of Tom Jones, a Foundling*
Fischer-Dieskau, Dietrich, *Auf den Spuren der Schubert-Lieder: Werden, Wesen, Wirkung*
——— (tr. Kenneth S. Whitton), *Schubert's Songs, a Biographical Study*
Flores, Angel, *An Anthology of German Poetry from Hölderlin to Rilke in English Translation*
Fontane, Theodor, *Effi Briest*
———, *Irrungen, Wirrungen: Roman*[22]
———, *Stine: ein Roman*
———, *Unterm Birnbaum*
Fordham's Narrative[23]
Forester, C.S., *Mr. Midshipman Hornblower*
Forster, E.M, *The Celestial Omnibus*
———, *Howard's End*
———, *A Passage to India*
Foss, Hubert J., *The Heritage of Music: Essays*
France, Anatole, Contes choisis[24]
———, *Les dieux ont soif*
———, *Le livre de mon ami*
Franklin, Benjamin, *The Autobiography of Benjamin Franklin* *
Freeman, Mary Eleanor Wilkins, *A New England Nun, and Other Stories*
Fritsch, Charles T., *The Qumrán Community: Its History and Scrolls*

Froissart, Jean, *Les plus belles chroniques de Jean Froissart, 1346–1393*
Frost, Robert, *Complete Poems of Robert Frost*
Fry, Christopher, *The Dark Is Light Enough*
Fuchs, Rudolf Herman, *Rembrandt in Amsterdam*
Fuerst, Norbert, *Phases of Rilke*
Fuller, Margaret, *Memoirs of Margaret Fuller Ossoli*
Gaskell, Elizabeth Cleghorn, *Cranford*
Gauguin, Paul, *Paul Gauguin (1848–1903). Text by John Rewald*
Geiringer, Karl, *Brahms, His Life and Work*
———, *Johann Sebastian Bach: The Culmination of an Era*
Geissendoerfer, Theodore, and John W. Kurtz (eds.), *Deutsche Meisternovellen*
Georges-Michel, Michel, *From Renoir to Picasso: Artists I Have Known*
Gerbault, Alain, *The Fight of the "Firecrest"*
———, *In Quest of the Sun: The Journal of the "Firecrest"*
Gernet, Jacques, *Daily Life in China on the Eve of the Mongol Invasion, 1250–1276*
Gibbings, Robert, *Sweet Cork of Thee*
Gibbons, Euell, *Stalking the Wild Asparagus*
Gide, André, *Journal, 1939–1949: Souvenirs* *
———, *La porte étroite*
———, *Travels in the Congo*
Giono, Jean, *Jean le Bleu*
Gissing, George, *Private Papers of Henry Ryecroft*
Glueck, Nelson, *The River Jordan, Being an Illustrated Account of Earth's Most Storied River*
Godden, Jon and Rumer, *Two under the Indian Sun*
Gogol, Nikolai Vasilevich, *The Collected Tales and Plays*
Gotthelf, Jeremias, *Geld und Geist*
———, *Gotthelfs Werke, Uli*
———, *Uli der Knecht*
———, *Uli der Pächter*[25]
Gould, John, *Farmer Takes a Wife*
Govan, Ada Clapham, *Wings at My Window*
Grace, Harvey, *The Organ Works of Bach*
Graves, John, *Goodbye to a River, a Narrative*
Graves, Robert, *The Anger of Achilles: Homer's Iliad, Translated by Robert Graves*
———, *Good-bye to All That*
Grayson, David,[26] *Adventures in Contentment*[27]
Greeley, Horace, *An Overland Journey*
Green, Julien, *Moira*
Grenfell, Sir Wilfred Thomason, *Adrift on an Ice-Pan*
Grout, Donald, *A History of Western Music* *
Guéhenno, Jean, *Caliban et Prospero, suivi d'autres essais*

————, *Voyages, tournée américaine, tournée africaine*
Guillemard, Francis Henry Hill, *The Cruise of the Marchesa to Kamchatka and New Guinea*
Hakluyt, Richard, *Voyages of the Elizabethan Seamen to America*
Hall, Charles Francis, *Narrative of the Second Arctic Expedition*
Hall, Leonard, *Stars Upstream, Life along an Ozark River*
Hamilton, Edith, *The Greek Way*
Hammarskjold, Dag, *Markings*
Hannaway, Patti, *Winslow Homer in the Tropics*
Harding, Walter, *Thoreau: A Century of Criticism*
————, *A Thoreau Handbook*
Harding, Walter Roy, *Thoreau, Man of Concord*
Harrison, Max, *The Lieder of Brahms*
Hauptmann, Gerhart, *Der Biberpelz: eine Diebskomödie*
————, *Die versunkene Glocke*
————, *Die Weber, Schauspiel aus den vierziger Jahren*
Havighurst, Walter, *Land of the Long Horizons*
Hawthorne, Julian, *The Memoirs of Julian Hawthorne*
Hawthorne, Nathaniel, *The American Notebooks* *
————, *The English Notebooks*
————, *Our Old Home: A Series of English Sketches*
————, *Twice-Told Tales*
Hayter, Adrian, *The Long Voyage*
Hearn, Lafcadio, *The Japanese Letters of Lafcadio Hearn*
————, *The Life and Letters of Lafcadio Hearn*
———— (ed. Henry Goodman), *Selected Writings*
Heine, Heinrich, *Die Harzreise*
————, *Sammtliche Werke*
Hemingway, Ernest, *The Old Man and the Sea*
Hémon, Louis (ed. Hugo P. Thieme), *Maria Chapdelaine, récit du Canada français*
Hesse, Hermann, *Gerbersau*
————, *Siddhartha*
———— (eds. Jacobson and Ascher), *Zwei Erzählungen: Der Novalis, Der Zwerg*
Heuss, Theodor, *Von Ort zu Ort: Wanderungen mit Stift und Feder*
Heyerdahl, Thor, *Aku Aku, the Secret of Easter Island*
————, *Kon Tiki: Across the Pacific by Raft*
Hickey, Joseph J., *A Guide to Bird Watching*
Higginson, Thomas Wentworth, *Margaret Fuller Ossoli*
History of Chinese Art[28]
Hokusai[29]
Hollar, Wenceslaus, Hollar's Journey on the Rhine[30]
Holmes, Edward, *A Ramble among the Musicians of Germany* *
Homer, *The Odyssey, with an English Translation by A.T. Murray*

Hough, Henry Beetle, *Country Editor*
———, *Thoreau of Walden: The Man and His Eventful Life*
How to Know & Predict the Weather[31]
Howard, Sir Albert, *An Agricultural Testament*
Howells, William Dean, *Literary Friends and Acquaintance: A Personal Retrospect of American Authorship*
——— (ed. Don Cook), *The Rise of Silas Lapham: Text, . . . Criticism*
Hubbard, Frank,[32] *Three Centuries of Harpsichord Making*
Huc, Evariste Régis, *A Journey through the Chinese Empire*
——— (Abbé Huc), *High Road in Tartary . . . 1844–1846*
Hudson, William Henry, *Far Away and Long Ago: A History of My Early Life*
Hulton, Nika, *An Approach to Paul Klee*
Hunter, Louis C., *Steamboats on the Western Rivers* *
Huxley, Thomas[33]
Irving, Washington, *Astoria*
———, *A Tour of the Prairies*
James, Henry[34]
James, Henry, *The Aspern Papers*
———, *The Bostonians*
———, *Letters*[35]
———, *The Spoils of Poynton*
———, *Washington Square*
——— (ed. Morton Dauwen Zabel), *The Portable Henry James*
James, William, *The Letters of William James*
——— (ed. Henry James), *Talks to Teachers*[36]
Jaques, Florence Page, *Canoe Country*
Jarrell, Randall, *The Lost World*
———, *Poetry and the Age*
———, *A Sad Heart at the Supermarket: Essays and Fables*
Jefferies, Richard, *Field and Hedgerow*
———, *Nature Near London* *
Jefferson, Thomas, *The Life and Selected Writings of Thomas Jefferson*
Jewett, Frances Louise, and Clare L. McCausland, *The Plant Hunters*
Jewett, Sarah Orne, *Strangers and Wayfarers* *
[Jones], *Life and Adventure in the South Pacific. By a Roving Printer*
Jones, Gwyn, *The Norse Atlantic Saga . . . Norse Voyages of Discovery and Settlement. . . .*
Jougkind[37]
Jusserand, J.J., *English Wayfaring Life in the Middle Ages*
Kalidasa, *Sakuntala*[38]
Kalm, Pehr, *Peter Kalm's Travels in North America*
Kane, Elisha Kent, *The U.S. Grinnell Expedition in Search of Sir John Franklin*
Kästner, Erich, *Als ich ein kleiner Junge war*

Katz, Richard, *Des Beste von Richard Katz: Eine Auswahl aus seinem Werken zum 80*
King, Hyatt, *Mozart in Retrospect: Studies in Criticism and Bibliography*
Kojiro, Yuichiro, *Forms in Japan*
Krutch, Joseph Wood, *Henry David Thoreau*
Kurtz, John William (ed.), *Drei novellen. Storm: Der Schimmelreiter. Keller: Die drei gerechten Kammacher. Kleist: Michael Kohlhaas*
Lacretelle, Jacques, *Deux coeurs simples*
Lambert, Constant, *Music Ho! A Study of Music in Decline*
Landowska, Wanda, *Landowska on Music*
Langland, William, *The Vision of Piers Plowman*
Langley, Dorothy, *Fool's Mate: A Sonnet Sequence*
Lansing, Alfred, *Endurance: Shackleton's Incredible Voyage*
Lao-tzu (ed. Witter Bynner), *The Way of Life according to Lao-Tzu*
Lawrence, T.E., *Seven Pillars of Wisdom*
Lee, Sherman E., *Chinese Landscape Painting*
Le Fort, Gertrud, *Hälfte des Lebens: Erinnerungen*
Lehmann, Lotte, *Eighteen Song Cycles: Studies in Their Interpretation*
Leichtentritt, Hugo, *Music, History, and Ideas*
Leopold, Aldo, *A Sand County Almanac*
Lessing, Gotthold Ephraim, *Minna von Barnhelm*
Levey, Michael, *A Concise History of Painting, from Giotto to Cézanne*
Lewis and Clark[39]
Liberman, Alexander, *The Artist in His Studio*
Lindbergh, Anne Morrow, *Gift from the Sea*
Lindsay, Jack, *J.M.W. Turner: His Life and Work, a Critical Biography*
Lorenz, Konrad, *King Solomon's Ring: New Light on Animal Ways*
Loti, Pierre, *Mon frère Yves*
———, *Le roman d'un spahi*
Lu, Yu, *The Rapier of Lu, Patriot Poet of China*
Lucian of Samosata (ed. Lionel Casson), *Selected Satires of Lucian*
Lucretius, Epictetus, Marcus Aurelius[40]
Ludwig, Otto, *Zwischen Himmel und Erde*
Lueders, Edward G., *Carl Van Vechten and the Twenties*
Luhan, Mabel Dodge, *Winter in Taos*
Luther, Martin (ed. William Hazlitt), *The Table Talk of Martin Luther*
MacClintock, Carol, *The Solo Song*
Macken, Walter, *Rain on the Wind*
Mackenzie, Alexander, *Voyages from Montreal on the River St. Lawrence. . . .*
MacKenzie, Finlay, *Chinese Art*
Malory, Sir Thomas, *Le morte d'Arthur*
Malot, Hector, *Sans famille*
———, *Par terre et par mer*[41]
Malraux, André, *The Voices of Silence*

Manly, William Lewis, *Death Valley in '49*
Mann, Erika, *The Last Year of Thomas Mann*
Mann, Thomas, *Die Betrogene: Erzählung*
————, *Buddenbrooks*
————, *Doktor Faustus*
————, *Die Entstehung des Doktor Faustus*
————, *Tonio Kröger*
———— (tr. Richard and Clara Winston), *The Story of a Novel: The Genesis of Doctor Faustus*
Manry, Robert, *Tinkerbelle*
Marcuse, Ludwig, *Heinrich Heine in Selbstzeugnissen und Bilddokumenten*
Marix, Jeanne, *Les musiciens de la cour de Bourgogne au XVe siécle*
Martin, John Bartlow, *Call It North Country: The Story of Upper Michigan*
Martineau, Harriet, *Retrospect of Western Travel*[42]
Martini, Fritz, *Klassische Deutsche Dichtung*
Maurois, André, *Lélia, ou, La vie de George Sand*
————, *Voltaire* *
Maxwell, Gavin, *Ring of Bright Water*
May, Florence, *The Life of Johannes Brahms*[43]
Melville, Herman, *Typee* *
Menzel, Adolph, *Das Flötenkonzert Friederich des Grossen. Einführung von Paul Ortwin Rave*
Meredith, George, *Diana of the Crossways*
————, *The Egoist*[44]
Meynell, Esther, *The Little Chronicle of Magdalena Bach*[45]
Miegel, Agnes, *Heimkehr. Erzählungen*
Molière, *L'avare*
————, *La critique de l'école des femmes*
————, *L'école des femmes*
————, *Le misanthrope*
————, *Tartuffe*
Montesquieu, *Lettres persanes*
Moore, George, *Evelyn Innes*
Moore, Gerald, *Singer and Accompanist: The Performance of Fifty Songs*
Moorehead, Alan, *The Fatal Impact: An Account of the Invasion of the South Pacific, 1767–1840*
Moorman, Mary Trevelyan, *William Wordsworth, a Biography*
Mount, Charles Merrill, *Monet, a Biography*
Mowat, Farley, *Never Cry Wolf*
Muir, John, *The Wilderness World of John Muir*
Musäus, Johann, *Volksmärchen der Deutschen*
Myrdal, Jan, *Chinese Journey*
Nansen, Fridtjof, *Farthest North: . . . Voyage of Exploration of the Ship "Fram" 1893–1896. . . .*
Niese, Charlotte, *Aus dänischer Zeit*

Noyes, Alfred, *Horace: A Portrait*
Nuttall, Thomas, *A Journal of Travels into the Arkansas Territory during the Year 1819*
Ogburn, Charlton, *The Winter Beach* *
Okudaira, Hideo, *Emaki: Japanese Picture Scrolls*
Olivier, Fernande, *Picasso et ses amis*
Olson, Sigurd, *The Lonely Land*
Ortega y Gasset, José, *The Dehumanization of Art*
Orwell, George, *Animal Farm*
———— (eds. Sonia Orwell and Ian Angus), *The Collected Essays, Journalism, and Letters of George Orwell.* Vol. 1, *An Age Like This (1920–1940).* Vol. 2, *My Country, Right or Left (1940–1943).* Vol. 3, *As I Please (1943–1945).*
Osborn, Fairfield, *Our Plundered Planet*
O'Sullivan, Maurice, *Twenty Years a-Growing*
Oxford Book of American Verse
Oxford Book of German Verse
Palmer, George Herbert, *The Odyssey of Homer, Books I-XII. The Text, and an English Version in Rhythmic Prose by George Herbert Palmer*
Park, Mungo, *Voyage dans l'intérieur de l'Afrique faite en 1795*[46]
Parrington, Vernon Louis, *Main Currents in American Thought*
Parrish, Carl (ed.), *Masterpieces of Music before 1750*
Parry, Charles Hubert H., *The Evolution of the Art of Music*
Partch, Harry, *Genesis of a Music: An Account of a Creative Work. . . .*
Paton, Alan, *Cry, the Beloved Country*
Patton, Frances Gray, *Good Morning, Miss Dove*
Peattie, Donald Culross, *A Natural History of Trees of Eastern and Central North America*
———— (ed.), *Audubon's America*
Pennell, Joseph, *The Adventures of an Illustrator*
Percy, William Alexander, *Lanterns on the Levee: Recollections of a Planter's Son*
Perrault, Charles, *Contes*[47]
Perruchot, Henri, *Cézanne*
Perry, Richard, *The Jeannette . . . Voyages and Expeditions to the North Polar Regions*
Pfeiffer, Ida, *Journey to Iceland*
Pidgeon, Harry, *Around the World Single-handed: The Cruise of the "Islander"*
Pike, Zebulon M., *The Southwestern Expedition of Zebulon M. Pike*
Piston, Walter, *Harmony*
Poncins, Gontran de Montaigne, *From a Chinese City*
Prescott, William Hickling, *Conquest of Mexico*, vols. 1 and 2
————, *History of the Conquest of Peru*
Proust, Marcel, *À la recherche du temps perdu.*[48] Vols. III–V, *À l'ombre des*

jeunes filles en fleur. Vols. VI–VIII, *Le côte de Guermantes.* Vol. IX, *Sodome et Gomorrhe.*[49]
Pumpelly, Raphael, *Travels and Adventures of Raphael Pumpelly, Mining Engineer, Geologist, Archaeologist and Explorer*
Ramsey, Carolyn, *Cajuns on the Bayous*
Rawlings, Marjorie Kinnan, *Cross Creek*
———, *The Sojourner*
Reischauer, Edwin O., *Ennin's Travels in T'ang China*
Renoir, Jean, *Renoir, My Father*
Rewald, John, *Histoire de l'Impressionnisme*
Rexroth, Kenneth, *Natural Numbers: New and Selected Poems*
———, *One Hundred Poems from the Chinese*
Richardson, Samuel, *Clarissa*
Richardson, Sir John, *Arctic Searching Expedition: A Journal of a Boat-voyage . . . in Search of . . . Sir John Franklin*
Richardson, Wyman, *The House on Nauset Marsh*
Richter, Conrad, *The Trees*
Riesenberg, Felix, *Cape Horn*
Rilke[50]
Rilke, Rainer Maria, *Duino Elegies*
———, *Das Stunden-Buch: enthaltend die drei Bucher. Vom moenchischen Leben, Von der Pilgerschaft, Von der Armuth und vom Tode*
——— (tr. C.F. MacIntyre), *Das Marienleben*
——— (tr. Greene and Norton), *Letters of Rainer Maria Rilke*
Robinson, William Albert, *Deep Water and Shoal*
———, *To the Great Southern Sea*
Roethke, Theodore, *The Far Field*
Roger-Marx, Claude, *Les impressionnistes*
Romains, Jules, *Bertrand de Ganges*
———, *Les hommes de bonne volonté*[51]
———, *Le moulin et l'hospice*
roman de la rose, le[52]
Rosegger, Peter, *Das Holzknechthaus*
———, *Das Holzknechthaus, eine Waldgeschichte*
———, *Der Lex von Gutenhag*
Rosen, Charles, *The Classical Style: Haydn, Mozart, Beethoven*
Ross, Andy, *Log*[53]
Rostand, Edmond, *La Princesse lointaine*
Rothenstein, Sir William, *Men and Memories: A History of the Arts 1872–1922* *
Rouault, Catalog of Modern Museum Exhibition[54]
Rousseau, Jean-Jacques, *Confessions*
———, *Discours sur les sciences et les arts. Deux lettres à Malesherbes. Les rêveries du promeneur solitaire* *
———, *Émile*

————, *Les pages immortelles de J.-J. Rousseau, choisies et expliquées par Romain Rolland*

Rowlands, John J. (illus. Henry B. Kane), *Cache Lake Country: Life in the North Woods*

Ruskin, John, *Diaries,* vol. 1, *1835–1847*

Sachs, Curt, *Rhythm and Tempo: A Study in Music History*

Saminsky, Lazare, *Living Music of the Americas*

Sand, George, *Les maîtres sonneurs*

————, *La mare au diable* *

————, *Marianne*

————, *La petite Fadette*

Santayana, George, *Persons and Places*

Sauer, Carl Ortwin, *Sixteenth Century North America. . . .*

Schendler, Sylvan, *Eakins*

Schildt, Göran, *In the Wake of Ulysses*

————, *In the Wake of a Wish*

Schiller, Friedrich, *Die Jungfrau von Orleans*

————, *Wilhelm Tell*

Schoolcraft, Henry Rowe[55]

————, *Travels through the Northwestern Regions of the United States*

Schrade, Leo, *Bach: The Conflict between the Sacred and the Secular*

Schweitzer, Albert, *Goethe, Four Studies*

————, *J.S. Bach*

————, *On the Edge of the Primeval Forest*

————, *The Philosophy of Civilization*

————, *The Quest of the Historical Jesus*

———— (tr. C.T. Campion), *Out of My Life and Thought: An Autobiography*

Scott[56]

Scott, Robert Falcon, *The Voyage of the "Discovery,"* vols. I and II

Scott, Sir Walter, *Rob Roy*

Shakespeare, William, *Antony and Cleopatra*

————, *As You Like It*

————, historical plays

————, *King Lear*

————, *Much Ado About Nothing* *

Shaw, Bernard, *London Music in 1888–1889. . . .*

Sherman, Paul (ed.), *Thoreau*[57]

Shikibu, Murasaki, *The Tale of Genji*[58]

Singer, Isaac Bashevis, *A Day of Pleasure: Stories of a Boy Growing up in Warsaw*

Sitwell, Sacheverell, *The Bridge of the Brocade Sash: Travels and Observations in Japan*

————, *Southern Baroque Art*

Slocum, Joshua, *Sailing Alone around the World*

Smeeton, Miles, *Once Is Enough*[59]

Smith, Olga Wright, *Gold on the Desert*
Smith, Preserved, *Erasmus: A Study of His Life, Ideals and Place in History*
Smollett, Tobias, *The Expedition of Humphry Clinker*
Snow, C.P., *The Affair*
Sophocles, *Electra*
——— (tr. Bernard Knox), *Oedipus the King*
Spalding, Albert, *Rise to Follow, an Autobiography*
Spears, Raymond, *The Cabin Boat Primer . . . on the Construction,
    Navigation and Use of House-Boats. . . .*
Spink, Ian, *English Song, Dowland to Purcell*
Spitta, Phillipp, *Johann Sebastian Bach*
Spohr, Louis, *Autobiography*
Stefansson, Vilhjalmur (ed.), *Great Adventures and Explorations*
Stephens, James, *The Crock of Gold*
Stephens, John Lloyd, *Incidents of Travel in Yucatan*
Stevens, Halsey, *The Life and Music of Béla Bartók*
Stevenson, Robert Louis, *The Amateur Emigrant*
———, *Essays of Travel and in the Art of Writing*
———, *Inland Voyage*
———, *The Letters of Robert Louis Stevenson* *
———, *Memories and Portraits*
———, *The Master of Ballantrae*
———, *Prince Otto: A Romance*
———, *Travels with a Donkey*
Stifter[60]
Still, James, *River of Earth*
Storer, John H., *Web of Life, a First Book of Ecology*
Storm, Theodor, *Auf der Universität*
———, *Immensee*
———, *Im Saal*
———, *Marthe und ihre Uhr*[61]
Stowe, Leland, *Crusoe of Lonesome Lake*
Stravinsky, Igor, and Robert Craft, *Conversations with Igor Stravinsky*
Stuiveling, Garmt, *A Sampling of Dutch Literature*
Sullivan, J.W.N., *Beethoven: His Spiritual Development*
Sutton, Denys, *Triumphant Satyr: The World of Auguste Rodin*
Suzuki, Shin'ichi, *Nurtured by Love: A New Approach to Education*
Swann, Peter C., *Art of China, Korea, and Japan*
Swift, Jonathan, *Gulliver's Travels*
Swinburne, Algernon Charles[62]
Szigeti, Joseph, *With Strings Attached: Reminiscences and Reflections*
Tambs, Erling, *The Cruise of the Teddy*
Tapié, Victor, *Chateaubriand par lui-même*
Taubman, Hyman Howard, *Music on My Beat: An Intimate Volume of
    Shop Talk*

Terry, Charles Sanford, *Bach, a Biography*
————, *Bach's Orchestra*
————, *The Music of Bach, an Introduction*
Thackeray, William Makepeace, *Henry Esmond*
Tharp, Louise Hall, *Saint-Gaudens and the Gilded Era*
Thayer, Alexander Wheelock, *Life of Beethoven*[63]
Thayer, James Bradley, *A Western Journey with Mr. Emerson*
Thomas, David, *Travels Through the Western Country in the Summer of 1816*
Thoreau, Henry David, *Autumn* *
————, *Cape Cod*
————, *Familiar Letters*
————, *The Maine Woods*
————, *Miscellanies*
————, *Walden*
————, *A Yankee in Canada*
———— (ed. Bradford Torrey), *The Writings of Henry David Thoreau*[64]
———— (ed. Laurence Stapleton), *A Writer's Journal*
Tillier, Claude, *Mon Oncle Benjamin*
Tolman, Francis Wyland, *Mosquitobush: Stories and Prints by Francis W. Tolman*[65]
Tolman, Newton F., *North of Monadnock*
Tolstoy, Leo, *War and Peace*
————, *What Is Art?*
————, *What Men Live by*
Tomlinson, H.M., *The Sea and the Jungle*
Torrington, John Byng, *The Torrington Diaries . . . Tours through England and Wales . . . 1781–1794*
Tovey[66]
Tovey, *Essays*[67]
Trollope, Mrs.[68]
Turgenev, Ivan, *A House of Gentlefolk*
————, *A Hunter's Sketches*
————, *Smoke*
Turner, J., *Sketches*[69]
Turner, John Gage, *Rain, Steam, and Speed*
Valentin, Erich, *Beethoven: Eine Bildbiographie*
Vallas, Léon (tr. Maire and Grace O'Brien), *Claude Debussy: His Life and Works*
van Gogh, Vincent, *Letters to an Artist: From Vincent van Gogh to Anton ridder van Rappard*
————, *Van Gogh: A Self-Portrait: Letters Revealing His Life as a Painter, Selected by W.H. Auden*
———— (ed. Irving Stone), *Dear Theo: The Autobiography of Vincent van Gogh*
van Rijn, Rembrandt, *Drawings of Rembrandt . . . [text by] Seymour Slive*

Vivas, Eliseo, and Murray Krieger (eds.), *The Problems of Aesthetics, a Book of Readings*
Voltaire, *Candide*
———, *Romans et contes*
von Goethe, Johann Wolfgang, *Aus Meinem Leben, Dichtung und Wahrheit*[70]
———, *Egmont*
———, *Faust*
———, *Das Märchen*
———, Poems[71]
———, *Die Wahlverwandschaften*
——— (ed. Frederick Ungar), *Goethe's World View*
von Hofmannsthal, Hugo[72]
———, *Deutsche Erzähler*
Voyages and Travels Mainly during the 16th and 17th Centuries. English Garner Series.
Voyages de Dixon[73]
Voyageuses au XIXe siècle, les[74]
Waggoner, Madeline Sadler, *The Long Haul West: The Great Canal Era, 1817–1850*
Waley, Arthur, Chinese Poems[75]
———, *The No Plays of Japan*
Walmsley, Lewis C., and Dorothy Walmsley, *Wang Wei, the Painter-Poet*
Walsh, Stephen, *The Lieder of Schumann*
Warner, Langdon, *The Enduring Art of Japan*
Warner, William, *Beautiful Swimmers: Watermen, Crabs, and the Chesapeake Bay*
Watkins, Anthony, *The Sea My Hunting Ground*
Waugh, Alec, *A Family of Islands: A History of the West Indies from 1492 to 1898.* . . .
Waugh, Evelyn, *Tactical Exercise*
———, *When the Going Was Good*
Welles, C.M., *Three Years Wanderings of a Connecticut Yankee . . . in South America, Africa, Australia, and California. . . . Also, a . . . Voyage around the World. . . .*
Westrup, J.A., *Purcell*
Wharton, Edith, *A Backward Glance*
White, Gilbert, *The Natural History of Selborne*
Whitman, Cedric Hubbell, *Homer and the Heroic Tradition*
Whitman, Walt, *Specimen Days*
Wiechert, Ernst Emil, *An die deutsche Jugend: Vier Raden*
———, *Das einfache Leben*
———, *Es geht ein Pflüger übers Land.* . . .
———, *Hirtennovelle*
———, *Jahre und Zeiten, Erinnerungen*
———, *Die Magd des Jürgen Doskocil*

————, *Das Mensch und sein Werk, eine Anthologie*
————, *Der silberne Wagen*
Wilde, Oscar, *Essays*
Wilder, Laura Ingalls, *The Long Winter*
Williams, Iolo Aneurin, *Early English Watercolours.* . . .
Woolf, Virginia, *Flush: A Biography*
———— (ed. Nigel Nicolson), *Letters of Virginia Woolf*
———— (ed. Quentin Bell), *The Diary of Virginia Woolf*
Woolman, John, *The Journal of John Woolman*
Yeats, William Butler, *Autobiography*
————, *The Collected Poems of W. B. Yeats*
————, *Irish Fairy and Folk Tales*
Young, Arthur, *Travels in France during the Years 1787, 1788 and 1789*
Young, Arthur Milton, *Troy and Her Legend*
Zola, Emile, *Germinal*

Notes to "Books Harlan and I Have Read Together"

*— Indicates a work appearing on the list more than once over a period of
  years.

1. AH's note: "a Skira book. A companion to the Chinese painting book
   we just finished reading."
2. Possibly Richard Walter, *Anson's Voyage round the World.*
3. Probably Robert John Goldwater, *Artists on Art: From the XIV to the
   XX Century.*
4. Several volumes in the Cincinnati Public Library are possible, including
   Rachel and Eleanor Holmes (tr.), *Memoirs of Hector Berlioz from 1803
   to 1865.* . . .
5. Unverified.
6. Binyon's *Painting in the Far East* is probably meant.
7. AH's note: "1879–80."
8. Unverified.
9. Possibly Berthold Litzmann (ed.), *Letters of Clara Schumann and
   Johannes Brahms, 1853–1896,* 2 vols.
10. AH's note: "(Chinese novels) v. 1."
11. AH's note: "(except last, prose tale)."
12. Possibly a 1932 collection, ed. Robert N. Linscott, *The Stories of Anton
    Chekhov*; or 1928, tr. Constance Garnett, *Short Stories.* AH spelled the
    name "Tchekov."
13. Probably *John Donne and the New Philosophy.*
14. No further information listed.
15. AH's note: ". . .1807–1809 being vol. IV of 'Early Western Travels:
    1748–1846' ed. by R. G. Thwaites."
16. Several collections are possible.

17. Unverified.
18. There is no indication whether series 1, series 2, or both are meant.
19. Essay.
20. AH's note: "(a selection)."
21. Unverified.
22. AH's note reads, "Werke, 'Irrungen, Wirrungen.'" "Werke" is probably *Werke in drei Bänden. Hrsg. von Kurt Schreinert.*
23. Possibly Elias Pym Fordham, *Personal Narrative of Travels in Virginia, Maryland, Pennsylvania, Ohio, Indiana, Kentucky.* . . .
24. Unverified.
25. Unverified.
26. Pseudonym of Ray Stannard Baker.
27. Book I of *Adventures of David Grayson.*
28. No further information listed.
29. No further information listed. Probably Charles S. Terry, *Hokusai's 36 Views of Mt. Fuji.*
30. Unverified.
31. Unverified.
32. Son of Harlan Hubbard's brother Frank.
33. No further information listed.
34. No further information listed. Possibly Henry James, *Henry James.*
35. Possibly Percy Lubbock's 1970 *The Letters of Henry James*, or Leon Edel's 1955 *Selected Letters.*
36. Probably *Talks to Teachers on Psychology and to Students on Some of Life's Ideals.*
37. No further information listed.
38. AH's note: "(in World Drama)," probably Barrett Harper Clark (ed.), *World Drama: An Anthology.*
39. Possibly a rereading of the DeVoto edition of the journals.
40. Unverified.
41. Unverified.
42. AH's note: "1838."
43. AH's note: "(intro)."
44. Either Meredith, *The Egoist: A Comedy in Narrative*, or a volume of annotated criticism by Robert M. Adams.
45. Read on their Licking River trip, May 1942. The first book on Anna's reading list.
46. AH's note: "v. 1 & v. 2."
47. Probably *Les contes de Ch. Perrault. Précédés d'une préface par P. L. Jacob.*
48. AH's note: "À la recherche du temps perdu vol 1. Du côté de chez Swann vol 2."
49. *Sodome et Gomorrhe* comprises vols. IX and X.
50. No further information listed.
51. AH's note: "XVIII, La douceur de la vie."

52. Many translations and commentaries are possible.
53. Possibly the log of AH's mother's brother Andy Ross, born 1883 in the Netherlands.
54. Unverified.
55. No further information listed.
56. Possibly Robert Falcon Scott, *The Voyage of the Discovery.*
57. Unverified. AH's note: "(Twentieth Century Views) This includes the poem 'Letter from a Distant Land' by Philip Booth."
58. Near the end of his life, HH told his friend Bob Canida that he and Anna had reread this book often (interview, Bob Canida).
59. An account of a voyage from Sydney to Valparaiso in a ketch.
60. Adalbert Stifter is meant. Probably *Stifters Werke: in zwei Bänden.*
61. Unverified.
62. AH's entry reads, "Swinburne's poems—selections." Possibly Gosse and Wise (eds.), *Selections from A.C. Swinburne.*
63. AH's note: "(Krehbul [?], ed.)"
64. AH's note: "I 1837-1846."
65. AH listed the subtitle as "Yankee Prints and Stories."
66. No further information listed. Probably Sir Donald Francis Tovey.
67. Probably Sir Donald Francis Tovey, *Essays and Lecture on Music.*
68. No further information listed. The author meant is Frances Trollope (1780–1863). Possibly AH meant *Domestic Manners of the Americans,* based on Mrs. Trollope's experiences living in Cincinnati.
69. Probably J.M.W. Turner, *The Sketches of Turner, R.A., 1802–20.*
70. AH's note: "and simultaneously, the English trans. by John Oxenford."
71. Probably *Goethe's Poems,* ed. Charles Harris.
72. No further information listed. Many works and collections are possible.
73. Unverified.
74. Unverified.
75. Possibly *Chinese Poems Selected from 170 Chinese Poems.*

Life in a Shantyboat

❧

Anna Hubbard
Milton, Kentucky

A former librarian, married to an artist and author, tells of quiet days on the Ohio and the Mississippi Rivers

There is ice on the water buckets this morning. A piercing cold gale from the west roars through the treetops above our hillside cabin and makes formidable waves out there on the river. Inside the cabin we are snug and warm with a wood fire blazing on the hearth and the sun shining in through the large windows. A rough day but with an exhilaration in it that reminds me of the many tempestuous days Harlan and I experienced when we were living on the river in our shantyboat. How such a wind as this would toss our little boat about!

The whole shantyboat adventure is fresh in my mind this morning because just last night Harlan was recounting it to the Women's Faculty Club of Hanover College, our neighbors a few miles upriver on the Indiana side. It was the publication of Harlan's book, *Shantyboat,* which had prompted their inviting him to speak to their club.

I was surprised to see these women, whose interests are so largely intellectual, listening with eager attention while Harlan told them how we built our boat on the Kentucky shore of the Ohio River and in the course of five years drifted down the Ohio and Mississippi Rivers from Cincinnati to New Orleans, stopping each summer in some remote country place to make a garden and fish and get acquainted with the farmers who lived near by. As I expected, they were interested in hearing about the paintings Harlan made while we were on the trip, since they had seen many of the oils and watercolor sketches in the exhibition of his work at Hanover College.

But their greatest concern was with my part of the shantyboat life and they crowded round asking me questions. They were frankly puzzled at my leaving the conventional life of a large city, Cincinnati—where I lived in a modern apartment, was a librarian in the Fine Arts Department of the Public Library, enjoyed attending symphony concerts and plays, and associated constantly with many friends interested in these things—putting all this aside to go and live on a shantyboat. As if there were necessarily some wide, unbridgeable gulf separating the two. There was not, of course, because it was our own boat we had built ourselves, it was our own life we had chosen to live in this comparatively simple, almost primitive way, and we brought to it every resource we had.

Far from leaving anything behind, we took with us all that was most worth-while out of our previous living. On the boat Harlan could paint the river in all its moods and in every season as he never had been able to do before. On the boat, as everywhere we go, Harlan kept his journal, and the log of the trip was the firsthand material he drew on for his book, *Shantyboat*. We had our music aboard the boat, Harlan's violin and viola and my 'cello, and there was time for playing together and with other music lovers we met along the way. We took with us a carefully chosen library of the most worth-while books, and these we enjoyed to the full, reading them aloud in the quiet evenings by the fire. If we wanted some special entertainment for any occasion, we invented something appropriate—I remember the little play Harlan wrote and read as his contribution to one of our Halloween celebrations.

Nor were we cut off from our friends. Many of them traveled long distances to visit us aboard the boat. And it seemed to us that we had the best part of our distant friends in the letters they wrote to us, that we came nearer an understanding of their ideas and their problems than we had in many years of personal association, with conversation so often confined to the most trivial matters.

All the way down the rivers we kept making new friends, most interesting people, fishermen, hunters, rivermen, farmers, all sorts. "Did you meet any people like yourselves, painters and musicians, living on boats?" one of the Hanover College faculty women asked me. No, we didn't. The musicians we met were living on shore in town houses.

Library Visits

The librarians, too, were to be found at our brief city stops, for of course we visited every library along the way. I was not surprised that the librarians took an interest in our voyage; I think there must be something of an adventurous spirit in any good librarian. They must have recognized, even before we did, that here was the stuff books are made of.

"Weren't you afraid when your husband sometimes left you alone on the boat?" Mercy, no! After a few years of living afloat, I no longer thought of our river life as an adventure or even anything unusual; it had become the normal thing for me. That tiny cabin was my home, after all. I rather welcomed the times when Harlan and the dogs went off for a long tramp ashore. I could concentrate on some letter writing. Or bake something special as a surprise. Or I could spread my sewing all over the floor.

I had sewing and mending to do, just as any homemaker anywhere has. Knitting wool socks for us both was another of my domestic occupations. Making the fish nets, dip nets, minnow dips, and the big hoop nets, while not as domestic, perhaps, also fell to my lot.

Naturally many of the questions asked me were about the details of keeping house aboard the boat. "How did you keep warm?" We were wonderfully cozy with a driftwood fire in the open fireplace in [one] corner of the cabin and a fire in the little cookstove in the opposite corner. "Wasn't the floor cold?" Not particularly. No wind could blow under the boat. The river under us was never as cold as the winter air. And, besides, the cabin floor was some nine inches above the bottom of the boat. The women were intrigued with our storing jars of canned food in the space between the floor and bottom, the floor being made in three sections that could be raised like hatches. Since nothing ever froze there, the hold was also an ideal place for storing the potatoes, turnips, parsnips, even sweet potatoes. In the hot summer, the dark hold was the coldest place on the boat and I used a special section of it as my refrigerator. The way we used every possible corner of the boat for storage appealed to the women.

It was important to have everything in the cabin fastened in place securely so no damage would be done when the boat rocked in the waves. When a section of the floor was raised, it was held up firmly by a wooden hook. This same hook automatically caught the oven door when I opened it, and held it open. A spring catch similarly held the lid of the drain open. A loop of leather on the wall slipped over a nail inside the lid of the woodbox to hold it up. The table that hooked to the wall under the window had a spike on the leg which fit into a corresponding tiny hole in the floor. A cleat held the broom from swinging on its nail. The lamps were safe in sturdy wall brackets. The string of red peppers I had hanging on the door of one of the "kitchen" cupboards was nailed in place at the bottom as well as the top.

"What did you have to eat when you couldn't go to a grocery store for weeks at a time?" We had the best of food. In the summer, fresh vegetables grown in our own riverbank gardens, wild fruits in abundance, fish freshly caught, and whatever else the neighborhood farms could supply. In the winter, our own canned fruits and vegetables and canned and smoked fish, nuts we had gathered, honey from our own bees we had with us on the boat, maple syrup we boiled down ourselves, and always, our own homemade bread.

These questions were far from being impertinent, because they apply equally to the life we are now living in the little house Harlan has built on the wooded hillside overlooking Payne's Landing on the Ohio. Here, as on the boat, Harlan grinds, in his hand gristmill, the wheat and soybeans and corn to make flour for our daily bread. Here we garden and fish, and gather wild greens.

In the summer we live almost entirely out of doors. We cook on an outdoor fireplace and eat our meals out in a shady spot from which we can watch the river. We wash clothes on the riverbank, rinsing them in the river. I say "we" because Harlan likes to have a hand in these things. We swim every day. In the evening I go out on the river with Harlan to bait up the trot line.

"You have a lot of fun, don't you?" was hardly a question. It was rather the conclusion of many of the women.

Why do we live as we do? In this remote hollow we have the peace of the quiet countryside, the joy of living close to the birds and to all growing things, the freedom of the out of doors. Our dogs, too, enjoy a good run over the hills. This beautiful little valley is as primitive as the wildest shores we touched at in our long shantyboat voyage. Yet, with a little effort, a mile climb up the steep, rocky path to the ridge or a row across the river, we are within easy reach of friends and neighbors and roads leading anywhere. Our farmer neighbors here in Trimble County, Kentucky, are the best of friends and we enjoy all our associations with them as well as the stimulating contacts with the college people.

This is a place in which Harlan can live as he needs to live in order to do his best work. Resting a moment from his wood chopping, or hoeing, looking up to the hills and the sky, he finds inspiration for his painting. Here he has time to paint, we have time to do whatever we feel worth doing.

It is no small thing for me to realize I have a part, though an indirect and intangible one, in Harlan's work. There is deep satisfaction for me in making the kind of home where we can live the same casual and spontaneous life we enjoyed in the shantyboat. We both find it richly rewarding.

And always, now as well as when we lived on the boat, there is the river we love.

Anna's Recipes

On February 17, 1947, the Hubbards completed their first winter of drifting down the Ohio River in the shantyboat and tied up at the spot where they would stay through November—Payne Hollow, Trimble County, Kentucky. They planted a garden, foraged for greens and wild fruit, and set out a trotline, and the local people came with farm produce to barter for fish.

On May 24 Anna began keeping a journal of menus and recipes sprinkled with narrative about visitors and activities. This is a minimally edited transcription of the original journal in the University of Louisville Archives, Harlan and Anna Hubbard Papers, box 18, folder 12. Some recipes of Anna's from other sources have been included at the end. The abbreviation T. stands for tablespoon; t., for teaspoon.

In this journal Anna made four consecutive entries in May and one in September 1947, at Payne Hollow; six scattered entries at Bizzle's Bluff on the Cumberland River in 1948; and just one entry, the last, at Bisland Bayou on the Mississippi River near Natchez in July 1949. Anna may have begun keeping the journal at Harlan's suggestion; the sparseness and dwindling of the entries suggest that it didn't capture her interest. But what she wrote captures a reader's interest—for instance, Skipper's first groundhog catch, the visit from Anna's sister Nella Mae and their mother, and Harlan's rejecting the cookies he said tasted as if they'd been bought in a health food store.

Payne Hollow

May 24, 1947

"Good dinner, Annie," says Harlan. And so it was. Eaten out on the deck, too: bacon and eggs, turnip greens, spoon bread, apple-celery salad, and tea. The bacon was country bacon from a slab Owen

Hammond had brought us as a thank-you for a generous mess of fish—not that Owen needs to thank us; we are indebted to him for letting us tie up here and make our garden on his land. The eggs were fresh country eggs, some of the three dozen the Boldery boy brought us, also in exchange for fish; he came rowing that ungainly old hulk of a johnboat down along the shore from Trout Bottom—and Wilmer Fresh had come with him—for fish, too, of course. No, it was his brother-in-law who came with him—Wilmer came in the same johnboat the next day, with Powell for a passenger—Powell giving us the squirrel he had shot on the way. Well, that's the way it is; they all come with their various offerings, to get fish. We like to have them come.

The spoon bread deserves special comment, as it was the first time I'd made any. As usual, I didn't quite follow the recipe—I made the mush with water instead of milk. The corn I used was the coarse corn meal that is left in the sifter after the fine sifts through: 3/4 cup coarse corn meal, made into thick mush by cooking it with 1–1/2 cups water, salted as for cereal. This mush mixed with 2 eggs well beaten and 1 teaspoon baking powder. The batter poured into the larger Pyrex baking dish, which had 2 tablespoons of sizzling hot bacon fat in it. Baked in a hot oven until it was light brown and drew away from the sides of the dish—served with a spoon from the Pyrex dish.

The turnip greens were from our garden—Harlan has been thinning out up there. We've been feasting on spinach and green salads. The first lettuce from our garden was Sunday April 27, when the Dunlaps and Lassie[1] had dinner with us—then it was background for tomato salad (our own canned tomatoes) with cottage cheese (our own make, from the skim milk Harlan gets up at the Marshalls' on the ridge), and mixed with the Marshalls' thick cream with dressing made of mayonnaise, cream, dried sweet basil; and the whole salad sprinkled with walnut meats. We have been having big green salads and will have another for supper tonight—lettuce, spinach, beets (the little plants Harlan thins out, tops and roots), carrots ditto, with ground nuts (leftover boiled ones, cut up) and toasted sunflower seeds, a little sweet pickle and pickle juice, lemon juice, and salad oil. Sometimes we have a hard-boiled egg to garnish this salad; sometimes cheese or cold beef cut up in it.

Apple-celery salad with the last of the hickory nuts we gathered at Brent last fall—when we went nutting one Sunday with George and Elisabeth [Potts], picnicking on the way. We gathered some two bushel of hickory nuts, and about _____ [blank not filled in] of black walnuts, our whole winter's supply.

May 25, 1947

Breakfast: cooked ground wheat that had been toasted previously in the corn popper over coals in the fireplace: 1 cup ground wheat mixed with 1/2 cup cold water, added to 1-1/2 cups boiling salted water. A little steaming over the bottom of the double boiler, after the cereal is almost cooked, thickens it perfectly without danger of burning; also makes the cereal perfectly tender. Served with brown sugar and condensed milk, and "sticky" raisins.

Fruit and cooked cereal has come to be our standard breakfast—but there are so many variations to this simple combination. Our fruit this morning was the last of the grapefruit we had purchased in Madison on our trip to town a week ago. Halved, the core removed, the little well filled with maple syrup. Harlan made _____quarts of most delicious thick maple syrup this spring: He tapped _____ trees [blanks not filled in] in a little grove on the steep wooded hillside just up the river from here and boiled each boilerful of sap down to about a quart of syrup. We used the syrup lavishly during the run, but put some away in canning jars. Delicious on pancakes, on hot corn bread, on rice cakes, on cereal; I made "pecan" rolls using maple syrup and walnuts in the bottom of buttered muffin pans—three 1–inch biscuits in each muffin cup. We also had maple frosting on our nut cake for our fourth anniversary celebration April 20.

Dinner: fish, mashed potatoes, spinach, stewed tomatoes, pear salad, and wheat nut bread and tea. Also fresh milk. The fish—two catfish Harlan had made into four steaks, dipped in fine cornmeal, fried in ham fat. The spinach—from the garden—steamed, and seasoned only with salt and butter today.

We like sweet basil as seasoning in tomatoes—the sweet basil now is dried, from last year's garden. We also like our stewed tomatoes thickened with bread crumbs, especially whole wheat bread—of our own baking. The tomatoes, cold packed from last year's garden, of course.

The pears too are those we canned last fall, served on lettuce leaves, so fresh now, with a dressing of mayonnaise and quite a lot of lemon juice, and sugar; the whole salad garnished generously with chopped walnuts. Cottage cheese adds a nice touch to this salad, when we have some.

This wheat nut bread was a Wheatsworth recipe—a quick bread made with sour milk—still moist after three days—and the flavor seems to improve with age.

The fresh milk was extra, as Wilmer and the young Marshall boy came by boat just before dinner, bringing us a gallon and a half of fresh milk. This time Harlan had no extra fish for them, as the river is rising and he has taken in his line for the present.

Supper: cream of spinach soup, lettuce salad, rice pudding, milk to drink. Because of all the fresh milk, we could have cream soup, made with the spinach juice left from dinner, seasoned with nutmeg. And at the same meal, rice pudding, "poor man's rice pudding," Mrs. Hollin's recipe: 3 T. rice, 3 T. sugar, 1/2 t. salt, 3 cups whole milk; and when this is almost baked, add raisins, lemon peel, nutmeg. Bake it in a slow oven, stirring it occasionally to stir in the Bessie's _____.[2] When the rice is tender, the pudding is done—it will thicken a little more as it stands. I baked the rice pudding while I was cooking dinner, so we had it cold for supper—we prefer it cold. Harlan likes to have cream on his.

The lettuce salad was quantities of lettuce with maple syrup, lemon juice, melted butter, and sunflower seeds.

May 26, 1947

Breakfast, on the beach: pancakes, bacon, maple syrup, fried apples, fresh milk to drink.

Pancakes were made from 1–1/4 cup hominy flour, 1/4 cup soy flour, 1/2 cup coarse-grind wheat flour, 1 t. baking soda, 1/2 t. salt. Stir in 1 egg well beaten and 2 cups sour milk. The bacon was some of the country bacon Owen Hammond brought us. The apples were a pint of our "pie pack" canned apples, sweetened with our "black strap" (as we call the last batch of maple syrup, which tastes more like molasses) and fried in bacon fat. The Marshall boy's milk, still fresh and sweet. We enjoy baking pancakes over a hot fire on the beach. We will be cooking out of doors more and more now.

A letter from Nell saying "Meet Mam and me at Clifty Inn Monday afternoon" took us away from the boat for the rest of the day. We took a snack with us, "as prudent sailors do"—toasted whole wheat mixed with walnuts; raisins; an apple. We had dinner with Mam and Nell at Clifty Inn, where they stayed overnight.

May 27, 1947

We were off early this morning to get Mam and Nell from Clifty and bring them down to the boat for the day. Mam is a good sport to come all the way here to see us and Payne Hollow—crossing the river in the johnboat and crossing back again. Now, at about five o'clock, they are on their way back to Cincinnati.

For lunch, for our guests, we served catfish soup; green salad; creamed eggs and poke on hot corn bread; pickled beets; wild grape jelly; raspberries and cream; and nutbread. Also Sinter Klaas cookies, and tea.

Catfish soup is milk soup, unthickened, seasoned with a teaspoon of butter and sweet basil. Green salad—lettuce, spinach, beet tops, carrot tops, with lemon juice, salad oil, sunflower seeds. I think our guests liked the cornbread as much as anything. Creamed eggs are one of Nell's favorite dishes. Our canned black raspberries—still our choicest fruit. The Sinter Klaas cookies Mam had brought—she is so thoughtful. She also brought us a metwurst, cheese, figs, bacon fat (not to mention recipes, magazines, Dutch books and papers).

September 7, 1947

Breakfast: rice, cold, with cream; peaches, fresh, with cream (we have canned most of two bushels of peaches, but saved out as many as we could to use fresh); whole milk to drink.

Dinner: scalloped potatoes with bacon strips (country bacon); baked acorn squash; lima beans; cole slaw with fresh tomato pieces; hot tea; peaches and cream.

Supper: muskmelon from our garden; cream of tomato soup; whole wheat nut bread toasted; plate of raw cabbage, carrots, parsley; milk to drink; chocolate cake—the birthday cake Harlan baked for me, trimmed with the candles we dipped last night.

Bissell's Bluff, Uncle Jim Joiner's place

May 1948

Baked eel—seasoned with bay leaf, cloves, mace, parsley, butter, and lemon—à la "the Browns." We find smoked eel is delicious, too.

June 5, 1948

Today Skipper brought home a young groundhog! We had him fried, like chicken. Yesterday we ate a big <u>old</u> groundhog that Harlan and Skipper dug out of his den under the stone wall along the garden—had him stewed—and will finish him in a meat pie tomorrow. Our whole wheat makes very tasty crust for meat pie—Wheatsworth recipe.

June 14, 1948

A new salad this noon—raw beets, fresh from the garden, chopped fine in the food chopper, mixed with an equal amount (almost) of raw chopped cabbage (2 medium-sized beets). Seasoned with vinegar, pickled beet juice, a squeeze of lemon juice, salt, sugar, mayonnaise, black walnuts. Served on crisp Bibb lettuce heads cut in half lengthwise.

And a new supper dish tonight, cooked over a fire on the shore, where we ate our supper just at sunset time—rice pancakes with elderberry blossoms in them: 1–1/4 cups cooked brown rice (left over) added to the liquid ingredients—1 egg beaten, about 1/2 cup sour milk (could have been a little more). Mix together the dry ingredients—1 cup whole wheat flour (Harlan's grind), 1/2 t. soda, 1/4 t. salt, 1 T. sugar, about 1 cup elderberry blossoms pulled off the stems (could have been more—we sprinkled more blossoms on the cakes in the frying pan before turning them). Add the liquid to the dry ingredients; stir. Fry, like rice cakes, in bacon fat, letting the cakes steam a very little while with the tight cover on. Serve with butter and brown sugar (or honey.)

Sunday June 27, 1948

This morning we baked two of the things Harlan has been urging me to try "Soy Crunch cookies" and elderberry blossom muffins.

The cookies: 3/8 cup shortening (Crisco); 1/2 cup brown sugar; 1/2 t. vanilla; 1/2 t. salt; 1 well-beaten egg; 1/2 cup soy flour (H's grind); 1/2 cup whole wheat flour [also H's grind]; 1/2 cup of our favorite breakfast cereal, which is toasted wheat and toasted soy beans coarsely ground; 1/4 cup chopped nuts (hickory). Cream shortening and sugar. Add vanilla, salt, and egg, and beat well. Add chopped nuts, soy and wheat flours, and toasted cereal. Mix well. Drop by teaspoonfuls on a greased cookie sheet (I used four pie tins). Bake 15 minutes in preheated 350° oven. Makes about 2 dozen.

Elderberry blossom muffins: 2 cups all-purpose flour; 3/4 t. baking soda; 1/2 t. salt; 1/3 cup sugar; 2 cups elderberry blossoms, cut from the stems; 1 egg; 1 cup sour milk; 1/3 cup shortening, melted. Sift, then measure, the flour. Sift twice with the baking soda, salt, and sugar. Then add the elderberry blossoms and stir in. Combine well-beaten egg, sour milk, and melted shortening. Turn the wet ingredients into the dry ingredients. Mix only until dry ingredients are dampened. Fill greased muffin tins 2/3 full. Bake in hot oven (425° F) 25 minutes. (I two-thirds-filled 6 small muffin tins, 4 larger muffin tins, and the sample bread tin). About 12 muffins, say.

October 1948

Very delicious persimmons from on the Bluff—mashed through the strainer to remove seeds and skins, and served, just so, with walnuts and cream.

December 23, 1948

A variation of the Soy Crunch cookies (Harlan said the others might have come from Parkes' Health Store): 3/8 cup shortening (Crisco), 1/4 cup brown sugar, 1/4 cup honey (from our own bees), 1/2 t. vanilla, 1/2 t. salt, 1 well-beaten egg, 1/2 cup whole wheat flour, 1 cup breakfast cereal (toasted wheat and toasted soy beans) ground as fine as flour, 1/4 cup chopped walnuts, 1/4 cup toasted sunflower seeds, 1/4 cup raisins, 1/4 cup candied orange peel. Cream shortening and sugar. Add honey. Add vanilla, salt, and egg, and beat well. Add other ingredients. Mix well. Drop by teaspoonfuls on a greased cookie sheet (we have one now, aluminum, just the size to fit into our oven). Bake 15 minutes in preheated 350° oven. Made about 3 dozen.

July 1949—Bisland Bayou

Tom[3] said gar was the best fish of all; and when I asked him how Rosie cooked it, he said, "She boils it and puts tomato paste on it." Following this clue, I worked out this dish:

I began steaming the gar in a heavy aluminum saucepan with a tight lid, but I soon found Rosie was right—it required boiling; so I added water and more water, and cooked it and cooked it until it did finally get tender. I salted it but little, as it had soaked in salt water. Meanwhile I had stewed some garden fresh tomatoes, but seasoned them only with a bit of salt—no sugar, no thickening. Meanwhile, too, I had been heating the casserole in the oven and browning in it some cut-up fennel stalks and parsley, also a small pepper, in butter. I put it all together in the hot casserole, finally, in this order: melted butter, boiled gar (the six pieces just covered bottom of casserole), two bay leaves broken up, juice and rind of one slice of lemon, the browned fennel and parsley, the stewed tomatoes, crumbs of whole wheat bread, dots of butter. Covered it and baked it a while. [End of Anna's shantyboat recipes journal.]

Anna's whole wheat biscuits (recipe reconstructed by Luella Newby).

Add 3/4 cup cold water to 1/4 cup powdered milk and mix well. With a paring knife, chip the peel off a lemon in flakes. Add the peel and 1 T. lemon juice to milk mixture. Combine 2 cups whole wheat flour, 2 to 3 T. brown sugar to taste, and 1 t. salt. Cut in 4 T. margarine. Add 1 t. baking soda to milk mixture and stir. Add milk mixture to flour mixture slowly and stir. Drop, in seven large spoonfuls, into a greased 9–inch pie pan. Bake at 400 degrees F. for 15 to 20 minutes or until a toothpick inserted in the center comes out clean. (Note: The coarser the flour and the higher the fat content of the margarine, the more the biscuits will resemble Anna's.)

Catfish soup recipe, paraphrased from "Anna Hubbard's Recipe for Catfish Soup," Madison (Indiana) Mirror, October 29, 1964, 2.

Remove the steaks from the bones. Simmer the backbone and the particles of meat clinging to it in 2 cups of water for 30 minutes. Cool. Remove any bits of meat still clinging to the backbone and add them to the soup stock. Add a cup of rich milk for each cup of soup stock.

Strengthen with a bit of cream. Salt to taste, and season with dried sweet basil.

Whole wheat bread recipe contributed by Anna to Savory Samplings, a cookbook compiled and published by Psi Iota Xi, Zeta Xi Chapter, Madison, Indiana, 1975 (2d printing). Reprinted with permission.

Before gathering other ingredients, stir 2 packages or cakes of crumbled bakers' yeast and 2 cups of warm water. Add at leisure 1/3 cup blackstrap molasses, 2 T. shortening, and 3-1/2 cups sifted, high-protein whole wheat flour. Stir until ingredients are combined, then beat 300 strokes. Do not be frightened by the beating, it takes only a few minutes. If an electric mixer is used, mix at low speed for exactly 10 minutes; gluten can be broken down by overbeating.

Combine and sift in 1/2 cup sifted high-protein whole wheat flour, 1 cup soy flour or 1 cup wheat germ, 1/2 cup powdered milk, 1 T. salt, and 4 T. vinegar. Stir well but do not knead.

Cover bowl, set in a warm place at 85 degrees or in warm water at 110 degrees. Let rise until double in bulk, or about 45 minutes. Stir dough until original size, and transfer to oiled 5- by 8-inch bread pan. You can let dough rise three or four more times, being careful to keep it warm and to stir it down each time. Put into moderately hot oven at 385 degrees and bake 45 to 50 minutes or until golden brown.

Three vegetable recipes from letters to Susan Bartnick.

Cauliflower cooked in milk (March 9, 1981)

Break the cauliflower into pieces. Cover them with milk in the cooking pan. Simmer about 15 or 20 minutes, until tender. Thicken the milk by adding cornstarch stirred into a little cold water. And of course sprinkle nutmeg on it when you serve it.

Steamed broccoli with herb butter (March 27, 1981)

Leave fresh broccoli stalks uncut; stand upright in utensil containing 1/2 cup boiling water; cover utensil with <u>tight</u> lid; steam until tender, or about 15 minutes. Herb butter: Heat 2 T. margarine or oil (1 minced clove garlic, salt, pepper), 1/4 t. basil or oregano, 1/4 cup lemon juice; pour over steamed broccoli. Or you can use broccoli cut up into small pieces—cut bud ends into 3/4 inch pieces; shred leaves and chop smaller stalks, peel any large stalks and cut into pieces 1/4 inch thick. Put broccoli pieces on rack, in basket colander or another smaller pan, and set in kettle. Add just enough boiling water to cover bottom of kettle, but not enough to touch the vegetable. Cover and steam until vegetable is tender, keeping the heat very low—on a simmer burner, for instance.

Corn pudding (March 27, 1981)

Open your can of corn. Pour the corn juice into your 2–cup measuring cup. Fill up the measuring cup with milk. Put the corn and most of the milk and juice into the casserole dish. Beat (with egg beater) 3 eggs into the rest of the milk and juice. Put this into the casserole. Add 1/2 t. salt. Mix everything together with a spoon. You can sprinkle a little summer savory on it all if you have some (or a very little pepper.) Bake in oven uncovered at 325 degrees Fahrenheit until firm, about 35 minutes.

Notes to Anna's Recipes

1. Miss Alice Dunlap of the Cincinnati Public Library; her sister, Miss Marie Dunlap; and Lassie Thompson, who lived with Marie in a Covington, Kentucky, boarding house.
2. Illegible; resembles "hempd." The allusion to "Bessie" is a mystery.
3. Tom ("Tomcat"), whose name was James Carter, and his wife, Rosie, were African Americans who lived at Pine Ridge. He is mentioned often in chapter 10 of *Shantyboat Journal*.

Notes

&

Published works are cited in the notes by author and title only. See "Selected Bibliography" for full bibliographic information. Quotations for which no published source is mentioned in text and no note is given are from interviews (see "Acknowledgments").

Unless otherwise noted, letters and other personal papers cited are located in the Harlan and Anna Hubbard Papers, University Archives and Records Center, University of Louisville, Kentucky (the University of Louisville Archives [ULA]). Letters are easy to locate with ULA's "Finding Aid" document.

The following papers archived at ULA were consulted often in the research; box and folder numbers are not given in the notes: Anna's accounts, B (box) 18, F (folder) 15; Anna's autobiographical sketch, a twelve-page, hand-written, unpublished memoir dated September 1982, B 32, F 23; Anna's 1926–39 Christmas card and gift lists, tucked into the little loose-leaf booklet of poems from Hilda, B 32, F 3; Anna's guest books, B 18; Anna's *Library Journal* drafts, thirty-two pages of handwritten drafts of the article published November 1, 1954, B 32, F 21.

Published works by Harlan Hubbard are abbreviated in the notes as follows: *HHJ—Harlan Hubbard Journals 1929–1944; PH—Payne Hollow: Life on the Fringe of Society; PHJ—Payne Hollow Journal; Sh— Shantyboat; SB— Shantyboat on the Bayous; SJ—Shantyboat Journal.* Also cited is Harlan's birthday-and-anniversary journal, ULA, B 18, F 12.

Shortened references are used in the notes as follows: FOH papers—Friends of the Hubbards papers, Duggan Library Archives, Hanover College. JW tape—Joanne Weeter's tapes (in ULA) of oral history interviews with HH from June to October 1987. VK tape—Vince Kohler's tapes (in his collection) of conversations with AH and HH in 1975–76. WH transcript—Wade Hall's transcript (in his collection) of his interview with HH in August 1987, which he used in producing *A Visit with Harlan Hubbard* (see "Selected Bibliography").

Harlan is referred to in notes as HH and Anna as AH, regardless of her marital status in the context.

Introduction

3   "amphibious race . . .": *Sh*, 2–3.

Chapter 1. In the Studio

9   "elfin streak": *Sh*, 96.
9   bright children: AH said so to Judy Moffett (interview, Judy Moffett).
10   "an attractive place . . .": HH, "A Hubbard Manuscript," February 1973, unpublished, 35, ULA, B 20, F 1.
10   "pristine, white cottage": George F. Roth Jr. to Robert Rosenthal, March 22, 1989, FOH papers.
11   "If you can get . . .": interview, Patricia Staebler.
11   "a solid, harmonious structure": *PH*, 45.
11   "To Anneke . . .": the photo is in ULA, B 26, F 13.

Chapter 2. Payne Hollow Summers

19   Harlan would climb: Luella (Lu) Newby (formerly Akers) saw HH do this once, "native-like, climbing up the unbranched tree" (interview, Lu Newby).
20   "We don't care . . .": AH, in David Hunter, "Payne Hollow Revisited."
21   Anna's favorite literature: HH, in WH transcript.
25   "on a sudden impulse . . .": *SB*, 69.
26   "Anna has done well . . .": *SJ*, 279.
26   "As you know . . .": HH to Herbert Fall, June 25, 1949.
27   "came home with . . .": AH, in VK tape, June 19, 1976.
29   "always thinking": AH, in VK tape, September 27, 1975.
30   "was too zealous . . .": *SJ*, 15–16.
31   "a job for all hands . . .": *SJ*, 98.
31   "could not be improved": *SJ*, 195.
32   "It's what goes . . .": AH, in taped interview with Christy Canida, 1985, Bob Canida's collection.
32   "too noisy . . .": HH, in Gene Logsdon, "A Homestead Venture That Works," 149.
34   "This very lamp . . .": AH, in VK tape, September 27, 1975.
35   "clean and prosperous . . .": *SJ*, 138.
35   "of Toggenburg breeding . . .": *PH*, 122.

Chapter 3. "She's So Dutch!"

38   "extremely neat . . .": Jacob van Hinte, *Netherlanders in America*, 985–86.
38   "I have too many . . .": interview, Patricia Staebler.
39   "The roughest . . .": *PH*, 35.

39   "Fortunately Anna . . .": *Sh*, 36.
39   "Each time . . .": *Sh*, 51.
40   "By good fortune . . .": *PH*, 146.
40   "simple, easily explained life": *HHJ*, 40.
40   "an eventful day": *SJ*, 36.
40   "We are quite pleased . . .": *SJ*, 238.
41   "Great fun!": AH to Bill and Rheta Caddell.
42   Payne Hollow gift list: in ULA, B 18, F 45.
42   van der Horst on uninvited guests: *The Low Sky*, 239–40.
43   "We give away . . .": *SJ*, 179–80.
44   "Oh, he's going . . .": interview, Susan Bartnick.
44   "To our dismay . . .": HH to John and Linda Hernick, August 3,
       1983, FOH papers.
44   added "naughts . . .": interview, Helen Spry.
45   "This isn't so hard . . .": interview, Bill Caddell.
45   sharp comments: interview, Ed Lueders.
45   "Just like a state park . . .": interview, Helen Spry.
45   "I think *I'll* just . . .": interview, Judy Moffett.
46   "Whoever comes . . .": *PH*, 141.
46   "the most unpromising . . .": HH, in JW tape 4, side 1.
49   "You've embarrassed me . . .": interview, Susan Bartnick.

Chapter 4. Little Dutch Girl

52   Summary of Dutch traits: based on van der Horst, *The Low Sky*.
53   "genuinely American": van Hinte, *Netherlanders in America*, 985–
       86.
54   "How I would . . .": AH to Mildred and Fred O'Nan, September
       20, 1979, FOH papers.
55   The eight children: named on the ship's passenger list, National
       Archives of the United States, microfilm pub. no. M-237,
       "Passenger List of Vessels Arriving New York," roll no. 611,
       1820–1897, June 6–24, 1893. Jan and Anna Wonder Ross had
       fourteen children in all. Three died before 1890 in the Nether-
       lands, ten lived out their lives in the United States, and one, the
       second oldest boy, Arie, died in Holland in 1935.
57   "withheld": interview, George Bartnick.
61   Instead she would send Anna . . . : HH said so to Wade Hall
       (interview, Wade Hall).

Chapter 5. Independence

63   Summary of AH's Ohio State curriculum: based on *The Ohio State
       University Bulletin, 1924–1925,* vol. XXVIII, nos. 20 (March
       22, 1924) and 21 (March 29, 1924). Her transcript is marked,
       in English, "with high distinction." In her autobiographical

sketch, however, written nearly sixty years later, AH wrote that she had graduated "summa cum laude" (with *highest* distinction). Perhaps AH's memory of a less-than-perfect performance had improved itself over time.

63   teaching French and German: AH, HH, and Etta all said AH taught French and German. However, the letter offering AH the position mentions French and English (Edward Dimnent, president of Hope College, to AH, June 26, 1925, Joint Archives of Holland), and captions under her pictures in the 1926 and 1927 yearbooks mention only French.

64   "didn't especially enjoy it": AH, in VK tape, June 19, 1976.

64   "stifling atmosphere": Etta to the Staeblers, May 20, 1989, their collection.

64   "felt terribly restricted": Etta to the Staeblers, March 16, 1989, their collection.

67   "Traits of a circulation . . .": AH, library training notes, ULA, B 32, F 12.

68   "Miss Miriam Rothenberg . . .": *Cincinnati Times Star*, April 9, 1935, 12.

Chapter 6. Turning Points

71   "My Annie dear . . .": in the little booklet of poems, ULA, B 32, F 3.

72   Loving friendships between women: for more on the cultural permissibility of those friendships in the Victorian era, and the change in attitude that occurred around World War I, see Faderman, *Surpassing the Love of Men.*

73   "Some friends . . .": AH to Lee Holden, February 26, 1933, the author's collection, courtesy of Helen Thiele Buran.

73   "The waves . . .": AH to Lee Holden, August 27, 1922, the author's collection, courtesy of Helen Thiele Buran.

75   "When I was upstairs . . .": AH to Lee Holden, September 18, 1932, the author's collection, courtesy of Helen Thiele Buran.

75   "Changes are always hard. . . .": AH to Lee Holden Thiele, February 26, 1933, the author's collection, courtesy of Helen Thiele Buran.

78   "My disappointment . . .": James Frederick O'Nan to Robert Rosenthal, 1989, FOH papers.

78   ". . . the young architect . . .": whether Charles E. Young was the same "young architect" of Taliesin whom AH mentioned later in her *Library Journal* drafts (see p. 69) is unlikely. A call to Taliesin did not turn up his name in the records.

79   Material on Paul Briol: from interviews with his daughter, Jan Briol Chinnock McLean, and her article "What a Father!" in the fall 1989 issue of *Queen City Heritage*, journal of the Cincinnati Historical Society.

79   photographing the library: eight images of the old library at 629
      Vine Street are among the thousands of Briol's negatives and
      prints now in the possession of the Cincinnati Historical Society.

83   open and cordial: Mary entertained Paul's women friends at dinner
      with Jan present. Jan remembers a tall, thin, quiet woman (AH)
      somehow connected with a female department-store detective
      (Etta). Mary inquired politely about AH in a letter to Paul from
      Tokyo on May 14, 1937 (Jan's collection). Mary and AH
      appear together in a photo taken by Paul in Pentwater, Michi-
      gan, at the lake cottage of friends (Jan's collection).

83   several of his own photographs . . . : the Crosley Field photograph,
      and others Paul made and gave to AH, are in Grand Rapids
      now with Susan Bartnick. AH gave them to Etta for safekeeping
      because HH would not have them around, and Etta later gave
      them to Susan.

83   Nun and pope costumes: in her Christmas card and gift lists, AH
      noted in 1938 that she received from Paul "new year's party
      including nun's costume." Paul's anti-Catholic bias stemmed
      from his father's experience preaching Calvinist doctrine in
      French-speaking Catholic Canada, where he hid in haystacks
      and was attacked with pitchforks.

86   AH's hysterectomy: written inquiries to the seven hospitals in and
      around the Clifton neighborhood about AH's 1939 medical
      records were unsuccessful; no records going back that far were
      still available.

Chapter 7. "And Then There Was Harlan"

90   Federal Public Works of Art: a project of the Depression-inspired
      Works Progress Administration, later called Works Projects
      Administration; HH wrote of it in *HHJ*, 91–92. The possibility
      that HH and AH met in 1934 was mentioned by George Roth,
      northern Kentucky chairman of the project, in part two of John
      Reiter's three-part feature series on the Hubbards in the *Ken-
      tucky Post* beginning January 5, 1979.

90   her little address book: one of two located in ULA, B 16.

91   "with a shy smile": AH, autobiographical sketch.

91   canoe trip down the Kentucky River: HH wrote to Frank Hubbard
      on September 3 about having just finished such a trip.

92   "Oh, that's nice": AH, in VK tape, June 19, 1976.

92   the playing didn't go well: HH, in JW tape 3, side 1.

93   "He didn't *ask* . . .": AH, in VK tape, June 19, 1976.

93   Thursday, January 16: of the possible Thursdays in January when
      AH and HH might have sat outdoors before going to the
      exhibition, January 16, the day after the opening, is the most
      likely; the temperature reached fifty degrees.

93 With a friend later: interview, Patricia Staebler.
94 Protestant, though not particularly religious: HH, in JW tape 8, side 1.
94 No signs of love: HH, in WH transcript, and in JW tape 1, side 1.
94 Relative ages of HH's brothers: Frank was born in December 1887; Lucien, in December 1889.
94 several seasons of art school: HH was enrolled in the art school of the National Academy of Art, New York, in 1918–19, 1920–21, and 1925–26, and in the Art Academy of Cincinnati in 1919–20. The dates are confirmed by museum staff of the two institutions.
96 the place he called his camp: HH wrote of his camp in *Sh*, 38. AH identified the town as New Richmond in a letter to the Staeblers (October 30, 1946, their collection).
97 "I think the fast water . . .": AH, Licking River log, ULA, B 32, F 8. Also used in reconstructing this trip was HH's letter to Frank dated June 16, 1942.
98 "At its best . . .": AH to Judy Moffett, September 25, 1964, JM's collection.
98 "Harlan is always working . . .": AH to Judy Moffett, January 5, 1965, JM's collection.
99 "He started to write": AH, in VK tape, September 27, 1975.
100 "but it didn't turn out . . .": HH, in WH transcript.
100 "Oh, I could . . .": told to the author by Don Wallis; the visitor who witnessed the event remains unidentified.
100 "What's that. . . ?": told to Susan Bartnick by Paul Hassfurder (interview, Susan Bartnick).
101 "I suppose . . .": AH, in VK tape, September 27, 1975.
101 He was beginning . . . : 42.
101 I do not think . . . : 61.
101 My one wish . . . : 63.

Chapter 8. Wedding Days

103 "Are you getting a dog?": interview, Susan Bartnick.
103 "went off to Buenos Aires . . .": Etta to Helen Spry, February 13, 1988, HS's collection.
103 "People always need soap": interview, Helen Spry.
104 Etta's career at Shillito's: Elaine Clapp, "Shoplifters Beware of Etta," *Grand Rapids Herald,* June 10, 1957.
106 The story of HH's proposal: HH, in JW tape 3, side 1.
106 "with a ceremony . . .": HH, birthday-and-anniversary journal, April 20, 1944.
106 Nearly forty years later . . . : in John Morgan, videotape, *Life on the Fringe of Society.*

107	Wartime crowds in Union Terminal: Allan M. Winkler, "The Queen City and World War II," in *Cincinnati Goes to War,* 12.
108	"No-o-o . . .": AH, in VK tape, June 19, 1976.
109	Mam had been shocked: interview, Susan Bartnick.
109	"didn't work, at all . . .": Etta to Helen Spry, January 24, 1988, HS's collection.
109	"shook up the whole Consistory": Etta to the Staeblers, January 22, 1988, their collection.

Chapter 9. The True Direction

110	"didn't take to Anna . . .": HH, in JW tape 3, side 2.
110	broke Rose's heart . . . : interview, Betty Hubbard Heasley.
111	"not a sharer . . .": HH, draft of commentary he added to his 1929–44 journals for publication in 1987 (*HHJ*), ULA, B 18, F 1.
112	She didn't seem to mind: HH, in JW tape 3, side 2.
112	The account of the eastern trip: from HH, eastern trip log, ULA, B 34, F 13, and his letters to Frank.
115	"There on the river shore . . .": HH, original journal, June 15, 1944, ULA, B 18, F 11.
115	"I hope that he . . .": AH, eastern trip log, August 9, 1944, ULA, B 32, F 4.
117	"We were returning . . .": HH, page of notes, ULA, B 18, F 12.
117	"This is the day . . .": *HHJ*, 199.
118	"setting the rude table . . .": *Sh*, 17.
118	"an event . . .": *SJ*, 15.
119	"We just thought . . .": AH, in VK tape, June 19, 1976.
120	"As usual . . .": AH, *Library Journal* drafts.
121	Why not visit. . . : HH, in JW tape 3, side 2.

Chapter 10. The Art of Living

122	"just as beautiful . . .": HH to Harvey Simmonds, January 6, 1977.
122	"We had so much fun . . .": *Sh*, 35.
122	"for other activities . . .": *SJ*, 29.
122	"time became as smooth . . .": *Sh*, 37.
122	"still tinkering": HH to Harvey Simmonds, January 21, 1974.
123	"alert enough . . .": *PHJ*, 102.
123	"To arise in the frosty morning . . .": *PHJ*, 154.
123	"tonight I am dressed . . .": *PHJ*, 127.
124	"little old-timey clips . . .": AH, in VK tape, June 19, 1976.
124	"Am I wrong . . .": AH to Judy Moffett, June 9, 1969, JM's collection.
125	"Oh, dear . . .": AH, in David Hunter, "Payne Hollow Revisited."

125   "<u>all wet</u> . . .": AH to Etta Crossley, February 8, 1984, the Bartnicks' collection.

125   Children not in HH's vision: HH, in JW tape 7, side 1, and in WH transcript.

125   "I had a minimum . . .": Etta to the Staeblers, January 8, 1990, their collection.

126   "I always imagined . . .": interview, Patricia Staebler. As the three Staebler children came along, AH's letters to Patricia and Warren were full of praise for the youngsters and admiration for the way Patricia managed things so that the quartet could have the maximum amount of playing time.

127   heaven on earth: AH said so to Bob Canida (interview, Bob Canida).

127   "Like the river rat . . .": AH, autobiographical sketch.

127   "Every time we come back . . .": AH to the Staeblers, December 30, 1953, their collection.

127   "Mercy, no!": AH, "Life in a Shantyboat" (see appendix, p. 196.)

128   "I'm just here . . .": interview, Lu Newby (formerly Akers).

129   "In fact . . .": HH, in VK tape, June 19, 1976.

129   Six months on two hundred dollars: interview, Wade Hall.

129   The bequest of $5,000: Diane Hubbard, Frank's daughter-in-law, quoting Frank's will, letter to the author, July 7, 1996. According to Etta (letters in 1988 to Helen Spry, January 24, and to the Staeblers, August 3, their collections), HH didn't want the money.

129   excited by the prospect . . . : HH, original journal, December 25, 1986, ULA, B 18, F 40.

129   approximately $310,000 . . . : Madison Bank and Trust Company, executor of HH's estate, statement of Kentucky assets, estate of HH, filed with Trimble County District Court, August 26, 1988.

130   "because I am afraid . . .": HH, in WH transcript.

130   "a wild existence . . .": PH, 84–85.

130   "I see Anna . . .": PHJ, 23.

130   "you establish a pattern . . .": HH, in VK tape, June 19, 1976.

131   "superfluous and conventional . . .": HH, original journal, June 8, 1986, ULA, B 18, F 41.

132   "truly a work of nature . . .": HH to Harvey Simmonds, June 19, 1986. The boulders and the white gravel were brought up to the house from the creek by Richard Strimple, Danny Bates, and George Thomas.

132   The thirty-inch hole: HH intended that the companion can of his ashes eventually be placed on top of the can containing AH's (interview, Richard Strimple).

132   The design on the gravestone, carved by Mike Skop: HH, in JW tape 7, side 1.

133   upset by the colostomy: HH said so to Judy Moffett (interview).
133   "clean and decisive break . . .": HH, in JW tape 9, side 1. HH
       spoke similarly to Wade Hall (WH transcript).
133   Emotional reticence a Hubbard trait: HH, "A Hubbard Manu-
       script," unpublished, February 1973, 32, ULA, B 20, F 1.
133   "can be sweet and tender . . .": *HHJ*, 183.
133   "I am surprised . . .": HH, journal (typescript), August 2, 1933,
       ULA, B 34, F 25.
134   Even in this first love. . . : HH, draft commentary for *HHJ*, ULA, B
       18, F 1; published version, *HHJ*, 67–68.
134   seduced him . . . : HH, in JW tape 10, side 1.
134   "something growing . . .": HH, original journal, May 17, 1943,
       ULA, B 18, F 11.
134   "pretty slapdash": HH, in JW tape 7, side 1.
136   "Harlan is wedded . . .": Mary Mitchell to the author, telephone
       conversation, March 11, 1996.
136   "Yes. He's good": AH, in VK tape, June 19, 1976.
136   "I'm just sick . . .": AH to HH, January 1946, the author's
       collection, courtesy of Don Wallis.
137   If the weather. . . : AH to HH, August 23, 1973, ULA, B 6, F 4.
138   "She's my courage": interview, Celia Mitchell Parrott.
138   "Her desires . . .": *PHJ*, 23.
138   "there would be weeks . . .": AH, in John Ed Pearce, "The Haven
       on Earth of the Hubbards at Payne's Hollow."
139   "never been averse . . .": HH to Gene and Lu Akers, undated letter
       postmarked September 2, 1971, collection of Lu Newby
       (formerly Akers).
139   "to pay Gene": HH to Lu Akers, May 18, 1972, collection of Lu
       Newby (formerly Akers).
139   "transportation division": HH, in VK tape, September 27, 1975.
139   "a good man": HH, in VK tape, June 19, 1976.

Chapter 11. Hidden

144   AH wanted to stay at Payne Hollow: interview, Don Wallis.
145   He hadn't noticed . . . : "The last two months have been hard for
       her—ebbing strength, weight and spirits" (HH to the Staeblers,
       April 3, 1986, their collection).
145   "Anna has held up . . .": HH to Helen Spry, March 16, 1986, HS's
       collection.
147   he knew things about her . . . : HH, in WH transcript.
147   "You seem very close . . .": HH, original journal, September 10,
       1986, ULA, B 18, F 41.
148   "A bad day . . .": HH, "Shantyboat Drifting," 135.
148   "a left handed day . . .": *SJ*, 230.

148   had had periods of depression: HH, in WH transcript.
148   others saw signs of depression: interviews, Bill Caddell, Don
          Wallis.
148   respect and duty: HH, in JW tape 10, side 2.
149   tragedies: the wren, *PHJ*, 124; the baby rabbits, *PHJ*, 50.
149   "The tragedy is . . .": *PHJ*, 85.
150   The imagining of going back to one's childhood home: based on
          John Bradshaw's "inner child" work with groups as the author
          remembers him doing it in one of his nationally televised PBS
          series. See John Bradshaw's *Homecoming: Reclaiming and
          Championing Your Inner Child*.

Chapter 12. Anna Always with Me

158   "a sense of wonder . . .": Celia Mitchell Parrott, presentation to
          Hubbard Symposium, Hanover College, April 29, 1989, CMP's
          collection.
158   "Sunlight streamed . . .": ibid.
164   "cut down everything . . .": HH to Susan Bartnick, May 23, 1986,
          SB's collection.
165   The mass of printed. . . : HH, original journal, September 20,
          1986, ULA, B 18, F 40.
169   "All your life . . .": AH to George Bartnick, March 1, 1984, GB's
          collection.

Selected Bibliography

❧

The following are the published sources I made use of in writing this book. The Hubbard sources included here do not constitute a complete Hubbard bibliography.

Especially helpful to me in my effort to portray Anna's personality were the following: Lillian Faderman, *Surpassing the Love of Men: Romantic Friendship and Love between Women from the Renaissance to the Present*; Julie Firman and Dorothy Firman, *Daughters and Mothers: Healing the Relationship*; Alice Miller, *Prisoners of Childhood: The Drama of the Gifted Child and the Search for the True Self*; Thomas Moore, *Care of the Soul: A Guide for Cultivating Depth and Sacredness in Everyday Life*; and Victoria Secunda, *When You and Your Mother Can't Be Friends: Resolving the Most Complicated Relationship of Your Life*.

By Anna Hubbard

"Life in a Shantyboat." *Library Journal* (November 1, 1954): 2062–65.

By Harlan Hubbard

Journals 1929–1944. Edited by Vincent Kohler and David F. Ward. Lexington: University Press of Kentucky, 1987.

Payne Hollow: Life on the Fringe of Society. New York: Eakins Press, 1974. Reprint, Frankfort, Ky.: Gnomon Press, 1985.

Payne Hollow Journal. Edited by Don Wallis. Lexington: University Press of Kentucky, 1996.

Shantyboat. New York: Dodd, Mead, 1953. Reprint, Lexington: University Press of Kentucky, 1977.

"Shantyboat Drifting." In *OYO: An Ohio River Anthology*. Edited by Don Wallis. Vol. 2, *River Journeys*. Yellow Springs, Ohio: OYO Press, 1988. A segment of Harlan's journal from January 1 to February 3, 1947.

Shantyboat Journal. Edited by Don Wallis. Lexington: University Press of Kentucky, 1994.

Shantyboat on the Bayous. Lexington: University Press of Kentucky, 1990.

The Woodcuts of Harlan Hubbard: From the Collection of Bill Caddell. Lexington: University Press of Kentucky, 1994.

About the Hubbards

Berry, Wendell. *Harlan Hubbard: Life and Work.* Lexington: University Press of Kentucky, 1990.

Caldwell, John. "The Happy Life." *Cincinnati Pictorial Enquirer,* Sunday, October 23, 1955. With photographs by Ran Cochran.

Greene, Jonathan. "Payne Hollow: A Story about Harlan and Anna Hubbard." *High Roads Folio* (spring 1983): 58–65. With photographs by Guy Mendes.

Hall, Wade. *A Visit with Harlan Hubbard.* University of Kentucky Libraries Occasional Paper No. 12. Lexington: University of Kentucky Libraries, 1996. Dramatic monologue.

Hunter, David. "Payne Hollow Revisited." *Cincinnati Enquirer Magazine,* Sunday, February 4, 1979.

Junker, Janet. "Walden-on-the-Ohio." *Cincinnati Pictorial Enquirer,* Sunday, August 24, 1958. With photographs by Allan Kain.

Logsdon, Gene. "A Homestead Venture That Works." *Organic Gardening and Farming* (July 1977): 147–62.

Moffett, Judith. "The Joy of Life in Payne Hollow." *Cincinnati Enquirer Magazine,* Sunday, October 27, 1974. With photographs by Allan Kain.

———. *Time, Like an Ever-Rolling Stream.* New York: St. Martin's Press, 1992.

Morgan, John. *Life on the Fringe of Society.* 1981. Videotape. Copies available from Behringer- Crawford Museum, P.O. Box 67, Covington, KY 41012–0067, tel. (859) 491–4003.

Morrissey, Jim. "They've *Stayed* Away from It All." *Louisville Courier-Journal Magazine,* Sunday, January 19, 1964. With photographs by H. Harold Davis.

Pearce, John Ed. "The Haven on Earth of the Hubbards of Payne's Hollow." *Louisville Courier- Journal Magazine,* Sunday, July 8, 1979. With photographs by Richard Nugent.

Reiter, John. "How to Beat the Rat Race a la Hubbards." *Kentucky Post,* January 5, 1979.

Wallis, Don. *Harlan Hubbard and the River: A Visionary Life.* Yellow Springs, Ohio: OYO Press, 1989.

———. "Harlan's Gift." In *OYO: An Ohio River Anthology.* Edited by Don Wallis. Vol. 2, *River Journeys.* Yellow Springs, Ohio: OYO Press, 1988.

[———]. "Life in Payne Hollow, Kentucky." *Vevay (Ind.) Reveille-Enterprise,* November 14, 1974.

About Cincinnati and Cincinnatians

Capitman, Barbara, Michael D. Kinerk, and Dennis W. Wilhelm. *Rediscovering Art Deco U.S.A.* New York: Viking Studio Books, 1994.

Cincinnati Historical Society. *Cincinnati Goes to War: A Community Responds to World War II.* Cincinnati: Cincinnati Historical Society, 1991.

Harlow, Alvin F. *The Serene Cincinnatians.* New York: Dutton and Company, 1950.

Hurley, Daniel. *Cincinnati: The Queen City.* Cincinnati: Cincinnati Historical Society, 1982.

McLean, Jan Briol Chinnock. "What a Father!" In *Queen City Heritage: The Journal of the Cincinnati Historical Society* 47, no. 3 (fall 1989): 3–8.

Perry, Dick. *Vas You Ever In Zinzinnati?: A Personal Portrait of Cincinnati.* Garden City, N.Y.: Doubleday, 1966.

Silberstein, Iola Hessler. *Cincinnati Then and Now.* Cincinnati: League of Women Voters of the Cincinnati Area, 1982.

Spiess, Philip D. II. "Sights and Scenes in Clifton: An Historical Tour." Cincinnati: Philip D. Spiess II, 1965. Pamphlet.

Stimson, George P. "River on a Rampage: An Account of the Ohio River Flood of 1937." *Bulletin of the Cincinnati Historical Society* 22, no. 2 (April 1964): 91–109.

Wagner, Richard M., and Roy J. Wright. *Cincinnati Streetcars. No. 7, Progress and Prosperity.* 1976. Second printing, Wyoming, Ohio: Trolley Talk, 1990.

Writers' Program, Work Projects Administration in the State of Ohio. *Cincinnati: A Guide to the Queen City and Its Neighbors.* Cincinnati: Wiesen-Hart Press, 1943. American Guide Series. Informally called the WPA Guide to Cincinnati.

About the Cincinnati Public Library

Board of Trustees of the Public Library of Cincinnati. *Annual Report of the Board of Trustees of the Public Library of Cincinnati for the Year Ending June 30, 1929.*

———. "50 Years: A Compendium of the Activities of the Staff Association of the Public Library of Cincinnati and Hamilton County, 1925–1975."

———. *Practice and Procedure Revised to July, 1941.* Public Library of Cincinnati and Hamilton County, 1941.

——— Public Library of Cincinnati. *Catalogue of the Public Library of Cincinnati.* Cincinnati: Press of Wilstach, Baldwin and Company, 1871.

Public Library of Cincinnati and Hamilton County. *A Decade of Service: 1930–1940.* Public Library of Cincinnati and Hamilton County, 1941.

About Grand Rapids, the Dutch, and the Netherlands

Elliott, Gerald. *Grand Rapids: Renaissance on the Grand*. Tulsa: Continental Heritage Press, 1982.

Lucas, Henry S. *Netherlanders in America*. Ann Arbor: University of Michigan Press, 1955. Reprint, Grand Rapids: Eerdmans Publishing Company, 1989.

Olson, Gordon L. *A Grand Rapids Sampler*. Grand Rapids: Grand Rapids Historical Commission, 1992.

van der Horst, Han. *The Low Sky: Understanding the Dutch*. Schiedam: Scriptum Books, 1996.

van Hinte, Jacob. *Netherlanders in America, A Study of Emigration and Settlement in the 19th and 20th Centuries in the United States of America*. 2 vols. 1928. Reprint, Grand Rapids: Baker Book House Company, 1985.

About Women and Parent-Child Relationships

Bradshaw, John. *Homecoming: Reclaiming and Championing Your Inner Child*. New York: Bantam Books, 1990.

Faderman, Lillian. *Surpassing the Love of Men: Romantic Friendship and Love between Women from the Renaissance to the Present*. New York: William Morrow and Co., Inc., 1981.

Firman, Julie, and Dorothy Firman. *Daughters and Mothers: Healing the Relationship*. New York: Continuum, 1989.

Heilbrun, Carolyn G. *Writing a Woman's Life*. New York: Ballantine Books, 1988.

Miller, Alice. *Prisoners of Childhood: The Drama of the Gifted Child and the Search for the True Self*. New York: Basic Books, 1981. Rev. ed., New York: HarperPerennial, 1997.

Secunda, Victoria. *When You and Your Mother Can't Be Friends: Resolving the Most Complicated Relationship of Your Life*. New York: Delta, 1990.

Smith-Rosenberg, Carroll. *Disorderly Conduct: Visions of Gender in Victorian America*. New York: Alfred A. Knopf, 1985.

Miscellaneous

Coon, Nelson. *Using Wayside Plants*. 4th rev. ed. New York: Hearthside Press, 1969.

Davis, Adelle. *Let's Cook It Right*. New York: Harcourt, Brace, 1947.

———. *Let's Eat Right To Keep Fit*. New York: Harcourt, Brace & World, 1954.

Lindbergh, Anne Morrow. *Gift from the Sea*. New York: Pantheon, 1955.

McDougal, W. Scott, M.D. *Prostate Disease*. New York: Times Books, 1996.

Meynell, Esther. *The Little Chronicle of Magdalena Bach*. London: Chatto and Windus, 1925.

Moffett, Judith. *Homestead Year: Back to the Land in Suburbia*. New York: Lyons and Burford, 1995.

Moore, Thomas. *Care of the Soul: A Guide for Cultivating Depth and Sacredness in Everyday Life*. New York: HarperCollins, 1992. Reprint, New York: HarperPerennial, 1994.

Snodgrass, Robert E., M.D. *Beloved Madison: A Pictorial Tour of Indiana's Historic Madison*. Madison: Jefferson County Historical Society of Indiana, 1990.

Viscott, David, M.D. *Emotional Resilience: Simple Truths for Dealing with the Unfinished Business of Your Past*. New York: Harmony Books, 1996.

Acknowledgments

❧

My first thanks go to Don Wallis, who encouraged and advised me from the beginning; read three drafts of the manuscript, editing minutely as well as substantively; and pressed me to keep probing and rewriting until I knew exactly what I thought and had expressed it clearly. He shared with me his love for and experience of the Hubbards and urged me to search for and write about the actual, human Anna and Harlan rather than the venerated figures they have become. As the Hubbards' literary executor, Don gave me unlimited permission to quote from the Hubbards' letters and papers.

Without the editing and other assistance graciously given by Georgiana Strickland, this book's publication history would have been quite different. She has my deepest gratitude.

Lynn Whittaker also gave me extensive, valuable editing. John Denton, Jonathan Greene, and John Ed Pearce read the manuscript, too, and offered helpful opinions. So did Judy Moffett, with long-haul, never-failing advice and encouragement. Anna's niece, Lynda Susan Bartnick, and youngest nephew, George Bartnick, turned the Bartnicks' Grand Rapids home inside out to show and lend me their Eikenhout family memorabilia. Patricia Staebler generously spent many hours on the telephone with me from 1995 till her death in April 2000, recounting her fifty-year friendship with Anna.

The following persons also went to extra lengths to share their memories of Anna and Harlan with me: Charles Bell, Florence Fowler Burdine, Bill Caddell, Charlotte and Bob Canida, Betty Hubbard Heasley, Anne Horner, Polly Hubbard, Vince Kohler, Edward Lueders, Jan Briol Chinnock McLean, Marcella Modisett, Luella Newby, Celia Mitchell Parrott, Helen Spry, and Carol and Richard Strimple. Priceless photographs were furnished by George Bartnick, Lynda Susan Bartnick, Helen Thiele Buran, Patricia Magaw Fuhs, Betty Hubbard

Heasley, Jan Briol Chinnock McLean, Don Wallis, Robert Webber, and William Webber.

Helen Thiele Buran and William Webber searched their homes for letters from Anna to their mothers, Lee Holden Thiele and Hilda Bell Webber. In the Netherlands, Gerrit de Gooyer facilitated the bit of genealogical research I added to what Anna had already done. He also took me to Anna's maternal grandmother's village and childhood house, and with his help in translating, the current owners of the house, Jo and Jacob Blokker, told me what they knew of its history.

Special thanks go also to librarians and archivists Thomas Moorman and Claire Pancero, Cincinnati Public Library; Bill Caddell, Frankfort (Indiana) Community Public Library; Laura Chace, Cincinnati Historical Society; David Chapman, Cushing Library, Texas A&M University; Bertha Ihnat, University Archives, Ohio State University; Katherine Burger Johnson, University of Louisville Archives; Dennis Kovener, Duggan Library, Hanover College, Hanover, Indiana; Anita Lamkin, Fairfax County (Virginia) Public Library, central branch; and Larry Wagenaar, Joint Archives of Holland, Michigan.

Museum and historical society personnel also gave me special help: Tom Dixon, Chesapeake and Ohio Historical Society, Clifton Forge, Virginia; Molly Russell Kendall, Mason County Museum, Maysville, Kentucky; and Laurie Risch, Behringer-Crawford Museum, Covington, Kentucky.

Darlene Kamperman, American Rose Society, Shreveport, Louisiana, gave me the leads I needed to locate Robert Basye. Kris Kindelsperger, Hanover College Office of Development, helped me locate former Hanover students and faculty members. Derek Knox, Federation of American Societies for Experimental Biology, Bethesda, Maryland, provided key biographical information about Barre Pritchett and put me in touch with her former co-workers.

I interviewed or, in a few cases, corresponded with, the following persons between 1995 and 1998; I am grateful to all of them: Diane Akers, Ruth Avram, George Bartnick, Lynda Susan Bartnick, John Paul Basye, Hans Bauer, Charles Bell, Tanya Berry, Jacob Blokker, Jo Blokker, Helen Thiele Buran, Florence Fowler Burdine, David Byrne, Bill Caddell, Bob Canida, Charlotte Canida, Shannon Clarkson, Connie McMahan Copeland, Malcolm Day, Honey Dowdy, Patricia Magaw Fuhs, Harry Garrison, Tom George, Yvette Gordon, Robert Gosman, Jonathan Greene, Wade Hall, Paul Hassfurder, Betty Hubbard Heasley, Anne Horner, Don Houseman, Polly Hubbard, Paul Kelly, Vince Kohler,

Philip Koplow, Sara Leslie, Ed Lueders, Judy Lueders, Henry G. Luhring Jr., Terry Madden, Cynthia Mapes, Daniel McDade, Jan Briol Chinnock McLean, Mary Mitchell, Marcella Modisett, Judy Moffett, John Muessel, Louis Munier, Lu Newby, Theresa Kolmschlag Noak, Gordon Olson, Celia Mitchell Parrott, David Payne, Bob Rosenthal, Betty Schenkel, Anne Schulte, James Schulte, George Seitz, Brother Benedict Simmonds, Kathy Skop, Mike Skop, Helen Spry, Jonathan Staebler, Patricia Staebler, Warren Staebler, Francesca Stead, Carol Strimple, Richard Strimple, Don Wallis, David Ward, William Webber, and Nita Webster.

James Cunningham, my husband, never doubted that I could write this book. Without his confidence in me I might not have made the attempt.

Index

❧

"Harlan Hubbard" is abbreviated HH, and "Anna Hubbard" is abbreviated AH, regardless of Anna's marital status in the given context. Notes are indexed, for example, "213 n (79)," the note itself being on page 213, and the text it refers to on page 79.

boating: AH's love of, 57, 60, 73–
74, 91–92; with HH, 96, 110,
111. *See also* camping trips
Brent, Kentucky: Mia and Dan at,
4, 8; Hubbards' trips to and
from, 106–8, 110–11;
shantyboaters at (*see* Detisch,
Andy and Sadie; Gander, Lou).
See also housekeeping, AH's: at
Brent; shantyboat: construction
of at Brent; —: living on, at Brent
Briol, Jan. *See* McLean, Jan Briol
Chinnock
Briol, Mary (née Emerson), 81, 82,
83, 86, 213 n (83)
Briol, Paul, 79–83, 84, 85–86, 96–
97, 141, 213 n (79), 213 n (83)

Caddell, Bill, 128
Cal Crim Detective Bureau, 103
camp: HH's, 96; Paul Briol's, 82–
83, 85, 96
camping trailer, 22, 35, 119–20
camping trips: through eastern
states, 112–14; on Licking River,
97–98, 134; in Michigan, 112,
115–17; on Ohio River, 110, 111;
after shantyboating, 3, 22, 120
cancer: AH's, 113, 131, 133, 143–
47; HH's, colon, 143–45; —,
prostate, 142–43, 166
C&0 (Chesapeake and Ohio
Railroad), 107, 112, 118
Canida, Ben, 126
Canida, Bob, 139, 166
Canida, Charlotte, 166
Canida, Christy, 126
canning: at Payne Hollow, 41, 154–
55; on shantyboat, 26
canoeing. *See* boating
Cayvan, Leo, 58, 73, 74, 97, 115,
116
Chesapeake and Ohio. *See* C&O
childhood: AH's, 5, 56–61; HH's, 1

children, Hubbards' views on, 125–
26, 216 n (126)
children's books, AH's love of, 21,
77, 157–58
children's hour, AH's, 58, 61
Christmas: at Payne Hollow, 124; in
Grand Rapids, 89
churchgoing, AH's, 102, 109
church weddings and HH, 106
Cincinnati: AH's apartments in, 11,
38–39, 64, 66, 75, 76; atmosphere of, in 1928, 64–65;
German influence on, 64–65, 67–
68; during Great Depression, 69;
music in, 65; Union Terminal,
107. *See also* Clifton; flood of
1937
Cincinnati Public Library, 16; AH's
resignation from, 111; AH working
in, 2, 64, 66–69, 78–79, 96
Cincinnati Reds, 57
City of Rivers and Hills, The (Briol),
79
Clifton (Cincinnati neighborhood),
60, 66
clothes, AH's, 12, 25, 39, 59–60
Collman, Sophie, 68, 84
concertgoing, 13, 36, 65, 106, 159
Coney Island, 118–19
cooking, AH's, 11, 28–32, 156,
199–208; biscuits, 28, 206 ;
breakfast cereal, 23, 201, 205;
cakes, 31, 203; catfish, 19, 203,
206–7; elderberries, 29–30, 204,
205; groundhog, 19, 204;
learned from HH, 29, 30; in
modern cottage, 144; on open
fires, 11, 28, 30; pokeweed, 30;
on stoves, 11, 28, 29, 30; whole
wheat bread, 31, 207. *See also*
foods
correspondence, AH's, 5–6, 46–48,
124, 141. *See also* letters from
AH; letters to AH